THIS
Bloody Deed

The Magruder Incident

LADD HAMILTON

WSU PRESS

Washington State University Press
Pullman, Washington

Washington State University Press, Pullman, Washington 99164-5910

© 1994 by the Board of Regents of Washington State University
All rights reserved
First printing 1994

Library of Congress Cataloging-in-Publication Data

Hamilton, Ladd.
    This bloody deed : the Magruder incident / Ladd Hamilton.
      p.   cm.
    Includes bibliographical references.
    ISBN 0-87422-107-2
    1. Murder—Idaho—Nez Perce County—Case studies.
2. Criminal justice, Administration of—Idaho—Nez Perce County—History—19th century. 3. Magruder, Loyd, 1825-1863. I. Title.
HV6533.I3H36   1994
364.1'523'0979685—dc20   94-11985
                                    CIP

Contents

For Pauletta

Author's Note

This retelling of an oft-told tale is based on a true case of crime and punishment, and all of the major characters and events are real. The destruction of Lloyd Magruder's pack train by road agents in the Bitterroot Range was reported in the newspapers of the day, as was Hill Beachey's pursuit of the suspects to San Francisco, their capture, and their return to Idaho Territory. The transcript of the trial of the outlaws—David Renton, Christopher Lower and James Romain—can be read in the Nez Perce County Courthouse, although with difficulty because it was written hastily in pencil.

For some parts of the story, however, there is no record, and in writing those parts I have set down what I thought probably happened or might have happened. For instance, the details of Hill Beachey's interview with the Governor of California and his visits to see the murderers in the San Francisco jail are undocumented, although they did take place. I had to imagine what probably occurred. This is also the case regarding the outlaw sheriff Henry Plummer's connection to the Renton gang. Plummer's role is unclear and some writers doubt there was any connection at all. But according to several sources, including Thomas Dimsdale, a Montana journalist of that period, it was Plummer who conceived the idea of stealing Magruder's gold. And it was Dimsdale's contention that a Plummer sidekick, Cyrus Skinner, had plotted the crime. I have tried to imagine how Skinner might have planned it and why his plan went awry when he lost contact with the actual robbers.

This may be as good a place as any to note that Dimsdale's book, *The Vigilantes of Montana*, for many years the standard source, is considered somewhat biased and not fully reliable by many modern historians. Yet because it is the one surviving contemporary account of the Magruder affair, and the basis of the folklore surrounding it, Dimsdale's book can hardly be ignored. It appeared in 1866 and was compiled from articles Professor Dimsdale wrote for the *Montana Post* (Virginia City) beginning with the August 26, 1865, issue. Readers interested in the wide variety of opinions concerning Plummer, William Page (the murderers' companion in the robbery), the vigilantes, and details of the crime should consult the Bibliography at the back of this book.

According to the version of the tale you are about to read, after Lloyd Magruder left Lewiston for the Montana mines Renton, Lower and Romain headed west in a feinting movement, and then turned east in pursuit of the pack train. That is how it was reported by, among others, the key vigilante chroniclers Nathaniel Pitt Langford and Hoffman Birney, but some later writers have argued that the trio approached Magruder directly from the east side of the mountains in what is now western Montana. And, there is disagreement in the sources as to how many men were in the gang that stole Magruder's gold. I have assumed that only three—Renton, Lower and Romain—left Lewiston and later joined Magruder on the trail. Some of the folklore has Lower joining Magruder a couple of days after the other two. Why? I have imagined that Lower fell ill on the trail. If so, it would have been natural for the others to leave him at Fort Lapwai to recuperate while they went on without him. We know that the murder suspects later were held at Fort Lapwai awaiting trial, and we know that the fort was the scene of frequent military balls; but although Magruder and the post commander were good friends, there is no record of Magruder stopping there with his pack string. I have imagined that he did.

William Page's involvement in the crime is a matter of controversy. According to his trial testimony, the unfolding of the plot by the murderers took the grizzled old mountaineer by surprise; according to some other accounts, he was in on the deal all along as a member of Plummer's gang; according to still others, there was no Plummer's gang at all.

I have given Cyrus Skinner a more important role, I'm sure, than he merits; there is no evidence I know of that he also pursued the murderers to San Francisco, as this version has it. But it seems likely that if Plummer had ordered the robbery, he would not easily have accepted the double-cross by Renton, Lower and Romain. He would have sent someone after that fleeing gold, and Skinner would have been a logical choice for the sinister mission.

Everything that happened aboard the ocean steamer carrying Hill Beachey and his prisoners from San Francisco back to Portland is fiction. Between these ports of call the record is blank, although we know that life went on. Furthermore, from Portland upriver to Lewiston, the record is scant. We know that Beachey picked up a military escort for his prisoners on the way back to Lewiston, but it is unclear whether the soldiers joined them at Fort Vancouver or Fort Walla Walla; most accounts suggest it was Vancouver.

It is also not clear whether Beachey's party arrived at Lewiston by stage or steamboat. Most sources favor the boat. Considering the number of persons involved, a sternwheeler seems to be the wiser choice, and the *Tenino* was a familiar sight on the upper river in those days.

To make the story credible, I have quoted people indirectly, without quotation marks, except where there is a record of their exact words. The transcript of the trial provides most of these direct quotations.

Concerning names: Hill Beachey's name is spelled Beachy by some, including some branches of his family, but it is Beachey in the transcript of the trial and it is Beachey in the Luna House ads that appeared in *The Golden Age*, Lewiston's weekly newspaper. David Renton was known to many as "Doc" Howard, but he was indicted and tried as Renton. Christopher Lower also was known to some as Lowry or Lowery, but he is Lower in the court record. As for James Romain, sometimes he spelled his name with an "e" (Romaine) and sometimes he didn't.

Lemuel Akins, the South Fork ferryman, is fictitious; John Silcott, the Lewiston ferryman, isn't. Bartender Dave Strait, the placer miners Pleasance and Sax, and the San Francisco police officers, Ames, Parker and Welch, are fictitious. But Captain Lees and Chief Burke of the San Francisco police department are real, as are the lawyers, Campbell, Coffroth, Thayer, Anderson and Grey. A number of the attorneys and judges in this story served in prominent roles in governmental affairs in 1863 and later.

I don't know that Charles LaFrancois, the former French Army captain, played the part I have given him in Beachey's confrontation with the lynch mob in Lewiston. But assuming the captain was present along with the rest of the citizens, I can't imagine him not coming to Beachey's aid.

According to some accounts it was Thomas Pike who accompanied Beachey to California in quest of the killers; according to some others it was Thomas Farrell. It is my opinion that Pike and Farrell were the same man. California and Idaho court documents give the name as Farrell, and therefore so have I.

We know who the eight men were that left Bannack with Magruder on the return to Lewiston in October 1863 and were involved, as victims or perpetrators, in the murders and the destruction of the mule train. The trial testimony is clear on that.

But who left Lewiston for Bannack with Magruder in the previous August? I have been unable to find any record of those names and have had to speculate as to who served in his crew going out. The record does provide some hints—

*Charles Allen, Magruder's chief packer, must have been part of that crew, since Lewiston residents assumed from the beginning that he was killed along with Magruder; the original charge against the fugitives listed both Magruder and Allen as the victims.

*The grand jury originally indicted Francis Creely, but his innocence was determined before the trial began and his name was dropped. Since there is no mention of Creely anywhere else in connection with the incident, this also suggested to me that he may have been a member of the crew that headed east. One writer (Welch; see Bibliography) suggests that Creely was a name Lower sometimes used, and that it may have been Lower's real name. That can't be true because Francis Creely, with several spellings, was mentioned in news items long after Lower was hanged (e.g., the *Northerner* of May 15, 1875, reported that "Frank Creeley has bought a dray and gone into the draying business").

*Regarding Jules Newburgh, another Magruder packer, the *Sacramento Daily Union*, on November 28, 1863, carried the following one-sentence item: "NOT MURDERED—Jules Newburg, who was reported killed by the murderers of Lloyd Magruder, arrived at Lewiston lately in good condition." Why would he have been reported killed unless he was assumed to have been with Magruder when the killings occurred? That was the basis for including Newburgh as part of the crew heading east in August (using the traditional spelling of his name because newspapers of that time were shamefully careless with names).

There may have been someone in the crew named Frank Moran, but the odds are greatly against it; I used the name in memory of a friend who worked as a cook for log drive crews on the Clearwater River in the 1950s.

Finally, a further word about Henry Plummer: most accounts say he was a cold-hearted desperado interested only in women, wealth and power, but a few writers claim he was a misunderstood lawman determined to bring order and decency to the mining camps. All of his biographers, however, agree on this: he was an ex-convict from California, he spent time in the Lewiston area, Bannack and Virginia City, and he was a charmer with a bad reputation, at least in some circles. Plummer and Lower both were imprisoned in California's San Quentin penitentiary and might have been there at the same time. If so, that would establish a connection that could have been resumed later.

In what survives of the murder trial transcript, there is no mention of Plummer. But Lower, on the gallows, declared that he had not told all he knew because it would have implicated someone dear to him. Could that someone have been Henry Plummer? We simply don't know. For the purposes of this narrative, I have assumed that it was. So let the reader beware: this much of the tale is surmise.

Actual Personages
August 1863-March 1864

Charles Allen
    Lloyd Magruder's chief packer.
J.W. Anderson
    Defense attorney in Renton, Lower and Romain trial.
(Captain) A.P. Ankeny
    Prominent Lewiston-area packer and merchant.
L.W. Bacon
    Mountain expressman.
Wilbur Bassett
    Member of Pierce party, 1860; discoverer of gold at Canal Gulch, W.T.
Hill Beachey
    Lloyd Magruder's avenger and owner of Luna House Hotel, Lewiston; subpoenaed to testify at Renton, Lower and Romain trial.
    Margaret "Maggie" Anne Early Beachey (wife) and children, including Early Beachey (2-year-old son; died of typhoid fever, September 28, 1864).

(Judge) John Berry
    Lewiston resident; subpoenaed to testify at Renton, Lower and Romain trial.
(Madame) Melaine Bonhore
    Owner of Hotel De France; married Captain Charles LaFrancois (1864).
        Eugene Bonhore (12-year-old son by previous marriage).
(Rev.) J.B.A. Brouilette
    Catholic priest.
Brown
    Walla Walla photographer.
(Chief) Burke
    San Francisco police chief.
Alexander Campbell
    Attorney who represented Renton, Lower and Romain in California.
R.P. Campbell
    Political activist from Boise City; Republican legislator.
John M. Cannady
    Political activist from Boise City; Democratic candidate for territorial
    delegate to the U.S. Congress.
Stanford Capps
    Pierce City legislator.
Tom Cassidy
    Lewiston saloonkeeper.
Horace and Robert Chalmers
    Brothers from Missouri.
(Officer) Clarke
    San Francisco policeman.
Jack Cleveland
    Desperado; shot in Bannack by Henry Plummer.
Clindinger
    Lloyd Magruder business partner.
Chester P. Coburn
    Luna Stables manager.
J.W. Coffroth
    Attorney hired by Hill Beachey in California.
Henry Crawford
    Bannack lawman; run out of town by Henry Plummer.
Frank Creely
    Lewiston area packer.
(Judge) E.B. Crocker
    California judge in Renton, Lower and Romain hearing.
William B. Daniels
    Idaho territorial secretary; acting governor after William H. Wallace
    resigned in 1863.
Mose Druillard
    Expressman; searched for Magruder party; testified at Renton, Lower and
    Romain trial.

Sidney Edgerton
> Bannack resident, supreme court justice, I.T.; later first governor of
> Montana Territory (1864).
>> Martha Edgerton (Sidney Edgerton's 13-year-old daughter).

Baptiste Escude
> Hotel De France chef.

Thomas Farrell
> Hill Beachey's companion during pursuit of the murderers to California.

(Sheriff) James Fisk
> Lewiston lawman.

Charles Frush
> Court reporter, Lewiston.

Bishop Goodrich
> Lewiston rancher; acquaintance of Billy Page; subpoenaed to testify at
> Renton, Lower and Romain trial.

(Officer) Greer
> San Francisco policeman.

Enos F. Grey
> Prosecuting attorney in Renton, Lower and Romain trial.

Leo Guion
> Luna House night watchman; testified at Renton, Lower and Romain trial.

Charles Harper
> Horse thief, hanged alongside road to Florence (1862).

Jim Haygood
> Lewiston resident.

James Hays
> Lewiston packing yard operator.

Hildebrandt
> Lewiston barkeeper, shot in 1862.

Louis Holt
> Bannack rancher; testified at Renton, Lower and Romain trial.

Charles Hutchins
> Nez Perce Indian agent.

(Dr.) Madison A. Kelly
> Coroner at the execution of Renton, Lower and Romain.

Milton Kelly.
> Boise City legislator, and assistant prosecuting attorney in the Renton,
> Lower and Romain trial.

Frank Kenyon
> Lewiston newspaper editor of *The Golden Age* (took over from John Scranton
> in 1863).

Shull Kenney
> Left Lewiston for Elk City in search of Magruder party; subpoenaed to
> testify at Renton, Lower and Romain trial.

(Captain) Charles LaFrancois
> Married Madame Melaine Bonhore of the Hotel De France (1864).

Timothy Lee.
>Testified at Renton, Lower and Romain trial.

(Captain) J.W. Lees
>San Francisco policeman.

Alonzo Leland
>Lewiston legislator (former editor of the *Times*, Portland); testified at Renton, Lower and Romain trial.

(Officer) Levatt
>San Francisco policeman.

Christopher Lower (Lowry, Lowery)
>Road agent.

W.W. McCarty
>Testified at Renton, Lower and Romain trial.

John Magruder
>Lloyd Magruder's brother.

Lloyd Magruder
>Merchant and packer; Elk City and Lewiston.
>>Caroline Elizabeth Pelham Magruder (wife); Sally Magruder (daughter who remained in Marysville, California); James "Jimmy" Pelham Magruder (son); John Carter Magruder (son); and Eliza Lloyd Magruder (daughter).

Emily Meredith
>Bannack resident.

L.C. Miller
>East Bannack legislator; testified at the Renton, Lower and Romain trial.

(Captain) John Mullan
>Former U.S. Army officer; noted for directing the building of the Mullan Road from Fort Walla Walla to Fort Benton.

Jules Newburgh
>Lloyd Magruder's friend and frequent traveling companion.

William "Billy" Page
>Companion of Renton, Lower and Romain; turned state's evidence in murder trial.

(Judge) Samuel Parks
>Supreme court associate justice, 2nd district, I.T.; presided at trial of Renton, Lower and Romain.

(U.S. Marshal) Dolphus Payne
>Affirmed the fraudulent Idaho Territory election results from Fort Laramie.

(Colonel) Charles Pelham
>Lloyd Magruder's father-in-law.

(Dr.) James Pelham
>Lloyd Magruder's brother-in-law.

Jeff Perkins
>Bannack resident.

William "Bill" Phillips
>Miner.

(Captain) E.D. Pierce
>Leader of party that discovered gold in Clearwater Mountains, 1860.

Henry Plummer
> Bannack County's outlaw sheriff.

(Lieutenant) Purdy
> Commander of soldiers at execution of Renton, Lower and Romain.

David Renton ("Doc" Howard)
> Road agent.

Indian Reuben
> Resident on Alpowa Creek.

William C. Rheems
> Bannack legislator, and assistant prosecuting attorney in Renton, Lower and Romain trial.

Bill Rhodes
> Montana miner.

James P. Romain (Romaine)
> Road agent.

John Scranton
> Newspaper editor, *The Golden Age*, Lewiston (sold to Frank Kenyon in 1863).

John Silcott
> Lewiston area ferryman.

Cyrus Skinner
> Bannack saloonkeeper; road agent.

(Judge) Alexander "Alleck" C. Smith
> Supreme court associate justice, 1st district, I.T.

(Rev.) Henry Harmon Spalding and Eliza Hart Spalding (wife)
> Presbyterian missionaries to the Nez Perce Indians, primarily 1836-47.

(Governor) Leland Stanford
> Governor of the State of California.

James Stuart
> Long-time western Montana pioneer and historical chronicler.

W.W. Thayer
> Defense attorney at the Renton, Lower and Romain trial.

(Chief) Timothy
> Nez Perce headman; owned land at the confluence of Alpowa Creek and the Snake River.

Vic Trevitt
> Lewiston resident.

(Major) Sewell Truax
> U.S. Army commander, Fort Lapwai.

William H. Wallace
> First governor of Idaho Territory; resigned in 1863 and won election as Idaho's delegate to the U.S. Congress.

John "Packer John" Welch
> Boise Basin packer.

Wesley H. Wickersham
> Lewiston lawman and Lloyd Magruder's business partner in Elk City.

James Witt
> Politically active Lewiston resident.

Bob Zachary
> Road agent.

Outlaws lynched in Lewiston, 1862—
> David English
> William Peoples
> Nelson Scott

*****

Lewiston area residents signing the 1863 petition soliciting Lloyd Magruder's political views.

The jurors at the Renton, Lower and Romain trial.

The discoverers of gold on Grasshopper Creek (Bannack), May 1862, and at Alder Gulch (Virginia City), summer 1863.

The vigilantes and road agents of the Beaverhead country.

Fictional Characters

Lemuel Akins
> South Fork ferryman.

Andy Clements
> Lewiston resident.

Jeff Grigsby
> Lewiston youth; volunteer messenger.

Frank Moran
> Packer.

Henry Pleasance
> Placer miner.

Eddie Sax
> Placer miner.

Gregory Schwartz
> California newspaper reporter.

James Spence
> Packer.

Dave Strait
> Luna House bartender.

San Francisco police officers—
> Ames
> Parker
> Welch

Lewiston, Idaho Territory
August 1863

Part One

1 Hill Beachey, a stout man of medium height and middle age, stepped off the veranda of the Luna House and into the afternoon sun, casting a hard, black shadow on the dusty street. Besides his broad-brimmed black hat, he wore a white shirt, a vest and a string tie, and on his right arm he carried, lovingly cradled, a fine Kentucky rifle. His stable manager, Chester P. Coburn, had a horse and buggy waiting. Beachey lifted himself onto the seat and carefully laid the rifle on the floorboard beside his foot. He snapped the reins lightly and set off down the street on an errand that he hoped might gain him, if nothing else, at least some peace of mind.

Five blocks away, Lloyd Magruder and his crew were loading mules for the trail that would carry them to the Beaverhead country some three hundred miles away, beyond the Bitterroot Range. The packing shed on this August day was a hot and noisy place, smelling of hay and sweat and manure and ringing with the racket of men and animals in cursing confrontation. In contrast to the blazing sun outside, it was dark—so dark that Beachey, coming with a warning for Magruder, had to pause at the door and ease the sun out of his eyes before he could get his bearings. In time he found a path through the confusion and made his way to Magruder, who was lifting a keg of whiskey into place on one side of a pack saddle while Charlie Allen balanced the load with another keg on the opposite side. The two men secured both with a diamond hitch, and then Magruder turned and noticed his friend Beachey at his side.

Beachey was carrying the Kentucky rifle, holding it tenderly with both hands. He presented it to Magruder, who seemed surprised. Take it, Beachey told him, he would need it. Still Magruder hesitated. Take it, take it, Beachey insisted. And Magruder did, with thanks. Beachey, feeling there was more to be said but doubting the use of it, turned without another word and found his way out into the blinding sun. He fanned his face with his hat, then climbed up onto the buggy seat and started back to the Luna House, the hotel that had been his place of business for these last two years.

Magruder grinned across the pack saddle at Allen, and nodded toward the street. A worrier, he said, giving a pull on the binding. Allen, who knew Beachey well, and liked him, returned the smile and slapped the mule out toward the light.

The packing sheds were built up against a bluff that separated the town flat below and the uninhabited, almost untouched sand-and-sagebrush bench above, from which one could look southeast to Craig's Mountain shimmering in the distance.[1] Craig's Mountain, which was not a mountain at all but another stair-step toward the Camas Prairie, would require the first of many climbs in Magruder's long trek from the Snake River almost to the Jefferson. It also offered a welcome view of timber, suggesting some relief from the heat once the traveler got that far. There was no timber less than twenty miles from Lewiston in any direction, and no trees at all unless one counted the willows that lined the creeks and shaded the watering holes. This was Indian country. Lewiston itself had been built on Indian land, and it was an Indian trail that would take Magruder's crew and its sixty-odd mules across the mountains to the new gold camps in what would soon become western Montana.

Magruder's goal was Bannack, where placer gold had recently been discovered in great quantities. Bannack was a good 300 miles away by trail, and Magruder figured he could get there in perhaps twenty days, averaging some fifteen miles a day. His mules would be carrying shovels, axes, flour, whiskey and other necessities to sell to the miners, who were too busy coaxing gold from the creeks of the Beaverhead to fetch their own supplies. It would be a profitable trip but a hard one. This was August 1863, near the end of the freighting season, and the route would take Magruder over the high Bitterroots where he could expect snow on the return trip in

September. Besides that, he would be short-handed. Other packers, some heading for the Salmon River country to the south, were
scrambling to get in one last haul before winter and snatching up
the available good help. That didn't worry Magruder as much as
Beachey thought it should. His experience told him that he was
likely to pick up other hands on the way. There would be more
than one traveler on the old Nez Perce Trail who would be glad to
tag along with Magruder's string and help with the animals in return for grub and companionship. Summer's end was not a good
time to ride alone on the Continental Divide, in danger not only
from road gangs but foul weather.

    In those mountains, he knew, the first flakes already could be
dancing among the firs—a hard thing to imagine here at the forks
in August, under a scorching sun. The packing sheds where
Magruder's animals were being readied for the trail, as well as the
warehouse where he kept the goods that came by steamer from
Portland, were strung out along a dusty, grimy main street that
would be ankle-deep in mud when the rains finally came. But
Magruder wasn't fooled. He knew that on days when Lewiston was
baking in the heat at seven hundred feet above sea level, the snow
might well be flying on the southern Nez Perce Trail where it was
not unusual to make camp at seven thousand feet.

    Beachey arrived back at the Luna House in time to see the
governor coming out onto the veranda carrying a newspaper in
one hand and a fan in the other. The governor, a large, bearded
man, was overdressed for the weather in a long coat, vest and tie,
and obviously uncomfortable. He waited, fanning himself vigor-
ously, as Beachey dismounted from the buggy. Governor William
H. Wallace greeted the innkeeper with a smile, raising the newspaper in salute without interrupting the rhythm of the fan. He supposed Mr. Beachey was used to this heat, he said, adding that he
wasn't and probably never would be. Nobody got used to this heat,
Beachey said. But he said a nip of whiskey could sometimes make
it more bearable, and he invited the governor to join him in the
Luna House bar. Governor Wallace declined with thanks. He had
come over only to buy a newspaper, since this was the stage stop,
and he couldn't stay. He had some documents to sign, he said, and
he had better get at it. The governor stared across the street at a
small log building which was to be the new territory's capitol. Some

men had been putting a false front on the structure but they were now lounging in the shade, talking and drinking from their canteens. Why wasn't anything being done over there? the governor wondered. Because it was too hot to work, Beachey told him. Anyway, he said, there was no hurry. The territorial government wasn't organized yet and the first legislature wouldn't meet until winter. That was true, the governor said. He certainly wouldn't care to be pounding nails in this heat.

Wallace bade Beachey goodbye, stepped into the street, and headed for the Hotel De France three blocks away, where he was living temporarily.

It rankled Beachey just a bit that the governor preferred the De France to his own hotel, and had once mentioned it to him jokingly. The governor had replied, in similar vein, that he had nothing against the Luna House but that he wouldn't feel comfortable among so many Democrats. Beachey could not deny that the Luna House bar was a hotbed of politics. But this was a political season, he pointed out, and Lewiston had become a very political town.

Beachey knew the real reason for the governor's preference, and it had nothing to do with politics. The Luna House could not match the splendor and comfort of the De France, which had opened that summer under the proprietorship of Madame Melaine Bonhore. This Parisian lady, on arriving the year before with an ailing husband, had turned up her nose at the Luna House and built what she considered a proper hotel.[2] Although Madame had found the Luna House wanting, by the standards of its time and place the Luna House was a good enough inn. It had a lobby, dining room, kitchen and bar plus living quarters on the ground floor and twenty rooms upstairs, including two that served as the town jail. Beachey had invested in a stagecoach line that ran between Lewiston and Walla Walla, and anyone arriving by that means had to stop at the Luna House first.[3]

Beachey went into the hotel, hung his hat on a rack in the lobby, and unbuttoned his vest. He took his seat on the high stool behind the registration desk, thinking to do some work on the accounts, but he could not concentrate. He worried about his friend Magruder, whom he had known since their days together in California. Magruder had told him many times there was no need to worry, but how could he help it? His friend was planning to carry a fortune in merchandise through a wilderness infested by outlaws. Then he was planning to carry back through those same dangerous mountains a fortune in gold. As he had told Magruder more than once, it was a foolhardy enterprise. On the other hand, he realized Magruder had done this many times before. He had never packed in to Bannack, to be sure, but he had taken his mule string into Florence and Warrens, in the Salmon River country, and to Elk City on the South Fork of the Clearwater, where he did a regular business. He had experienced hands to help him. He understood men and animals. He could take care of himself. And Beachey realized it was a recent nightmare that had him upset and on edge; he would have to dismiss it from his mind.

Beachey got up and went through a side door to the Luna Stables, which adjoined the hotel on the east, looking for his stable manager, Chester Coburn. He wished to tell Coburn not to unhitch the horse, for he would be using the buggy again. It was almost time to go see Magruder off across the mountains.

2 Beachey found the stableman in the dim interior of the shed repairing a piece of harness with waxed twine and a leather punch. He told Coburn he and Mrs. Beachey were going to ride up to Montgomery Street to see Magruder off. In that case, Coburn said, he would not unhitch the horse. As for himself, he was staying here in the stable where it was cooler.

Beachey understood. He liked it here too, among the earthy smells and familiar sounds that eased his tensions. Often, when he felt nervous and at odds with himself, he found some reason to come out here and have a talk with Coburn. He admired Coburn because he was comfortable with whatever he was doing. Beachey's nervous energies had him forever racing, mentally and physically, toward some distant object. Coburn took life a minute at a time, devoting his full attention to that moment's task, whether it was splicing a picket rope or tending a sick animal. He never was rushed, yet Beachey had never seen him doing nothing. Even when sitting in the little "office" up front where he kept his account book or pausing somewhere among the stalls, his hands were doing something useful, like mending harness. Beachey was overweight and hyperactive. Coburn was scrawny and deliberate. He moved with all the pace and passion of thick syrup. For a while, as they chatted about this and that in the soft light of the stable, Beachey was unworried and at peace. When it was time to go, he returned to the hotel to get Margaret and found her on a chair in a corner of the kitchen darning stockings.

He told her Lloyd was about ready to leave and that they should go now and pick up Mrs. Magruder and the kids. He also told her about the rifle. Margaret had said earlier that she saw no point in giving Magruder his favorite rifle since Magruder surely had one already. But Beachey had said this was a better one and he'd feel easier if Magruder had it with him.

Margaret took off her apron and went to get her hat. Then the two of them went out into the hot sun, stepped into the buggy, and drove the few blocks to pick up Caroline Magruder and the Magruder children, John, James and Eliza. Caroline was worried, she told the Beacheys, but then she always worried. Beachey kept his own concern to himself and he didn't mention the rifle. Caroline was a tall, angular woman—every bit as tall as her husband—with dark brown eyes and hair, and pale skin which she protected on this day with a broad-brimmed, black straw hat. She was a Pelham, the daughter of a well-do-do Arkansas sugar planter, and she trusted that this frontier settlement would not be her permanent home.[4] But while she was here she would make the best of it, and she did. The Magruders and the Beacheys drove together frequently to the dances at Fort Lapwai, a dozen miles distant, and Caroline was a favorite of the post commander, Major Sewell Truax. She had a strong sense of civic duty, and was a leader in the town's frequent, usually unsuccessful efforts to attract a school teacher. She had an air of competence about her and a store of talents that she would pull out and display now and then like heirlooms from the attic. After Madame Bonhore installed her new piano in the lobby of the De France, Caroline had startled the Beacheys by sitting down and playing the latest Stephen Foster hit, a lovely, sad song called "I Dream of Jeannie," completely from memory.

Unlike Margaret, who'd had few brushes with the finer things of life, Caroline had enjoyed a good education on the Pelham plantation in Arkansas. She had been tutored in Latin and French as well as music, mathematics and art before her marriage at age sixteen. It pleased and puzzled their men that these two such different women should get along so well together. For Margaret was older and tougher, and hardly educated at all in the formal sense, although she knew how to run a business; she and her husband had operated two hotels in California before building the one in Lewiston.

If Caroline was worried today, she gave no sign of it when the buggy arrived on Montgomery Street to see Magruder off.

Sixty mules, loaded with merchandise, were strung out along the dusty street and Magruder and his crew were making a final check of the packsaddles and bindings. It was hot, but it wouldn't be so bad when the train left town and gained some elevation. Beachey, driving his buggy past mule after mule from the back of the train to the front, realized there was no way Magruder could leave quietly, as he had once suggested. A couple of dozen people, mostly men and boys, were here already to enjoy the excitement and to give Magruder messages for friends prospecting beyond the mountains. Most packers charged for this service but Magruder didn't, thinking that he might need a favor some day from just about anyone here.

Magruder finally was ready to go. He watched the children clamber down from the buggy, then picked up Eliza, the youngest, and lifted her into the saddle of his horse, Bud, holding her there as he chatted with the Beacheys and Caroline. The crew had gathered in a knot at the head of the string, everybody joking and laughing. Caroline knew most of them and joined in the banter. Beachey, in the midst of the gaiety, felt a chilling sudden fear, approaching panic, but he tried not to show it. Instead, he reminded Magruder that he had promised to scatter some Luna House advertising posters around Bannack. Magruder replied with a wink to the others that he would expect a cut of any business from that direction. A bystander loudly declared that there wouldn't be any whiskey left for the miners when the train reached Bannack, and one of the crew called out that he sure hoped not. Eliza, growing restless, wanted down. Magruder pulled her from the horse, kissed her on the forehead, and set her on the ground.

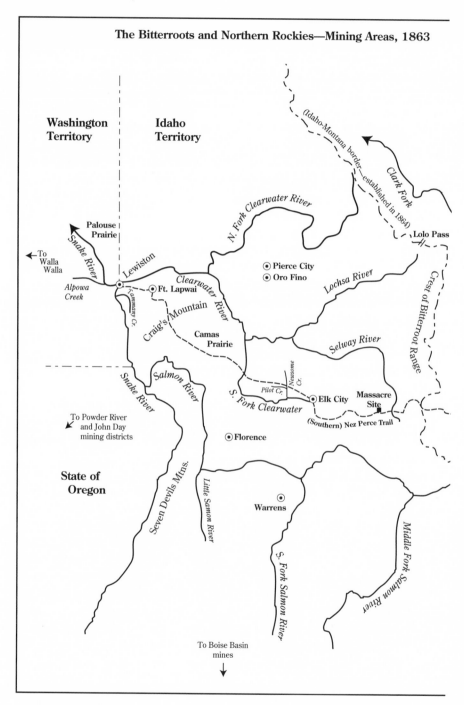

The Bitterroots and Northern Rockies—Mining Areas, 1863

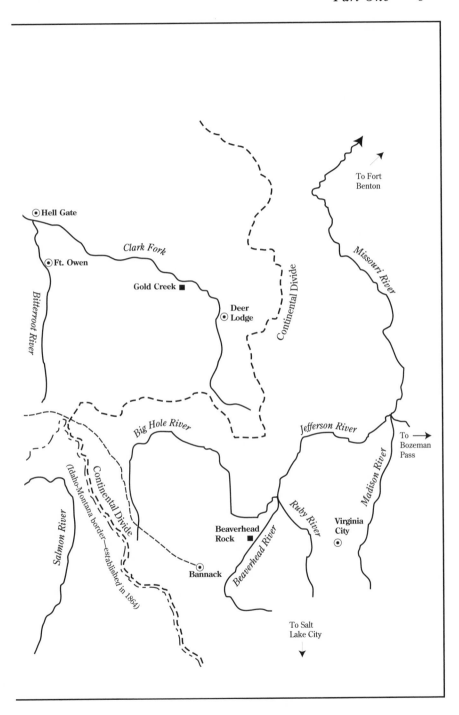

He lifted himself into the saddle, indicating it was time to go. Caroline stepped in close, turned her face up, and pulled back the brim of her hat. Magruder leaned down far enough to give her a quick kiss on the mouth, and then shook hands with Beachey. He raised his hat as a signal to move out, then noticed that Jimmy was dancing in the dirt with arms outstretched, crying for attention. Caroline lifted the boy up, Magruder set him on the horse with legs on either side of the pommel, and the string began to move. The Beacheys, Caroline and the other two children climbed back into the buggy and drove alongside the pack train as it moved up Montgomery Street heading east. The buggy, the mule train and a dozen men on horseback moved sedately along in a solemn file for three blocks. There, on the outskirts of town, Magruder pulled over, waving the others on, and stopped long enough to hand Jimmy down to Caroline. She took him without a word, the buggy turned around, and Magruder rode back to his position at the head of the string. Within minutes the men, mules and horses had left Lewiston behind and begun an easy ascent from the Clearwater River valley to the first of a series of rises that would carry them to higher, cooler country.

The Beacheys drove Caroline and the children back to their small house, and Margaret told Caroline that she should not worry about Lloyd. They both knew the men in his crew; they were all stout, competent hands who knew how to protect themselves. In all of Lloyd's trips through the mountains he had never once been set upon by thieves. Magruder and his men were safer in those woods, Margaret declared, than they would be here in town on any Saturday night. She reminded Caroline of the German saloon keeper, a man named Hildebrandt, who had been shot to death the year before as he slept behind his bar. Caroline herself could remember times when she wouldn't let the children out of the house because of the armed drunks roaming the streets.

Margaret gave Caroline a hug, and left with Beachey for the Luna House. Margaret went directly inside, but Beachey helped Coburn take care of the horse and buggy, and then sat down with him in his tiny office to play a game of cribbage. There would be a stage coming in, which meant he would be needed in the hotel soon. But for a little while, he would let the cards and Coburn's company take his mind off his foolish apprehensions.

*****

From Lewiston Magruder followed a trail that turned to the southeast, up a narrow gully and onto a broad, grassy flat well above the Clearwater.[5] The bunchgrass rustled in a light breeze. A few warm-weather clouds relieved the monotony of the August sky, and the air was cooler by about five degrees than it had been in the town. The pack train was moving slowly through a world of blue and tan— the blue of sky and distant mountains and the tan of dry grass interrupted here and there by the faint, ghostly dance of a brown dust devil. Magruder breathed deeply of the scented air, savoring the smells of leather, dust and aromatic weeds. Ahead in the distance, looking closer now, he could see Craig's Mountain, which he would reach tomorrow. Off to his right, out of sight between its high banks, the Snake River moved northward on a sluggish course, and beyond the Snake rose the mountains of eastern Oregon. To his left, Magruder could make out the valley of the Clearwater and the richly timbered mountains thrusting up on either side. In that direction, some 80 miles away, lay the mining camps of Oro Fino and Pierce City where, three years earlier at about this season, Captain E.D. Pierce's men had made the first big strike.

At a point midway across the flat the trail turned to the east, and here Magruder's outfit—well strung out to keep the dust down—proceeded parallel to but out of sight of the river the whites called Clearwater and the Nez Perce Indians called Kooskooskee, their word for the same thing. Off to the left now were the tawny, rounded buttresses that rose voluptuously from the river's edge to the high northern prairie the Indians called the Palouse. The going was easier here for Magruder's men and animals because the sun was at their backs. The wind was too, but it forced them to breathe their own dust, and a few of the men had pulled their kerchiefs up over their noses.

In spite of the August heat, Magruder felt good. It was good to be moving, good to be out of the hurly-burly of the town, good to smell the dry grass of the countryside and to soak up the familiar sounds of a pack string on the move: the whoofing breath of the animals, the monotonous tramp of hooves in the dirt, the squeak of leather, the occasional light-hearted chatter of the crew. It would be a long trip, going and coming back, but Magruder didn't mind. He had a sailor's attitude about long journeys: ignore the distance yet to go and measure only the distance traveled. Bannack lay some 290 miles southeast of Magruder's train that afternoon as it dropped down toward Lapwai Creek, but Magruder preferred to note that he had already made ten miles.

The pack train descended from the flat through a rocky gulch that opened at the bottom into a valley about a mile across and bordered on each side by gently rising hills. The valley ran roughly north and south. Through it meandered a creek that still carried water, despite the season, toward the Clearwater River a couple of miles away on the left. Where the creek joined the river was the site of the former Presbyterian mission of the Rev. Henry Harmon Spalding who had proselytized among the Nez Perce Indians, teaching them to farm. The mission had closed in 1847 after the outbreak of the Cayuse War.[6] From where Magruder was riding the old mission was out of sight. Laid out beside the creek were Indian-owned fields of stubble where wheat had been recently harvested and patches of dry, rustling corn stalks now bereft of their ears. Scattered about the valley were wooden houses and Indian lodges, fenced horses and unfenced chickens and dogs. To the right, in a clump of cottonwood trees, was Fort Lapwai, and beyond it was the Indian agency, housed in a plain wooden building with an attached shed and outhouse. The fort, now dozing in the late afternoon sun, consisted mainly of a two-story white wooden building that served as officers' quarters and troop barracks. Between it and the smaller headquarters building were horse barns, a guard house and a parade ground.

Magruder had friends here. It was his custom, when traveling this road, to spend the first night at the fort, talking politics with Major Truax and enjoying the hospitality of the Army of the Columbia. The Indian agent, Charles Hutchins, would almost certainly drop over after dinner for a glass of whiskey and the latest news from "the outside." Meanwhile, Magruder's men and animals would be fed and housed, and in the morning the whole outfit would begin the first full day's journey rested and refreshed. And a good thing, too, for ahead of them was the long, hot climb to the Camas Prairie.

Both Truax and Magruder were veterans of the Mexican War, and these occasional meetings gave them a chance to share experiences. Their wives were friends as well, and so it would not do for Magruder ever to pass by the fort without stopping. Since a sixty-mule train can't arrive anywhere without being noticed, the Indian agent was aware of Magruder's presence and, as expected, came over after dinner for a glass. Hutchins fretted about the problems the gold rush was bringing to the reservation. The major assured him that he was a worrier, reminding Magruder of Beachey, and Magruder declared that there were some things no human could stop. A gold rush, for instance, or the tides. But he sympathized and wished the agent well.[7] After an hour of talk about Mr. Lincoln's war—which the major was glad to be out of—the Indian agent began to doze off and the meeting ended. The major offered Magruder a cot in the officers' quarters but Magruder, as usual, said he'd rather bed down in the horse barn with his crew.

By sunup the next morning the pack string was making its way up the Lapwai Valley toward the foot of Craig's Mountain. After several easy crossings of Lapwai Creek, almost dry at this time of year, the party would reach the head of the valley where the foothills formed a kind of culdesac.[8] This was one of the places Beachey had in mind when he told Magruder he would need that rifle. And Magruder also was aware of the danger that might await the unsuspecting traveler arriving at this place. It was well known as a "shebang," a road gang hideaway. Magruder, out of curiosity, had once asked if any of his packers knew why it was called that. Frank Moran had said it was a corruption of the Irish word shebeen, a worthless, low-class building in which people outside the law sold unlicensed liquor. On this frontier, a shebang was pretty much that—a rundown shack where lawless men gathered to rest and connive, and where somebody running from the law could find shelter for a while.

There were several of these in the region: this one at the foot of Craig's Mountain, another near the far end of the Camas Prairie on the trail to Florence, and still another on Alpowa Creek on the road to Walla Walla.[9] People familiar with the country knew better than to pass these places unarmed. So Magruder now rode back along the string, advising his men to load their rifles and keep them handy. En route to the mines, hauling goods still untraded, he was not as tempting a target as he would be on the return trip, carrying gold. But as he had often told Beachey, the best way to avoid trouble was to expect it.

3 Henry Plummer's name was signed with a single "m," when he registered at the Luna House on July 24, 1862, the day he arrived in Lewiston.[10] In California, he had been a town marshal and there he also had killed two men—one a jealous husband who surprised him in the boudoir and the other a young fellow who had knifed him in a quarrel over a prostitute. He spent some time in San Quentin for killing the husband but was released on a bad-health pardon. After the second altercation, he walked out of the jail where he was being held for trial and headed north.

Plummer was probably twenty-eight years old when he arrived in Lewiston. San Quentin prison records describe him as five feet, eight and a half inches tall with a light complexion, light brown hair and gray eyes. He had apparently had a good education for he spoke well, with an eastern accent that set him apart from most of those he would deal with in Idaho Territory; a majority of the whites who populated the region in the wake of the gold rush were from the southern states.[11] Everyone who knew him agreed he was a great hand with the ladies. Always well-dressed and carefully groomed, Plummer (as he usually spelled it) quickly became a member of "the better element" of the town.

He didn't spend all of his time in Lewiston. He went to Florence, in the Salmon River country, to scout prospects there, but he happened to be back in Lewiston with friends the weekend the German saloonkeeper, Hildebrandt, was murdered as he slept behind his bar. And it was Plummer who happened to be in the crowd that gathered afterward to demand that something be done about this outrage. After several voices called for a vigilance committee to hunt down and hang the culprits, Plummer raised his in opposition. Stepping forward, he addressed the crowd with a sincere and reasonable air. He agreed that something ought to be done to protect law-abiding citizens from ruffians like these. But he suggested that a vigilance committee might be the wrong answer. Did the people of Lewiston really want the town to become known as a place where vigilante justice ruled? No. Let the sheriff investigate this sordid crime and make his arrests in due course. Plummer's eloquence quieted the crowd and the meeting broke up. Nobody was ever arrested for Hildebrandt's murder.

Plummer, meanwhile, had not only been making new friends in Lewiston and Florence but renewing old acquaintances from his California days. One of these was a local tough named Christopher Lower—or Lowry, as he sometimes called himself—and another was Bob Zachary, an historically shadowy character with a bad reputation. These and others whom Plummer had befriended were frequently in trouble over drunkenness and petty crimes, but Plummer's good name remained intact—at least in Lewiston. Hill Beachey was pleased to see him in the Luna House bar because wherever Plummer went others followed. The ladies found him charming. Madame Melaine Bonhore, as her new hotel was going up, gave Plummer a tour of the lobby and dining room and sought his advice on stocking the bar.

From Lewiston he went to Oro Fino but did not linger there. He went to Elk City, a busy mining camp on the South Fork of the Clearwater, on the trail from Lewiston to the Beaverhead country. He moved on again after recognizing a couple of men who had caused him trouble in California.

This time, Plummer went to Bannack in what was later to become western Montana. With him was Jack Cleveland, an old compatriot with whom Plummer had fought and made up more times than either could remember. They took rooms in separate hotels; Plummer had no wish to be identified with Cleveland if Cleveland should get into trouble. He did a little prospecting, invested in some mining claims, and, again, attracted a loose-knit band of associates all of whom he publicly disowned.

This was still Idaho Territory. The new boundaries, dividing Idaho and Montana at the Bitterroots, would not be established for another year. And the law that created the original Idaho Territory did not include a legal code, and would not until the new supreme court had got around to approving one. Thus it was that between early 1863 and the spring of 1864, there technically was no law in the territory. In the better organized mining districts, such as those at Oro Fino and Pierce City, the people made their own laws and enforced them. In the absence of an official judiciary, they established informal miners' courts. If they needed a sheriff, the miners held a meeting and elected one. In most of the mining districts, most of the time, the system worked quite well.

Bannack was a different matter. The place attracted many more gold-hungry people than the diggings on the Clearwater—so many that the creeks could not support enough claims to satisfy the throngs. Those who could not buy claims of their own turned to other means of support, and crime flourished. As a marshal in Nevada City, California, Plummer had shown a talent for organization. On the Beaverhead, he used this talent effectively to organize and direct a gang of thieves and cutthroats while conducting himself as an upstanding citizen of the town.

One of the territory's new supreme court judges was Sidney Edgerton, of Bannack and Virginia City, and later to become the first governor of Montana. It was Edgerton's daughter, Martha, who said afterward that "Henry Plummer . . . looked more like a gentleman than any man in Bannack."[12] Martha Edgerton was only thirteen years old when she met Plummer, but she never forgot how beautifully he danced.

Plummer's way with the women caused the final, fatal rupture between him and Jack Cleveland. Plummer spent some of his well-known charm on a woman who was keeping company with Cleveland, and refused to back off when Cleveland warned him away. When Cleveland found the two together in a Bannack saloon, he pulled a knife on Plummer and in the scuffle that followed he cut both Plummer and the woman, neither seriously. Others pulled them apart and Cleveland stormed out of the place, leaving Plummer and the woman wiping blood off their arms. Cleveland now had reason to believe he was doomed. Plummer assumed that Cleveland, who had a notorious temper, would find some way to get even. Each man within a couple of days became convinced that the other was out to kill him.

That was the state of things when Cleveland walked into the bar of the Goodrich Hotel for a morning drink, unaware that

Plummer was sitting with friends out of sight behind an iron stove. Several people, including a man named Perkins, were lounging at the bar and another man was sleeping in a barber chair in a corner of the room.[13] Cleveland strode over to where Perkins was standing and said he wanted the money Perkins owed him. Perkins said he had paid Cleveland everything he owed. Cleveland demanded to know whether Perkins was calling him a liar. Perkins said he wasn't calling anybody names, but neither was he going to pay anybody money he didn't owe. And Perkins moved down the bar away from Cleveland, pushing his glass ahead of him. Cleveland followed, glaring at Perkins, and again demanded money. Someone at the bar told Cleveland to go sober up and come back later. Cleveland declared that no son of a bitch was telling him what to do. He stepped back and took a gun out of his belt.

Plummer walked out from behind the stove and said to Cleveland, "I'm tired of this." Cleveland whirled around to face Plummer and Plummer shot him in the stomach. Cleveland staggered back against the bar, Plummer shot him again, and Cleveland crumpled to the floor. Two men carried Cleveland into a back room and laid him down on a cot. The man in the barber chair woke up and asked, of no one in particular, what the hell was going on.

It was agreed that Plummer had shot in self defense. Sheriff Henry Crawford by now had begun to suspect that Plummer was not all he seemed to be. If his suspicions were correct, then Plummer might soon be stalking him. After several days of brooding on this possibility, Crawford followed Plummer on foot down the main street of Bannack, ducked behind the corner of a building, and took a shot at him from some distance with a rifle. The rifle ball hit Plummer in the right arm and spun him around but did not hurt him badly.[14] Crawford lacked the nerve to finish the job, but knew better than to stay in town, and he was out of Bannack by nightfall. To the vast amusement of those who knew him best, Plummer was then elected sheriff in Crawford's place.

Meanwhile, on the other side of the mountains, two men who had been into various scrapes in California arrived in Lewiston from the John Day River country of Oregon, and became acquainted with Christopher Lower. One of these newcomers was James Romain; the other was David Renton. They and Lower quickly became a threesome, and sometime in the summer of 1863 Cyrus

Skinner was giving them orders on behalf of his boss back in Bannack.[15]

*****

The shebang, a long, low building, was almost hidden behind tall pines, but from a corner window Cy Skinner could see about half a mile down the trail. He sat on a kerosene box, watching the pack train slowly approaching from the northwest. On his lap was an army-issue telescope. Skinner put the glass to his eye and noted that the horseman at the head of the string was indeed Lloyd Magruder and that Magruder was about where he ought to be on the second day out of Lewiston. Skinner had no schooling, but he was good at keeping track of people who interested him; he knew, for instance, that Magruder almost always spent the first night on the road at Fort Lapwai, jawing with the commander and dining on government food. Skinner noted also, and without surprise, that Magruder was carrying a rifle across the saddle. He moved the glass down the line of mules. Yes, each of Magruder's crew also had his rifle out, clearly expecting trouble. There would be no trouble today, Skinner could have told them.

A couple of the other men in the hideout joined Skinner and the three of them watched in silence as the mule train approached, passed by some sixty yards from them, made a turn to the left and began the climb out of the valley, rifles still at the ready. Once the pack string was out of sight, Skinner fetched his horse from a pine grove where it had been hidden and prepared to leave for Lewiston. He would be back in a day or two, he told his companions. In the meantime they could do as they wished as long as they stayed out of sight of that mule train.

In Lewiston, Skinner would be looking for David Renton, the man he knew as Doc Howard, and Chris Lower, whom he knew as Lowry. He was used to dealing with Lower, who had worked for Plummer before, both in Lewiston and Elk City, and Lower already had agreed to this assignment. All Skinner knew about Renton, on the other hand, was that Lower liked him and had recommended him.

Lower, however, did not like Renton's partner James Romain. He considered him stupid and childish, and he had told Renton that Romain talked too much. Lower wanted Bob Zachary to join them instead but Renton had insisted on Romain because he said Jimmie would do anything he was told to do and he knew how to shoot. Lower had given in, hoping that Skinner would overrule Renton and let him have Zachary.

This decision awaited Skinner as he left the shebang for Lewiston. He spurred his horse down the valley toward Lapwai, eager to get his venture under way and trusting he would have no trouble finding his three allies.

*****

Magruder had seen the sunlight glinting off a window in a pine grove to the right of the trail but noticed that no one seemed to be hanging around. All was quiet. There would be no men there without horses, and if there were any horses, they were out of sight. Even so, Magruder and his men would keep their rifles handy until they were well out of the valley.

Where it made the turn at the culdesac, the trail crossed a small creek and snaked up toward the Camas Prairie over an ascending series of rolling hills. It was an easy climb through patches of pine separated by straw-colored meadows.

A half hour beyond the culdesac, Magruder passed word back that the rifles could be put away. Two hours later he ordered a halt, to give men and animals a rest. They were now almost at the top, in scattered pine. Ahead of them to the east, a gentle rise of a hundred yards or so led to the edge of the prairie. Behind and far below, in the afternoon sun, lay the Lapwai Valley. Beyond it, Magruder could see the yellow grassy flat he had crossed yesterday and beyond that, barely visible, the smoke of cookstoves rising above Lewiston. Of all the vistas that presented themselves in the country around the forks, this one pleased him the most.

He dismounted and walked to a familiar rocky ledge. He took out his pipe and filled it from a small cloth bag as a couple of his crew joined him, using their bandanas to wipe the dust and sweat from their faces. Somewhere out there under the smoke was the cabin where Caroline might now be cooking supper for Jimmy, John and Eliza. The town itself was out of sight under its bluff. In his mind's eye, Magruder could see not only the cabin but Montgomery Street and the packing sheds, Silcott's ferry, the Luna House and the saloons. How far away the town seemed—farther even than it would when he had put a mountain between them. Magruder tilted his hat down in front to shade his eyes against the descending sun and continued to gaze into the west, toward home, until his pipe went out. Then he knocked the ashes loose on the heel of his boot and strolled back to his horse.

The mule train followed the trail for a few more miles, and once out of the trees Magruder made camp. There was plenty of grass here for the animals and a year-'round spring that also had attracted a party of Nez Perce women and men. The Indians had spent the day digging late-harvest camas bulbs and already had a cooking fire going when Magruder's party arrived. There were about a dozen Nez Perces in this group and they apparently had been here for some time; they had put up two tepees, something they wouldn't have bothered to do for a couple of days' shelter.

Magruder, according to custom, dismounted and without pausing walked to where the Indians were lounging and talking in crackling Nez Perce. One of the men rose to meet him, and they shook hands. The Indian looked to be about Magruder's age—maybe forty years old. He wore moccasins, a pair of old army pants and a tall, wide-brimmed hat that shaded his face. His black hair, flecked with white, fell from under his hat in a pair of braids. He was bare from his waist to his head except for a large red kerchief around his neck. Gripping Magruder's hand, he smiled broadly and in English welcomed the whites to the campground. Magruder, pointing to a bulging gunny sack nearby, said he hoped the camas harvest was good this year. Very good, the other said. The man turned and spoke briefly to one of the women, who then poured some of the bulbs into her skirt and from her skirt into Magruder's extended hat. Magruder carried the hat over to one of his crew and returned with a chunk of bacon, which he presented to the woman. He explained to the man that his party would spend one night here and then move across the prairie in the direction of the South Fork. After another handshake, the formalities ended.

Magruder's crew, in the meantime, was unloading the mules, hobbling the horses, and getting the kitchen equipment unpacked. It took some time. Unloading a mule required two men; with one on each side they lifted the pack and proded the mule out from underneath. Everything the mule carried was lashed to a wooden packsaddle balanced across the animal's back. The merchandise remained on the saddle, and in the morning the whole thing would be hoisted back onto the mule and strapped down. Two experienced men could load and unload twenty mules a day if necessary. The mules, once unloaded, would be turned loose with the horses to graze on the tall prairie grass.

The crew tonight would eat fresh pork, compliments of Major Truax, with boiled potatoes and turnips washed down with black coffee. They would save the camas for emergencies since they didn't relish the starchy bulbs as much as the Indians did. Every man was expected to share in the cooking chores and later take his turn at guard duty. It was Magruder's custom to post two armed men each night to watch the animals and keep a lookout for road agents. The first man would be relieved at midnight and the second would keep the watch until dawn. Magruder frequently took the first watch because he said it gave him "a feel" for the night that let him sleep easier when midnight came.

By dusk, most of Magruder's men were asleep in their blankets under a clear sky, and there was no sound from the Nez Perces camped on the other side of the spring. The presence of the Indians would discourage any thieves who might come by, so Magruder decided to post only one watch tonight. He left Frank Creely and Jules Newburgh to finish the supper cleanup. Then, after lighting his pipe from the last coals of the cooking fire, he walked to a small hillock on the edge of camp, carrying an empty kitchen box in one hand and the Kentucky rifle in the other. He sat on the box, laid Beachey's gift across his lap, and watched the night fall.

4 Magruder awoke before sunup to the rattling sound of breakfast being cooked. Down at the spring some of his crew were washing up, filling canteens and chattering, and some others were

getting mules loaded and ready for the trail. In the direction of the tepees, all was quiet; the Nez Perces were out of sight somewhere, already engaged in the day's harvest of camas. Magruder came upon some of them later, a quarter of a mile down the trail, as he led his pack string out of camp and toward the rising sun. Three women were digging in the prairie with short-handled, hoe-like implements and tossing camas bulbs into little sacks on their hips. They were all dressed the same, in long, dark skirts, plain cotton blouses and bandanas. As the pack string approached, they straightened up and stood silently watching. Magruder touched a finger to his hat brim in response and the women bent again over their diggers. Magruder saw none of the Indian men; they and the rest of the women were apparently occupied elsewhere.

Magruder's party was traveling now toward the southeast, across rolling prairie dotted with groves of pine. Some thin, high clouds had drifted in during the night, but the day was promising. A light wind teased the prairie grass. The air was cool for August and the travel was easy over the broad, well-worn Indian trail. Magruder was glad for that. After two weeks of sleeping in a bed, his first night on the ground had left him a bit stiff. Would another night or two cure the aches, he wondered, or was he feeling his age? He was 38 now, and beginning to notice his joints. A couple of more seasons of this, perhaps, and he would give Bud a rest. He could open a store in town, he could practice law, he could go into politics, where he had some experience. There were other things he could do that would keep him closer to home and to his family— once he had banked enough money doing this.

But Caroline could have told him he was not the kind to settle down. His roots were in the clan MacGregor and the MacGregor blood had in no way been diluted by the Magruder strain. To the Magruder side he owed intelligence and his robust good health. From the MacGregors he acquired his restlessness and sense of adventure. And from someone in his Scottish background he inherited a knack for politics.

He was born July 7, 1825, on the family plantation, Locust Grove, in Montgomery County, Maryland. In 1845, on the eve of his twentieth birthday, he went to Arkansas and joined his brother Charles in Batesville. He worked there briefly as a surveyor, studied law for a while, then enlisted in the Army and went off to help fight the war with Mexico. As a private in the Quartermaster Corps, Magruder handled the mules that pulled the supply wagons and thereby learned the trade that he would later put to good use. After serving out his one-year enlistment, he joined the regular Army as a second lieutenant and in 1847 was ordered back to Batesville to recruit for his regiment.[16]

On August 10th of that year, he married Caroline Elizabeth Pelham, then sixteen years old, the youngest sister of his brother Charles's wife and the daughter of Colonel Charles Pelham, a prominent sugar cane planter. After four months of settled married life in Batesville, the lieutenant took his recruits to Mexico City and remained there until the following spring, when the war officially ended. His first daughter, Sally, was born in Batesville in July 1848.

There may never have been a better time to be a white man footloose in America, with or without a young family. Magruder found himself fresh out of the Army just as the California gold rush began. The excitement of the westward movement proved irresistible. He and a brother-in-law, Dr. James Pelham, left for California by the overland stage, planning to meet his brother, John, who had gone there earlier. They met in Marysville, a town on the Feather River of central California not far from Sutter's Mill, where the great gold strike had been made the year before. Marysville, they were told—and had every reason to believe—would become the prime metropolis of California. The brothers wintered there and in the spring Magruder sent for his wife and daughter.

In California, Magruder tried his hand at mining but didn't do well. He turned to the mercantile business, buying goods to sell in the mining camps, and invested his profits in Marysville real estate. His timing was bad, for Marysville, like other mining towns of the time, began to decline as the easy gold ran out and miners started leaving for new diggings. Magruder moved his family to the small but promising mining town of St. Louis in the Sierra Nevada and opened a store. He was making money again when fire destroyed the town and wiped out the store and all his stock. He decided to get out of the retail business, move back to Marysville, and enter politics. He ran for the office of Yuba County clerk, and won. He also began practicing law and served as a justice of the peace. He made friends easily and became a popular figure in the community. At the summit of his career in California, he was a prominent member of the Assembly, the lower house of the California legislature. And during those years he and Caroline had three more children—John Carter, James Pelham and Eliza Lloyd.[17]

It was during this time also that Magruder bought an interest in a newspaper, later described as "very Democratic," and he became not only part owner but editor. The paper did so well that the owners decided they should remodel and improve their offices. One of the plasterers hired for the job was a young fellow named James Romain. He had learned the trade in New York and now made an occasional living at it in California while looking for something better. Romain and Magruder became acquainted, but only briefly, and neither had reason to believe that he would ever see the other again.

In the late 1850s, reports were received of gold strikes far to the north—in the mountains of western Canada, as well as on the east side of the Cascade Range and in the upper Columbia River country of Washington Territory. Sizeable numbers of California miners, along with men from western Oregon and Washington, flocked into the new gold fields.

Magruder had been in Marysville twelve years when rumors began drifting down about other new gold explorations in the north—this time in the more easterly parts of Washington Territory. The rumors were vague but enticing. The placer mining in California, the cheap kind of mining that anyone could do, was drying up. By 1860, the gold claims of the Feather River district were pretty well worked out and a new gold rush—someplace, anyplace—was waiting to happen. By the winter of 1860, rumors were confirmed: a prospecting party led by Captain E.D. Pierce, another Mexican War veteran, struck gold at a place called Canal Gulch on Oro Fino Creek in the Clearwater range of Washington Territory. The mountains remained inaccessible in winter, so nothing could happen until spring. For Californians hungry for that once-in-a-lifetime bonanza, the wait proved excruciating. Magruder caught the fever, but Sally was in school now, his family was settled, and he had business and political commitments to honor.

By February, some prospectors already were moving north toward Portland, some overland by way of Red Bluff, Weed and Yreka, some by boat out of San Francisco. At Portland, the *Times* reported great prospects in the mountains to the east. One of the paper's editors, Alonzo Leland, received the word personally from a friend of his who had been a member of the Pierce party. That was Wilbur Bassett, who claimed to have panned the gold that started it all. Bassett, Pierce and several others returned from the Clearwater just before winter set in to buy supplies, and Bassett told Leland there was enough gold in those mountains to keep five thousand men busy for ten years. Leland's reports in the *Times*, picked up by the *Oregonian*, the *Sacramento Daily Union* and the *San Francisco Bulletin*, among others, went a long way toward emptying the mining camps of California.

By March, Portland teemed with men restless to continue on. Seven hundred California prospectors disembarked from a single ship in early March, all intending to head in the same direction: east, up the Columbia.

Marysville, once touted to be the next great metropolis of California, shrank fast. Magruder, dividing his time between business in Marysville and politics at the state capital in Sacramento, watched the exodus with dismay. He was thinking no longer of a political career in the Golden State, which he was beginning to find dull. What beckoned now was the north country and the prospect of adventure on a new frontier. The MacGregor blood was rising in him. Caroline recognized the signs—his impatience with the children, his sudden lack of interest in the legislature, his ravenous hunger for news from the north. She wrote to her father in Batesville, saying that if Lloyd insisted on leaving for the north, she might decide to return with the children to her former home. The reply, arriving some weeks later, was that they all would be welcomed there, of course. But Colonel Pelham told her that if she did decide to let her husband go on this adventure alone she might later have cause for regret. Since her father did not elaborate, she found his reply no help at all.

By the end of March, the rush to the new mines began. A great cavalcade of bedazzled gold hunters, some accompanied by their wives and children, traveled by boat, by wagon, on foot and horseback, overland or by sea to Washington Territory. Most commonly, gold hunters proceeded up the Columbia into the interior, via Portland to The Dalles, to Walla Walla, and from there on into the

Clearwater Mountains. Large mining camps sprang up at Oro Fino and Pierce City. Somebody found gold on the South Fork of the Clearwater and suddenly Elk City arose.

Alonzo Leland caught the bug himself, abandoned his desk at the *Times*, and struck out for Oro Fino.[18]

In June, Magruder began seeing reports of a new town flourishing at the confluence of the Snake and Clearwater rivers. By midsummer, he decided that he would go there in the following spring and check out the possibilities. The thousands of people in the new mining camps would need regular supplies of tools, food and clothing, and Magruder had some experience in that line. He also understood, from his years on the Feather River, that there was more to be made serving the miners than being one. As he explained to Caroline, he could supply the mining camps from a warehouse in Lewiston, and the family would be safely and comfortably at home in a good-sized town. In fact, he said, in another year there would probably even be a school there.

Caroline felt quite relieved. Lewiston sounded not much different from Marysville, and if the place was going to amount to anything, the Magruders would be there to take advantage of it. She wrote to her father, informing him that Lloyd would travel to Washington Territory in the spring and that the family, with the possible exception of Sally, would follow later if the prospects there looked good. Sally was fourteen now, and Caroline thought it might be better if she stayed in school; she could live with Charles' family. Colonel Pelham wished he could leave everything and go with them, he said, but he had a plantation to run.

Magruder bought a string of mules, and he and a friend, Wesley Wickersham, started north from Marysville in company with several other parties, driving their mules over the Siskiyou Mountains into Oregon. They proceeded north to The Dalles and from there eastward to Lewiston.[19]

It was July 1862. Magruder and Wickersham, scouting out the region, discovered that Oro Fino and Pierce City already were declining, and that the best prospects now were on the South Fork of the Clearwater River at Elk City and on the Salmon River to the south. Magruder decided to establish his store in Elk City, which was only a few days travel from Lewiston on the trail to Florence and Warrens on the Salmon. He and Wickersham took on a third investor, a man named Clindinger, and opened the Elk City store that summer. Magruder wrote to Caroline in Marysville, instructing her to bring the family, except for Sally, to Lewiston. They would live there, he said, and he would supply the Elk City store out of a Lewiston warehouse.

For the Magruders, Lewiston had more to offer than simply economic opportunity. Hill and Margaret Beachey, with whom they had become fast friends in Marysville, had moved to Lewiston the year before, and Caroline could look forward to a joyous reunion. Leaving Sally with the Pelhams, Caroline and the other three children traveled by stagecoach down the Sacramento Valley to San Francisco, and from there by sea to Portland. Coming up the Columbia and Snake, the weather was fair and the rivers were still high enough that except for short portages around the treacherous Cascade Rapids and Celilo Falls, the family travelled all the way to Lewiston by steamboat. Lloyd, meanwhile, built a temporary shelter which the family could occupy until fall. He also purchased more mules, harness and packsaddles, and rented a canvas-covered building on Montgomery Street for use as a warehouse. He had put in a stock of tools, clothing, flour and tobacco and had begun packing his merchandise to the mining camps.

Before the summer was out, Magruder packed into Oro Fino, Pierce and Elk City as well as Florence and Warrens in the Salmon River country to the south. Having acquired a substantial herd of mules, he developed a good business relationship with suppliers on the lower Columbia, and had won the friendship and respect of his fellow townsmen. When fall arrived, Magruder was able to build a real house for his family about three blocks from Beachey's hotel, in the teeming heart of a community bursting with energy and bright with promise. Magruder was confident that he had come to exactly the right place at just the right time.

On July 27, 1862, three days after Magruder rode into Lewiston, a group of prospectors travelling north from Denver camped for the night beside a creek in the Beaverhead drainage. It was hot, dry sagebrush country thick with grasshoppers. The next day, as usual, the men grabbed their gold pans and tested the gravels. They found loose placer gold in several places and by evening realized they had struck it rich.[20]

By early September, some seventy miners were working rockers and sluice boxes on Grasshopper Creek and its tributaries. By fall, when mining halted for the winter, the new diggings had yielded some $700,000 in gold. As cold weather approached in that high country, the miners built huts, cabins and a saloon, and called the town Grasshopper. By spring they had changed the name to Bannack.[21]

5 On the Camas Prairie, the westerly breeze had turned suddenly cool. It was afternoon. The camas diggers were far behind, and the pack train moved monotonously along the broad trail toward the valley of the South Fork. To Magruder, the cold touch of the breeze on his cheek foretold a change in the weather. He turned and gazed into the west, trying to read the sky for signs of storm. Blue tree-clad hills formed a ragged border on the western rim of the prairie, and above the hills Magruder could see dark thunderheads forming. Above and to the south and east, the sky was still a brassy blue.

Magruder felt his spirits rise. He could use a weather change, or anything else that might break the monotony of this long, plodding trek across the broad and undulating prairie. He'd had too much time to think, and for a man approaching middle age with so much yet to do, that was no great comfort.

With surprising speed, the clouds mounted higher into the sky. The wind freshened. Behind him, Magruder could hear his crew calling to one another and making bets as to what this weather change might bring. A flock of small birds scudded across the grassy plain as though hurrying to some rendezvous. Within moments, the whole sky was dark and Magruder, anticipating rain, fumbled in his saddlebag for a slicker. But there was no rain. Instead, the wind changed suddenly to southwesterly and tiny white pellets, pinhead size, began to appear on the chocolate brown head and neck of his horse. The hailstones became larger, like white peas falling, and Magruder could hear them hitting his hat and feel them against his hands and wrists. Hailstorms were not unusual on the prairie in August and of no great concern. Magruder preferred hail to rain because it made less trouble, and he was rather enjoying this brief respite from the late summer heat.

The hailstones continued to fall and to grow. They were as big as cherries when one of Magruder's men rode up to the front of the string and suggested a halt. Why? Magruder wanted to know; men and animals were going to be hit by hail whether moving or standing still. The hailstones were becoming a cannonade. Magruder looked around for some sign of shelter but he could see no trees within a couple of miles, only flat land and bunchgrass. On the trail and between the grass clumps, the ground was white and inches deep in melting ice. Magruder could turn off the trail and head for that grove of pine trees some two miles away. But he was apt to find when he got there that the hail had stopped and he would have taken the pack train four miles out of its way for nothing. Or he could continue on into the storm, which by now was hurling the stones at the right front of the train, and hope for the best. While Magruder was pondering his next move, the lead mule, Susannah, made the decision. She stopped in her tracks, turned her rump to the wind and stood there, head down. The mule behind did the same. Two of the men rode up and tried to turn the mules back, but it was too late; the whole string had stopped, turned away from the storm, and were as motionless as statues. Magruder called out to leave them alone. The pack animals had instinctively adopted the only shelter they could find, and he would accept that. Once the reins were released, the horses did the same. The men dismounted and crouched down on the ground between the animals, their only shield now against hailstones as big as robins' eggs.

No one traveled in the mountains these days without a gold pan, and several of the men had lashed theirs to the tops of the packs where they could get at them quickly. Now, under the onslaught of the hailstones, the pans became tin drums, creating an earsplitting racket that amplified the fearsomeness of the storm. To Magruder and his men, huddled on the ground under their ample hats, the pelting and the banging seemed to go on forever.

Then it stopped. For a little while, the men and animals remained motionless in a mottled white and silent world. Magruder stood up and examined his horse. He brushed the melting white stuff off Bud's rump and shoulders, felt his head, and found no damage. Magruder and the other men checked the mules and their loads, laughing and shouting in relief and wonderment over this outburst of nature. The mules, willing once again to be led, reformed the train. Men and animals soon moved down a path now solid white between the yellow and white of smashed grass and hail.

Within a half hour, the gray-black sky had turned to blue and the hail was melting quickly under a warming sun. Magruder, who had never seen a hailstorm quite this severe, was thinking now he wouldn't have missed it for the world. It seemed to have changed everybody's mood; from behind him Magruder could hear more joshing and hilarity than he had heard since leaving Lewiston. Even Bud seemed to be stepping more lively than before.

*****

In late afternoon, the pack train arrived at an outcropping of rock and scattered pine that marked the southeastern edge of the Camas Prairie. From here the trail wound downhill through increasingly thick pine and fir, across meadows mean with mosquitos and, finally, down still farther to the valley of the South Fork. The river at this point was some thirty yards from bank to bank. There stood two poles, one on each side of the river near the water's edge, linked by a steel cable running about forty feet above the river. The pole on Magruder's side was braced by a guy wire secured to a large stump. A similar guy wire on the other side was wrapped around the base of a tree. The cable between the poles, combined with the river's current, provided the power that ran Lemuel Akins' ferry. The ferry itself and the shack Akins lived in were on the other side—usually the case, as Magruder had found out in his travels.

At the edge of the river the pack train halted and Magruder, cupping his hands to his mouth, called out the traditional signal: "Ho, the ferry!" The river's chuckling roar almost drowned him out and he had to call again before Akins appeared on the opposite bank and waved. Across the swiftly moving river, Magruder saw Akins untie the ferry, jump on board and fiddle with certain ropes. Then the ferry was moving toward him across the river. It was attached by a line to the overhead wire and it looked like what it was: a wooden raft about thirty feet long and ten feet wide with a railing on either side and a board four feet high across each end. When the ferry reached the shore, Akins jerked on a cord and dropped the forward board onto the sand. It now served as the gang plank. Magruder nudged Bud in the flanks and the horse splashed through shallow water and nervously tapped his foot a few times on the board. Magruder had to urge him across the board and onto the ferry. Then he dismounted and helped his crew coax four mules onto the ferry behind Bud. Akins pulled up the board, then turned to greet for the first time in several weeks the good customer he knew as "Gruder."

Akins was a skinny, toothless little man, probably in his sixties, with sparse gray hair under a shapeless hat and a permanent, tobacco-stained white stubble. He had tried prospecting without much luck and a year ago had spent every ounce of dust he had, plus a few ounces of Gruder's, to buy this ferry. Magruder had been glad to help because his business needed the crossing and he knew Akins to be honest and reliable. The ferry's first owner had been willing to sell out cheap after a nasty accident that killed five loaded pack mules and almost killed him. The overhead cable had broken during the spring runoff and the ferry had drifted into some rapids and swamped, throwing the mules overboard. Akins had fixed the cable, repaired the ferry, and now earned more money carrying miners than most of the miners were making in the gold fields.

Akins tightened one rope and loosened another on the upriver side. That allowed the current to push the shoreside end of the craft downstream by about four feet, putting the ferry at an angle to the current, which then began pushing it along the cable toward the other side of the river. Depending on how he angled his boat, Akins could make the current work for him in either direction. Magruder had seen the same system in operation in California and on the Clearwater at Lewiston, where John Silcott ran a similar ferry to Akins'.

The ferryman was a gratifying source of news because he shared gossip and mining information with customers traveling both ways. As the current nudged the ferry across the sparkling river, Magruder gave Akins the latest news of the forks, and Akins filled Gruder in on the people he'd seen and most of what they'd told him. For one thing, there had been new gold strikes east of Bannack, in the Stinking Water country, and for another, Bannack had a new sheriff by the name of Henry Plummer. Magruder told Akins he should thank his maker that he wasn't doing this in Lewiston in the August heat. Akins, who was from Ohio and a Northern sympathizer, asked for the latest news of the war and Magruder filled him in as best he could on the basis of news reports that were sometimes two weeks old. On the far side of the river, Akins dropped the end-board and Magruder walked his horse off the ferry. The mules followed, and Magruder prepared to make camp for the night while Akins switched his ropes around and started back for another load. It took an hour and a half to move the whole pack string from one bank to the other, after which Akins went into his shack for a pencil and a piece of paper. His rate was one dollar to cross a loaded pack animal and a dollar and a half to cross a man and horse. As Akins figured it, Magruder owed him seventy-two dollars. Magruder paid in gold dust weighed out on a scale in Akins' shack. The charge was fair, and about what he would have paid at any ferry crossing in the region.

Anyone who knew the country well enough could ford the South Fork upstream from here, and avoid paying Akins' fee. Magruder had done that a couple of times while the ferry was out of commission, but since he had helped Akins buy the ferry he thought he ought to patronize it. Besides, he liked Akins and looked forward to crossings like this one and the gossip that went with them.

One traveler who had used the upstream ford a few days earlier was Cy Skinner on his way from Bannack to the culdesac. Skinner wasn't trying to avoid the fee; he simply preferred not to be seen by any more people than necessary. So Akins, chatting with Magruder about all the customers he'd carried lately, never mentioned Skinner.

It wouldn't have mattered; Cy Skinner's name meant nothing to Magruder. Henry Plummer's name did, however, and Magruder told Akins that evening that he found it hard to imagine Plummer as a frontier sheriff. He had known him at Lewiston as a smooth-talking, obviously educated professional gambler. But Akins, who seldom forgot anything he heard, said Plummer had been a marshal in Nevada City, California, before moving north. But he sure didn't look like a lawman, Akins agreed. He was a small fellow, even delicate looking, and he talked like a school teacher. On the other hand, he had heard that Plummer killed a couple of men in California. You can't always tell about people, Akins said, slipping a pinch of chewing tobacco into his cheek.

Magruder's men unloaded the animals and turned them loose to graze in a meadow some distance above the river, and Magruder asked Akins to join them for supper. The evening was cool under a clear sky and for some reason the mosquitos were no great nuisance on this side of the river. Jules Newburgh had a fiddle, which he kept in a canvas bag, and after supper he pulled it out and played some reels and jigs. Akins, unable to resist the music, jumped up and started to dance. Magruder joined him after a few turns, and before long every man was on his feet, dancing and whooping as the fiddler scraped away and the cooking fire burned down. The party ended when Newburgh pleaded exhaustion and put the fiddle away. As darkness fell, the men picked out their beds and rolled into their blankets. Magruder asked Charlie Allen to take the first watch and said he would take the second. He posted Allen on the meadow above them where he had a clear view of the trail and the ferry. Then he walked Akins down to the ferryman's shack and poured each of them a shot of brandy out of a small leather flask.

They talked about mines and miners and mules and the river, and Akins expressed great pleasure in the evening's company. As Magruder started back to his own bedroll, Akins asked him to linger a moment. He wanted to show him something he would need to know, just in case. Just in case what? Magruder asked him, but Akins didn't answer. The ferryman lit a kerosene lantern and led Magruder out of the shack and down the riverbank a few yards. It was almost dark now, and there was no moon yet. Akins laid his hand on a large boulder about hip high, some ten feet up the bank from the river that was muttering aimlessly below them. Then, handing the lantern to Magruder, Akins bent down and turned over a flat rock, exposing a hole in the ground about ten inches across. Akins bent down on his knees and thrust one arm into the hole almost as far as the armpit and pulled out a one-quart mason jar. Inside this jar, he said, was his store of gold. He daren't keep it in the shack, he said; he would surely be robbed. And if anything happened to him he wanted Magruder to know where it was. He put the jar back in the hole and replaced the flat rock. Remember to look for the big boulder, he told Magruder; the hole was right behind it.

Magruder understood. He would remember, he said. As they walked back to the shack, he asked Akins who ought to have the gold. Well, Akins said, that would be for Magruder to decide; he didn't care since he had no kin that he knew how to find. Magruder had a wife and kids; he could use the gold. Then Akins spat a stream of tobacco juice and laughed. Magruder could buy Jules a new fiddle, he said happily. The one he had was putting out a lot of bad notes.

6 Madame Melaine Bonhore, in starched white blouse and black skirt, walked across the red-carpeted lobby of the Hotel De France, heading for the kitchen in search of her chef, Baptiste Escude. Since dinner was about over, she was not surprised to find him instead in the bar. He was still wearing his apron and chatting with three young men who looked as though they would have been more comfortable in one of the town's other hotels. She caught Escude's eye from the doorway and he joined her in the lobby. She told him, in French, that he was wanted at one of the tables where a couple of obviously distinguished guests had just finished dinner. The two gentlemen from Boise City wished to compliment the chef on his *filet de veau*. But before sending him into the dining room, she advised him to change his apron. These people were important looking, and she hoped they would stay on for a few days. She also asked the chef who those young men were at the bar. She recognized one of them as a town rowdy who had caused trouble there before, but the other two were strangers. A couple of fellows from up the Clearwater, he told her, who had been prospecting and had their fill of it. Stopping at Lewiston en route to the coast. Portland, they had told him. She would be glad to see all three of them go, she said; one of them was too young to be drinking anyway.

Escude went quickly to the kitchen, donned a clean apron, and presented himself to the two gentlemen, who were having cigars with their after-dinner cognac. They told him they had never tasted better roast veal and said they were not surprised to learn that he had developed his talents in the kitchens of Paris. Escude accepted the accolades with a charming mixture of pleasure and humility. He hoped the gentlemen would return for dinner tomorrow evening and taste his young salmon with caper sauce. It was quite probable that they would. And in the meantime, could the chef tell them where in town was the best place to go for political conversation?

Escude knew where to send them—to the Luna House—but he dared not. So he said they could do very well without even leaving the building. Just cross the lobby to the bar, where they could be assured an evening of lively political talk with the De France's friendly clientele.

The two took the chef's advice and adjourned to the bar. They were not encouraged by the three rough-looking young men who were leaving as they went in, but once inside they found a dozen or so people standing or sitting and talking about everything from the price of gold to Lincoln's war in the East. And politics. No one needed to look far for political conversation in Lewiston, the capital of Idaho Territory, in the election year of 1863. Lincoln had signed the bill creating the territory earlier in the year, and that meant there would be much political jostling and maneuvering as the new territorial government was formed. For one thing, the territory was entitled to a delegate in congress. He would have no vote but some influence. And he would be first in line to become a senator should statehood follow.

The visitors introduced themselves as R. P. Campbell and John M. Cannady and said they hoped to find out who the leading contenders might be in this end of the territory. They heard several names. Captain John Mullan, who had built the military road from Fort Benton to Walla Walla, was interested. So was John Scranton, a real estate agent and editor of Lewiston's weekly paper, *The Golden Age*. Some suspected that the territory's new Republican governor, William H. Wallace, had his eye on it. Local Democrats thought highly of one Lloyd Magruder, a prominent merchant and packer who had been a member of the California legislature before coming north. But Magruder hadn't expressed any interest, and he was out of town a lot. Someone said the new delegate, no matter who he was, would probably be from the northern part of the territory, since that was where most of the voters were. True for the moment, one of the visitors said. But he observed that new gold strikes in the Boise Basin were causing a population shift from north to south. By November, when the votes were counted, the north's current advantage could be diminished. On one aspect of it, all agreed: the big question was the Civil War, and how that would affect Democratic and Republican fortunes here and elsewhere in the West.

As the gentlemen from Boise City prepared to leave, the bartender told them the story of the hotel guest who had arrived not long ago on a steamboat that also was carrying an accused murderer. The traveler had to watch with horror as the poor fellow was dragged off the boat by a lynch mob and hanged from the end of a beam pushed out through one of the windows of the Luna House. Recounted with marked disapproval, the tale had the effect of establishing the speaker's devotion to law and order while leaving a vague distaste for the other hotel. Why should that surprise anybody, one of the gentlemen said. This wasn't San Francisco or Salt Lake City, after all.

The two left the bar. It had been an interesting hour, they agreed, but they didn't yet have all the political talk they wanted.

*****

Hill Beachey, looking up from his register at the Luna House, saw three men—two men and a boy, really—come in the door and walk through the lobby toward the bar. Later, he remembered only that they had been talking among themselves, a bit loudly, about leaving the next day for Portland. Beachey's bartender, Dave Strait, recalled later that the three had ordered whiskey and inquired about the road west, saying they were on their way to the coast.

Other customers of the Luna House bar that evening included the usual mixture of merchants, professional men and miners plus a couple of gentlemen from Boise City—important people, judging by their clothes—who were expressing an interest in the coming territorial election. They talked politics with other customers for an hour or two, mentioning the names they had heard at the Hotel De France. James Witt, who knew almost everyone in town, said his personal choice would be Lloyd Magruder, if Magruder was interested in running as a Democrat. For the first time, they heard Hill Beachey's name. Beachey would be a strong Democratic candidate, several thought. Beachey himself, appearing in the bar a bit later, said he'd be tempted if he didn't have a business to run. As it was, he hoped Magruder would try for it even though he and Magruder didn't see eye to eye on some things. Beachey and Magruder had often talked politics, but if others wanted to know how Magruder felt about such things as secession, slavery and the war, they would have to find out for themselves.

Jim Witt, who by now had been in the Luna House bar for several hours, was urging that something be done quickly to feel out Magruder. Problem was, he was out of town and not expected back until near the end of September. Then write him a letter, Jim Haygood suggested. Mail it to Elk City, where Magruder had a store, and ask him to respond by express. Witt liked that idea. He proposed to call a meeting of Nez Perce County Democrats to draft a letter of support which he would mail to Elk City. Magruder would be there soon and would surely spend at least a couple of days before packing in to the high mountains. No point in calling a meeting, Andy Clements said. Why not just write the letter here and now, and then get some others to sign it? Witt would be glad to do it, he said, and went out to the front desk for some paper, a pen and a bottle of ink.

He and Clements and Haygood sat down at a table in the bar and ordered a cup of coffee. Witt sat for a few moments rubbing his cheek and scratching his head, then started to write. He wrote that "your friends" in Nez Perce County would welcome Magruder's positions on current politics and wanted to know whether he would be available to run for the Democratic Party nomination for delegate to congress. Several in the bar signed it on the spot, and Haygood said he would get more signatures tomorrow before putting it in the mail. Witt invited the gentlemen from Boise to sign if they wished, but both declined. Campbell said he couldn't sign the letter in good conscience since he had never met Magruder and thus could hardly qualify as "your friend." Cannady said he would rather not sign it since he was thinking of seeking the nomination himself. But he said that if he decided not to run, Magruder seemed to be the kind of candidate he could support. Cannady told the group he realized that Magruder had many friends here; but if Magruder showed no interest in the office, then perhaps Magruder's friends might be interested in his views on the issues of the day. And Cannady proceeded to share those views with the company in the Luna House bar.

As the meeting was breaking up, Campbell asked Dave Strait if it was true about the man getting off the boat and then being hanged from a window of this hotel. Well, partly true, Strait said, but it was three men. And they didn't get off the boat here, they arrived by stage. And they weren't hanged from a window of the Luna House but from a makeshift gallows a block away. Otherwise, what they'd heard at the De France was a true story—as true as anything they were likely to hear at the De France. Strange how a tale like that gets started, Cannady remarked amid the laughter, but the bartender thought it was not so odd, really. It could have happened at the Luna House, he pointed out, since this was the only building in the block with a second-story window.

*****

For John Silcott, the ferryman, it had been a slow morning, and he was pleased to see two men and a teen-aged boy lead their horses aboard his ferry on the Lewiston side of the Clearwater. One of the men told him they were headed for the coast and unfamiliar with the country west of here. Silcott said he also owned the ferry that would take them across the Snake River some six miles to the west, and that he had a package deal: he would charge them once for both crossings.

As the ferry followed its cable across the wide river, Silcott tore three tickets off a roll and gave one to each of his three passengers. Those tickets would pay their way across the Snake downriver. From there, he said, the road went up Alpowa Creek and thence across some rolling hills to Walla Walla. He advised them to ride the first few miles with caution; one of the road gangs had a shebang some distance up the creek not long ago and might have still. He took care to collect a total of six dollars before lowering the splashboard on the other side of the river. As the three rode out of sight down the north bank of the Snake, Silcott wondered how they had come into this country. As he said later, they should have known about the road to Walla Walla since almost nobody arrived here from any other direction.

7 Cy Skinner had found no sign of Renton, Lower or Romain in Lewiston, where he was supposed to meet them. He needed to tell them that Magruder had passed the shebang at the culdesac en route to the Camas Prairie. Where could they have gone? According to the plan, the three were to follow Magruder through the mountains to Bannack, separately make contact with him there, and arrange to join his crew for the return to Lewiston. Once they had his gold, they were to return directly to Bannack and check in at Skinner's saloon. If they were already on the trail behind Magruder, Skinner would have met them. Maybe they had decided to go to Elk City ahead of Magruder and wait for him there. That made no sense at all to Skinner, but he decided that tomorrow he would start for Elk City anyhow, just to find out. In the meantime, he thought it wouldn't hurt to poke around a little. He went into the Luna House bar, ordered a drink, and asked if anyone had seen some friends of his. He described them, and the bartender recalled that a man he knew as Lowry had been in the place the night before with two others, and that Lowry had been talking about going to Portland.

In that case, Skinner said, he wouldn't plan to see them soon. He finished his drink and left the bar wondering what was going on. He rode down to the ferry crossing, thinking to ask the ferryman whether he had carried the three across the Clearwater, but when he arrived he found that Silcott and the ferry were on the other side. Skinner decided not to wait. The other three wouldn't be going to Portland; Lower must have been drunk. So Skinner spent that night in Beachey's hotel and the next morning rode out of town toward Lapwai en route to the culdesac.

After a night in the shebang at the culdesac, Skinner rode up to the Camas Prairie, using a route that would take him some distance to the east of Magruder's pack train, and traveled as far as the South Fork of the Clearwater. He made good time, unencumbered by pack horse or mule. To avoid Lem Akins, whom he considered the worst gossip in the district, he stayed out of sight of the river until reaching a ford a mile upstream from the ferry. He splashed across the South Fork there and spent the night in a pine grove that provided some cover while giving him a good view of the river as far downstream as Akins' shack. He broke camp early the next morning and reached Newsome Creek that afternoon. As Skinner was scouting out a place to camp, Magruder was leading his pack string down the hill to the South Fork and the approach to Akins' ferry.

The next morning, as Magruder was getting his pack train under way, Skinner was on the trail from Newsome Creek to Elk City, which he reached that evening. He checked in at one of the town's two hotels, washed up and ate a hearty supper. He started back upstairs to bed, thought better of it, and instead walked across the street to the livery stable where he had left his horse. He told the boy that he had changed his mind and he would take the saddle with him after all. He took it off the rail where it sat with several others and carried it back across the street and upstairs to his room. Skinner was a careful man. In the language of a later time, he might have been called paranoid. He had robbed a few people in his day and more than one renegade had tried to rob his saloon in Bannack. He had lost a good saddle once, although not as good as this one, out of carelessness. Since then it had been his custom, when leaving his horse with someone overnight, to keep the saddle with him. This time, in his eagerness to get a room and supper, he had left it in the stable. A mistake, he realized later. Now that he had it in his hotel room, he felt better and would sleep well. He took off his boots, lay down on the bed without getting undressed, and fell asleep.

In the morning, he went downstairs to the lobby of the hotel to inquire about some friends of his. Nobody was around, not even a room clerk. Skinner went to the desk and slapped his palm down on the bell. There was no response. He picked a newspaper up off one of the lobby's plain wooden chairs and sat down with the still-folded paper on his lap. He sat looking out the window at the shabby, early-morning street, occasionally slapping the paper nervously against his knee.

Somebody rode by in the street, kicking up a little puff of white dust. Then Skinner heard squeaking, scraping sounds and saw that the room clerk was at last behind the desk. Skinner walked over and said he was trying to locate three friends who may have been through here recently. They were two men, Chris Lowry and Doc Howard, and a youngish looking man named Jim Romain. The room clerk couldn't recall any such. But he said there was another hotel in town as well as a half dozen saloons, and advised Skinner to ask around. He did, but found no one who could recollect seeing any of Skinner's three friends. Skinner returned to his hotel, checked out, and walked across the street to the livery stable, carrying his saddle over one arm and his saddlebags over the other. He paid a stable hand two dollars for overnight care and feeding of his horse, and rode out of town.

Magruder, meanwhile, had put Newsome Creek behind him and was leading the mule train into higher, rougher country. He was on a wide and well-worn trail, one the Indians had used for generations in their periodic travels to and from the buffalo country east of the Bitterroots. There was game in the pine forests and fish in the streams—trout the year around and salmon in season—and in the mountain meadows that lay cupped in the valleys there was good grass for horses and cool spring water. Here and there along the creeks, Magruder came across miners working their claims or the signs of old claims that hadn't paid off.

The day before at Pilot Creek, Magruder had sent the train on ahead while he paused to visit with a couple of men who had worked for him as packers in the past. Henry Pleasance was shoveling gravel into one end of a twelve-foot sluice box and Eddie Sax was pouring in water by the bucketful out of the creek. The water would wash the gravel downhill through the length of the box and the heaviest material would sink and get caught in the riffles on the bottom. In the stuff lodged against the riffles, if they were lucky, Pleasance and Sax might find some flecks of gold.

So far they hadn't found much, they told Magruder. Sax was trying to talk Pleasance into giving up here and trying their luck at Bannack, but Pleasance didn't want to move so late in the season. So they would probably stick it out on this claim until winter. Magruder suggested they look him up in the spring; he would need hands and they could pack into the Beaverhead country with him. They'd think about it, they said, getting back to work. Magruder turned Bud around and caught up with the train as it wound through dry grass and scrub pine toward Newsome Creek.

Lawrence Bacon, carrying the express between Lewiston and Elk City, caught up with the Magruder party a couple of days later.[22] Bacon, along with about a hundred other people in Nez Perce County, knew about the letter Jim Witt had written and that Jim Haygood had mailed to Elk City. Since Bacon did not sort the mail, he could only assume that he was carrying that letter. Therefore, when he overtook Magruder on the trail, he could not promise that the packer would find a letter waiting for him in Elk City. He did say that Magruder should check first thing at the post office, which was in the lobby of the Grand Union Hotel, if there was nothing for him at the store. To get the postal contract, Bacon had been required to swear that he would never tamper with the mail in any way, and he took the oath seriously. Even if the bag weren't locked, and even if he knew Magruder's letter was there, Bacon would not—could not—have delivered it on the spot. It was addressed to Elk City, and to Elk City it would go. Although Bacon had heard what was in the letter, he didn't think it was his place to say. For all he knew, the oath might cover that as well. So the expressman simply told Magruder, whom he considered a friend, that there might be a letter waiting for him in Elk City. And Bacon continued on his way, having interrupted for as long as he dared the faithful discharge of his sacred duty.

He had done Magruder no favor. His friend, now certain there was a letter for him in that mailbag, had to wonder for many miles ahead who might have mailed it. Caroline, probably, since she knew he was going to Elk City. But Caroline wouldn't write to him there unless it was important. Was one of the children sick? Had something happened to Sally in Marysville? A few minutes of this and Magruder was ready to abandon the pack string, race to wherever Bacon might be by now and snatch the mailbag off the back of his horse. Instead, he lit his pipe and got control of himself. If it was bad news, he would get it soon enough.

Some twenty-four hours later, Magruder's party descended into a pleasant river valley and came in sight of Elk City. It was a bustling little town of one main street and a half dozen cross streets, built on a flat between the South Fork and the forest with a population that fluctuated between two hundred and two thousand, depending on the season and the latest reports of new diggings. On a rolling meadow beyond the nearest trees, a miner down on his luck had said the hell with it and established a horse ranch. Magruder would leave his animals, together with a couple of his men, here for two nights while he did business in town. He would restock the store, get a business report from Wickersham and Clindinger, and then pay a visit to each of the town's merchants. But first he would find that letter. There was no mail for him at the store, a log building midway down the main street, but there was a letter waiting for him in the lobby of the hotel, which was also the post office. Haygood, who had mailed it, couldn't remember the name of Magruder's store and so he had simply written Elk City on the envelope. Magruder carried the letter back to the store, and into the small room at the rear which he used as living quarters when he was in town. He noted with some relief that the letter had not been mailed by Caroline. It wasn't only the handwriting; she would never have addressed him as "The Hon. Lloyd Magruder, Esq."

The envelope suggested nothing of great importance, so Magruder tossed it onto the narrow bed and went outside to draw a bucket of water from the town well. Back in his room, he took off his hat and shirt, washed his face, then splashed some water on his head and combed his hair. He carried the letter and a chair over to the window and sat down to read.

The letter told him that a number of the Democrats of Nez Perce County would like to know how he stood on the primary issues of the day and whether he would accept the party's nomination to be the territory's first delegate to congress should the party be inclined to nominate him. It was signed, "Your Friends."[23] Magruder read it with surprise and pleasure. He recognized all but a few of the names as those of good friends, among them Jack Martin, George Edgar, Jacob Hoffman, Thomas Kirkpatrick, William White, John Vickers, Elisha Whitley and John Proctor. Magruder ran his finger over the list, counting the signatures. There were fifty. He pursed his lips and softly whistled. He would have to think about this, but he already felt a little surge of excitement. Washington, D.C. It would take him back almost to where he'd come from, in Maryland. He could show Caroline off to his family and show Locust Grove to Caroline and the children. Even though as a delegate to congress he would have no vote, he would have influence and a clear shot at one day becoming a senator. But of course he was counting chickens now.

He dug into his duffel bag for a clean shirt and went up front to confer with Wickersham about the stock. Tomorrow he would go out to the horse ranch and bring as much of his merchandise to town as the store needed. Then he would make the rounds of the other merchants, to renew his business relationships and find out what they needed that he might be able to provide. He tried not to notice the little thrill of expectation that now thrummed in the back of his mind. After all these months, the prospect of a new political challenge was lifting his spirits and threatening to dominate his thoughts. That wouldn't do; he had a business to run, and many hard miles to go in running it. Of course he would answer the letter. And then he'd get on with his work.

At day's end, he found three of his crew in one of the saloons and bought a round of whiskey. Then he ate a quiet supper at the hotel and returned to his room in the back of the store. It was dark by now. He lit a kerosene lamp and took it to a small bedside table. He found the paper, pen and ink he always carried in the duffel bag, and sat down on the edge of the bed to write.

"Gentlemen," he wrote. "Your favor of the 18th inst. is before me, and in reply thereto suffer me to thank you kindly for the honor you propose for me. The position referred to is one of the most honorable within the gift of a free people, and one which I will be proud to occupy, if my views on the vital issues of the times correspond with those of my fellow citizens."[24]

No one had replenished the kerosene, and at this point the lamp went out, leaving a wisp of acrid, black smoke rising from the charred wick. Magruder cursed and dug into his bag for a candle. Nobody traveled in the mining country—or elsewhere in the West, for that matter—without a stock of candles since the hotels were notoriously stingy with lamp oil. He went into the store looking for a holder. Finding none, he lit the candle, spilled some hot wax off the top of it onto the table and stuck the candle in the wax. He dipped the pen in the ink and resumed writing.

"I therefore authorize you to use my name as a Democratic candidate to represent Idaho Territory in the ensuing Congress, subject to the action of a Democratic convention, should one be held prior to the election."

As for his politics, he said, he believed "the Union should remain as it was, the Constitution as it is . . . I am opposed to the war policy of the administration because it is a political war, led by political generals, carried on for political purposes and warring upon an institution of the country recognized by the Constitution of the United States." He added that "if we succeed in subjugating the seceding states it will require an immense standing army to keep down dissension and anarchy in the conquered territory; thus converting sovereign states into subjugated and dependent provinces (occupying about the same position that England has to Ireland) . . . Another evil incident thereto will be the liberating of four million of African slaves and making them political equals of the white man and bringing their labor in competition with the white labor of the north; thereby inflicting an injury upon both races . . ."

He opposed the Lincoln Administration, he wrote, "because it has suspended the great writ of habeas corpus—that writ which every lover of civil liberty should hold sacred and inviolate; a right which was wrung from King John by the people of England centuries ago. It has prohibited the press from discussing the polity of its measures, denied the right of free speech and arrested and hurried into prison, in foreign states, American citizens for daring to express opinions upon public affairs which are not in accordance with its own . . .

"I have been opposed to the war since its beginning. As a question of policy the resort to war was, in my judgment, an error. Our government was conceived and formed in a spirit of concession, and only thus can it be perpetuated as our fathers formed it."

An hour later, he was astonished to find he had written six pages. He brought the letter quickly to an end and signed it as "your most obedient servant and fellow citizen, Lloyd Magruder."

He found an envelope, sealed it, and addressed it to "Jacob Hoffman and others, c/o the Luna House, Lewiston, I.T." He would mail it in the morning. What he needed now was sleep.

But sleep would not come. Magruder lay in the dark, staring into the night and wondering if he had sealed the envelope too soon. Other ideas, other ways to say the things he had said, were racing across his mind. He heard voices in the street outside and strained to see if he could recognize any as those of his crew. He wondered if the men and animals he had left at the horse ranch were all right. Was his inventory safe out there? Would Caroline be pleased to hear about the letter he had received this day? He would write to her first thing in the morning and tell her. On the other hand, she probably knew already. How secret could a letter be if fifty people had signed it? He hoped Sally was doing well in Marysville, and he missed her. If there were a school in Lewiston, he would send for her. Maybe he would anyhow. No, that wouldn't be fair. If he went to Washington, D.C., they could all be together. Best not to think such thoughts. It could never happen.

Still, fifty signatures . . .

8 Christopher Lowry, David "Doc" Howard and James Romain are the names they used much of the time, but two at least were names of convenience. Lowry also went by the name of Lower, which probably was his true family name; it is, at any rate, the name by which he later would be identified in the territorial court records.

Howard's real name was Renton, and nobody who knew him as Renton called him Doc. Some who knew him as Howard said he was called Doc because he had once performed surgery on a friend's dog and the dog recovered; some others said it was because he claimed to have attended the Yale University School of Medicine. Both Lower and Renton had spent time in prison in California before arriving in Lewiston.[25]

Renton had left New York state in the 1840s and wandered down to New Orleans, where he met and became friendly with Romain. Although well educated and intelligent, according to those who knew him, Renton had a weakness for money and a penchant for getting into trouble. From New Orleans he drifted west to St. Louis and was arrested there on a charge of helping to rob the National Bank of Missouri of some $60,000. He served a ten-year prison sentence and in 1857 or 1858 turned up in Marysville, California. There, under the name of Howard, he opened a livery stable. Before long, Romain was in Marysville also, but he didn't stay. He and Renton came under suspicion of robbery and both left the state. Renton, however, returned in 1859 and was caught robbing a bank in Sacramento. After serving time for that conviction, he left California again and went with Romain to Oregon.[26]

Romain was a brash, reckless ne'er-do-well from New York state who had been trained as a plasterer but was making his living

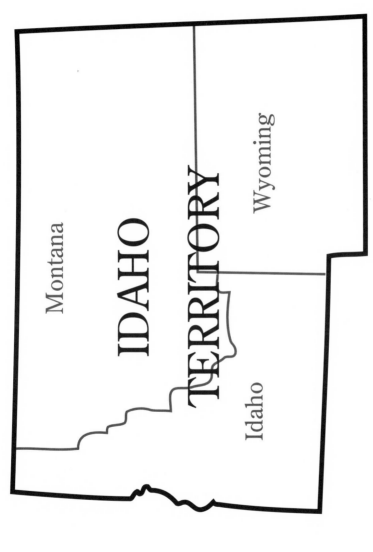

When Idaho Territory was established, March 3, 1863, its boundaries included the future states of Idaho, Montana, and Wyoming. Idaho was reduced to its present size in the following year.

An 1862 view of Lewiston, looking northward toward the Clearwater River. At the right is Hill Beachey's Luna House hotel with its original cloth roof. Lewiston had been established in the previous year. *Nez Perce County Historical Society*

Hill Beachey, the innkeeper whose nightmare sent him to California in pursuit of Lloyd Magruder's murderers. *Nez Perce County Historical Society*

The Luna House after a roof was added. This is how the hotel appeared in 1863-64, at the time of the Magruder incident. *Nez Perce County Historical Society*

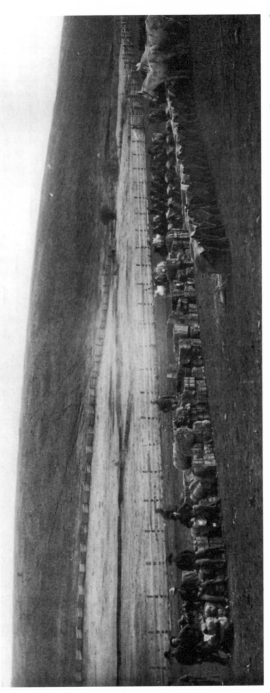

An Army-contracted pack train in camp on the Camas Prairie during the 1877 Nez Perce War. This view shows the vast amount of goods that could be transported by packers like Lloyd Magruder. *Lewiston Morning Tribune*

John Silcott's ferry, used by Lloyd Magruder's murderers to cross the Clearwater River from Lewiston en route to Walla Walla—and later used by Hill Beachey and Thomas Farrell in pursuit. A few miles to the west, Silcott operated a second ferry on the Snake River. *Nez Perce County Historical Society, John Luedke Collection*

After fleeing down the Columbia with the stolen gold, the outlaws took the passenger steamer *Sierra Nevada* from Portland to San Francisco. *Oregon Historical Society, OrHi 3498*

A typical miner's cabin. This photo was taken in 1872 at Warrens, Idaho Territory, one of the camps visited by Magruder and other packers. *Lewiston Morning Tribune*

in California also as a "dust runner"—a fellow who lured miners to certain brokers where they exchanged their dust for legal tender. The brokers usually cheated the miners, and they paid Romain a percentage of the take.[27] Although probably in his middle twenties by the time he and Renton arrived in Lewiston, he looked much younger. Several of those who knew him in Lewiston and Bannack thought him a teenager, and some accounts of the Magruder affair give his age as about sixteen.

Little is recorded of Chris Lower. He was an ex-convict and known as a hot-tempered troublemaker. He and a pal, Bob Zachary, were thrown out of more than one saloon during his short residence in Lewiston and it was Lower that Madame Bonhore had recognized as a town rowdy. Others have described him as a large, powerfully built blond man with long hair and an unkempt beard.[28]

*****

After riding some six miles down the north bank of the Snake, the three used the ferry tickets John Silcott had given them to cross the river near the mouth of Alpowa Creek where a small group of Nez Perces led by Chief Timothy had a farm and cattle ranch. It was a bright, warm morning. A low cloud bank in the west offered some hope of relief later in the day, but the August heat was already baking the sandbars along the river and the weather-worn lava cliffs that rose on the southern edge.

An old Indian woman and a couple of children were picking some kind of dark colored berries in the front yard of Timothy's small wooden house and Romain, who liked to do the talking, asked the woman if he could buy some. She held up a basket full. He told her he couldn't carry a basket full of berries on horseback. Could she put them in something else? Her English was not good enough for that much talk, and she remained silent. Lower dismounted and pulled a bandana from a saddle bag. He held it loosely in front of the woman at waist level and she poured the berries into it. Lower tied the four corners together into a knot and tossed the bag to Romain. Lower reached into his pocket, gave the woman a twenty-five cent piece, remounted the horse, and the three rode up the trail beside Alpowa Creek.

They did not go in that direction very far, however. Once well out of sight of the river and the farm, they turned to the left and rode back toward Lewiston across a rolling prairie some three miles south of the Snake. Lower was familiar enough with the country to remember an old Indian trail that led from Alpowa Creek to the Snake River above the forks. In less than a day on this trail, they could reach the Snake south of Lewiston, swim the horses across, and be on their way up Tammany Creek going east. That route would bypass Lewiston at a safe distance. That way, they would easily fool not only the folks at Lewiston who thought they were going to Portland, but anyone who might be waiting for them in the hideout on Alpowa Creek.

Headed now in the direction they wanted to go, their spirits rose. They rode easily and steadily, pausing occasionally to enjoy the shade of stream-side willows and to pass the berry bag. Most of the creeks were dry this time of year but there was enough water in some to satisfy the horses, and the men had their canteens. The clouds that had been hanging low in the west in early morning had dissipated by noon and the sky was pure blue from one horizon to the other. There was a bit of a breeze up here outside the deep valley of the Snake and the traveling, all agreed, was not bad.

Romain was the first to become ill, in mid-afternoon. He slid off his horse, cursing and tugging at his pants, hobbled a few yards and squatted in the grass. The other two laughed and rode on, saying Romain could catch up when he was through. A few minutes later, Lower told Renton he didn't feel so good and had to stop. Renton took one look at him, reached behind Lower for the berry bag, and threw it as far as he could. Lower had turned a sickly pale and was holding his stomach. Renton helped him down from his horse and Lower fell to his knees on the ground. He began to moan. He stood up, saying he felt somewhat better, just before the dam burst and he too was squatting miserably in the weeds.

Renton now knew what to expect. He tied the two horses to a willow branch and found some shade. Then he put some tobacco in his cheek, prepared himself, and waited.

When Romain rode down, looking washed out, he found Lower, with nothing on but his boots, standing by the horses and wiping himself off with his shirt. Renton was sitting under a willow bush gazing gloomily into the distance, still waiting.

Neither Lower nor Romain felt like riding, but they needed water. If they could find a spring, or a creek still running, they would camp for the night and continue in the morning. Renton had decided that if he were going to get sick he would have by now. But he felt fine. So he suggested that they all move on down the trail and see how far they could go before evening. They found water in the late afternoon—a little stream that came out of the ground, ran down the middle of a dry bed for twenty feet and disappeared again. It was good enough. They filled their canteens, the horses drank, and Lower laid his soiled clothes in the stream below camp and piled some rocks on them. He didn't feel like eating and neither did Romain.

Renton built a small cooking fire in the dry streambed above the spring and put a pan of water on to boil. From his pack he took a chunk of fresh pork, purchased that morning in Lewiston, and cut it into pieces with a Bowie knife. He dropped the meat into the pan and while the meat cooked he unloaded his horse. He took off the bedroll, then a couple of saddlebags and finally the saddle and turned the horse loose to graze. Lower and Romain watched all this activity with mixed envy and disgust. They had talked it over and both by now suspected that the old Indian woman had poisoned them on purpose—just as she probably poisoned the other white people who came by the ranch in season, out of plain spite. They also began to wonder why only they became sick and not Renton. Maybe he had just pretended to eat the berries, knowing they were dangerous, and was now waiting for them to die so he could have their horses and their packs.

But they evidently were not going to die, at least not yet. By the time supper was ready they had unloaded their gear and were feeling better, although Lower could tell that he still mustn't eat. Instead, he lay down with his head against his saddle and monitored the state of his stomach while Renton and Romain sucked noisily on tough boiled pork and soggy bread.

In the morning, Lower ate his share of bacon and bread, soaked this time in coffee, and an hour later was sick again. Renton was beginning to lose patience. Romain, now feeling fine, no longer shared the misery of his former fellow-sufferer. Both Renton and Romain were determined to proceed and continued on eastward toward the Snake River, letting Lower follow as best he could. Lower, after frequent stops to relieve himself, was a good half-mile behind at mid-morning when Renton and Romain reached the river. Since they would need Lower later, they let him catch up before crossing and went into the water with his horse between the other two. The Snake at this point and in this season was shallow except for a narrow channel close to the Idaho side. The three were able to ford the river for most of its width and had to swim the horses only for some twenty yards. The spring had not done much for Lower's soiled clothes the day before, and now, on the east bank, he dismounted and washed them in the river. Then he draped them over the horse's rump and with some difficulty, because he was feeling dizzy, he remounted. When he reached the flat at the top of the bank, Romain and Renton had turned up Tammany Creek and were out of sight.

Since Lower was unable to keep up, and obviously growing weaker, the other two had to make a decision. They couldn't go on without Lower; he was a necessary part of their plan, and if he were left behind and found by somebody else, he might say too much. They couldn't continue as they had been because Lower was too severe a drag in his condition. It was Renton who suggested that they get Lower as far as Fort Lapwai and leave him there while they went on. Lower could get rest and treatment at the fort and join them later.

They stopped and waited. When Lower rode up, Renton told him everything would be all right once they reached Fort Lapwai. To Lower by now, nothing much mattered; he would do as he was told. So the three continued on up Tammany Creek, at Lower's speed, and camped that night at the head of a narrow ravine that would take them down to the Lapwai Valley in the morning.

*****

At Fort Lapwai, Major Truax and some others were preparing to go to Sunday services when Renton, Romain and Lower arrived. Renton explained that they were on their way from Lewiston to Elk City and wondered whether Lower could remain at the fort while recovering from a sudden attack of dysentery. Lower, lying, said he was sure he would be able to travel again in a day or two. The major didn't have to point out that the fort had no doctor. There were few physicians on the frontier and most military posts got along with a shelf of common remedies and a few medical books. At Fort Lapwai, when surgery was called for, the major sent to Lewiston for Dr. Madison A. Kelly. Lower's case probably would call for dosing with paregoric and fennel to ease the stomach pains and a heavy liquid intake to relieve dehydration. And rest, for Lower was so weary by now he could barely stand. The major agreed with Renton that his friend was in no shape to ride over the mountains to Elk City, but he wondered why they hadn't taken him back to Lewiston when he became sick. Renton was considering an answer to this question when the major dismissed it with a wave of his hand and climbed into the buggy. Lower could stay until he was able to travel, he said, and turned the sick man over to an orderly.

Renton and Romain left Lower in the care of the United States Army and rode up the Lapwai Valley toward the culdesac. Instead of following the trail past the shebang, as Magruder had, they turned off a good mile to the west of it and drove their horses up a steep slope that intersected the main trail near the edge of the Camas Prairie. They had made sure that anyone in the hideout who might have been watching the trail would have seen nothing. They paused briefly at the top to rest their horses, and Renton mentioned to Romain that you could almost see Lewiston from here. Renton also pointed out signs indicating the recent passage of a large pack train. When they emerged from a fringe of pines onto the prairie, in the afternoon, they came upon a spring and two Indian tepees. A woman was sitting in the shade of one of the tepees watching a couple of children playing in the grass and a middle-aged man in braids and a tall hat was leading a pair of horses down from the woods.

The man paused as Renton and Romain approached, and he waved the woman and the two children into the tepee. The white men did not dismount. Romain asked the Indian if anyone had passed this way recently and the Indian said yes, some white men with a large pack train had camped here three nights ago and then moved on. To Renton, this meant that he and Romain were only three days behind Magruder. They had plenty of time. Renton told Romain he would like to spend the night here, where there was good water, and take it easy for a day or two. Romain said he would rather not. It made him nervous to be around Indians. Renton understood the feeling and agreed to continue on and camp elsewhere. After watering their horses and filling their canteens, the two men waved to the Indian and rode on across the prairie, past several women who looked up only briefly as they went by and then returned to their digging.

9 After two full days in Elk City, Magruder had disposed of roughly a quarter of the merchandise he had carried out of Lewiston. That meant that by rearranging some of the packs, he could temporarily retire about a dozen mules. He left them and their pack-saddles at the horse ranch, collected as many of his crew as he could find, and on the early morning of August 22 continued on into the Bitterroot mountains.

He was not surprised to find himself short-handed after two days and three nights in Elk City. Packing crews were notoriously prone to disappear at such times. Since the men owned their horses and gear, they felt free to come and go much as they pleased, so long as they were willing to give up some wages. Magruder had lost three of his crew in Elk City—perhaps because they had decided to do some prospecting, or because they hadn't sobered up enough to find their way back to the horse ranch. One or two of them might show up later, and if they didn't Magruder might be able to pick up some other hands along the way. However that may be, he knew that when he started back to Lewiston sometime in the coming month, he might very well have a completely new crew. He would rather it were otherwise, but you couldn't fight human nature. And it was natural to want to go prospecting when everybody else was going and the excitement was high.

The route turned south at Elk City, followed the Red River to its headwaters, and then mounted the main ridge between the Clearwater and the Salmon.[29] On the afternoon of the first day, Magruder and his men were traveling at five thousand feet under a cloudless sky, on a comfortable trail through fir and cedar interspersed with patches of aspen, now turning bright yellow. On their left, off to the north, the blue forested ridges fell away one after another to the Clearwater and beyond. Far away to their right, hidden in its own deep canyon, the Salmon flowed westward toward its union with the Snake. The party camped near a spring in a wide meadow surrounded by Alpine fir.

On the second day out of Elk City, two young fellows came up the trail behind the string, trotted their horses to the head of the train and passed the time of day with Magruder. One of them was a short and slender, dark-haired man wearing a mustache who appeared to be in his early thirties; the other was much younger, blond, of medium height, with a slight build and an unlined, childish face. They were on their way to the Beaverhead country beyond the mountains, they said, because they had heard of new gold strikes there. They'd be glad to join Magruder's train and help with the animals in return for grub. They also had noticed that Magruder seemed to be a bit short-handed. It was true, Magruder said, but he was doing all right.

Magruder looked the two over shrewdly. The younger one looked familiar but he couldn't place him. Had he come from California? Magruder asked him, and yes, he had. He'd been in Marysville most recently. It was Romain who made the connection first. Hadn't he met Magruder at the *California Express* when the paper was remodeling? That was it. Magruder then remembered Romain as the lath and plaster man, and they shook hands. Romain introduced his friend as Doc Howard, and after a bit of small talk Magruder said they could string along with him if they liked. The two men thanked him and moved back down the line of mules, chatting easily with others in the crew. Although they obviously were easterners, judging by the way they talked, they seemed to know what they were doing and they both had good, strong horses. Magruder felt pleased with the way things were turning out.

The broad back of the high ridge became sharp and rocky, and the trail more difficult. Magruder found himself leading the train along a narrow track that dropped off sharply first on the left and then on the right as it passed from one side of the ridge to the other through narrow saddles. In one of these, after a day's progress of some 15 miles, the party made camp. Although the sky remained clear, the temperature was dropping and the men had to dig out their woolen coats for night guard duty. Still, even at 6,000 feet, the days were pleasantly warm. Flattering, Magruder called this day-time weather. It made mountain travelers feel so comfortable and so easy and then turned on them the moment the sun went down.

*****

Renton and Romain had been three days with the mule train when Lower appeared one late afternoon just as Magruder was preparing to camp in a high mountain meadow. Lower gave no sign of recognizing either of the other two, and they seemed not to know him. Magruder didn't need another man now, and even if he did, Lower had a sickly look about him; Magruder doubted he would be much help with the animals. Lower said he was meeting friends in Bannack and would rather not be traveling alone. Magruder understood. At another season, it would be possible to travel with the Nez Perce Indians, who used this trail as a main route between the buffalo country to the east and their winter villages in the river valleys to the west. But at the end of August, the Nez Perces were traveling from east to west—in the wrong direction to do Lower any good. Magruder told Lower he could ride with the mule train and help with the cooking and guard duty in return for his meals. Lower assured Magruder that he was a pretty good camp cook. He would earn his keep, he said, and then some. After supper, Magruder gave Lower a chance to begin. He assigned himself and Lower to the first guard watch.

The meadow was several acres in size, roughly circular in shape, and surrounded by a dense forest of mixed larch and fir. The trail ran through the middle of it, parallel to a small creek that was fed by a spring a short distance back in the trees. The mountain arose on three sides, heavily timbered and black in the growing dusk. Magruder posted Lower near the trail at one end of the meadow and he placed himself at the other end. He found an old tree that had blown down long ago and sat there with his rifle leaning against the trunk. The camp sounds were fading by now and the animals were grazing quietly. Here and there above the mountain's black silhouette, stars were twinkling. A lovely evening, Magruder thought, buttoning his coat more tightly.

He was satisfied that he was on schedule and would reach Bannack on about September 5. If things went as well there as they had in Elk City, he would be ready to begin the return journey on about the 12th. He filled his pipe and lit it, and sat smoking and thinking of things far away. He assumed that Caroline and the children were all right. He had to assume that or go crazy. He wondered what he would find in Bannack: a bustling little town or cold ashes? Bannack was a gold camp, and gold camps were short-lived. He doubted that in ten years anyone would even remember Elk City. There were no mines in Lewiston but Lewiston would outlast them all, he suspected, because it was the point of supply. And his thoughts returned to the thing he had been trying for several days not to think about: that letter. Had his answer yet found its way to Lewiston? He tried to picture his fellow Democrats reading it and discussing it. He should be there now, not here in the far-off mountains guarding a pack string. He was beginning to realize that he wanted very much to be Idaho Territory's delegate to congress.

The next morning, as Magruder rolled out of his blankets, he noticed that the three newcomers were up before him and conversing around the breakfast fire like old friends. More important, he noticed that the weather had changed overnight. A cold, gray sky lay over the mountain, its clouds dripping down in ragged streamers and enveloping the tree tops. A damp wind was sighing in the woods and rippling the animals' manes. Well, it was time: it was almost September.

The snow began to fall at mid-morning, a few small flakes at first then blinding big ones that turned the air around them white. The wind had died and the snow floated straight and silently down. Within minutes, the men and animals at the head of the string were out of sight of those at the rear. Shortly thereafter, when Magruder turned around in his saddle, he could not see farther than four mules back. He called a halt and told the crew to tie the mules together, front to back and about six feet apart. That would tighten the string and keep the animals from wandering off the trail. Magruder took off his hat, shook the snow from it, and used it to brush Bud's mane and rump. He and the other men, using their hats, brushed the snow off the packs, and would have to do it periodically to keep them from getting even heavier than they were.

Once under way again, Magruder kept the pace slow. Although the trail was well marked and broad, the land dropped off sharply on the left and in heavy, falling snow even mules could lose their bearings.

Magruder had hoped to reach the pass through the Bitter-roots today and possibly descend for some little way down the other side. That was now out of the question. The mule train plodded on through deepening snow as the men continued to swing their hats across the tops of the packs and brush the snow off themselves. It was a windless, silent world they moved through, the sounds damp-ened by countless soft and gathering bits of fluff. Magruder knew his men were calling to one another down the line behind him, but he could not hear them. All he could hear was the muffled crunch of hooves in snow, the breathing of the animals and the squeak of harness—all pleasant sounds. And it was not awfully cold. In fact, Magruder felt quite comfortable in his woolen coat, his vest and his hat.

He decided that it would be best to camp as soon as he found good grazing for the animals and then try to reach the pass some time tomorrow. If he waited too long before stopping, the snow would cover the grass and make grazing difficult. He felt confident that once over the pass he would be out of the snow, and then he could make good time again. His luck was holding surprisingly well. In mid-afternoon, still climbing, the mule train rounded a corner of the mountain and entered a narrow valley that twisted, snakelike, between high, steep slopes covered with fir and cedar. As Magruder proceeded up the valley the storm began to subside. Then the snow stopped falling altogether. Magruder could see just over the moun-tain on his right the blurred disc of the sun behind thinning clouds and then a patch of blue sky. At almost the same time, the trail made one final twist to the left, the mountain on the right fell away, and Magruder was looking across the Bitterroot Valley into the heartland of Idaho Territory, soon to become Montana.

Ahead under a bright sun lay the ridged and fir-covered foot-hills of the Continental Divide and out of sight beyond them the Beaverhead country, a lacework of streams that once produced another kind of gold—the furs that drew the first white men here. Behind was the crest of the Bitterroots, still cloaked in clouds.

Once the whole mule train was out of the pass, Magruder ordered a pause. He and his men gathered at the head of the string and gazed out across a terrain that stretched as far as they could see, ridge after forested ridge falling away like waves into the hazy blue distance. Out there somewhere was Bannack and Grasshopper Creek and the Bozeman Road and Deer Lodge. To adventurous, gold-hungry men, the names were magic. There were fortunes to be made in the gravel beds of those creeks—and in other ways as well. James Romain, Christopher Lower and David Renton stood quietly staring into the east along with the rest of the men. Magruder saw his fortune out there also, and he felt a twinge of pity for those of his crew who would launch themselves happily into that glory hole only to come out of it broke and broken. His was the better way. The merchant who supplied the miners, like the town that nourished his inventory, could be counted on always to come out a little bit richer.

*****

The letter Magruder had mailed from Elk City accepting the nomination to congress, should it be proffered, reached Lewiston just as Magruder was approaching the pass. Beachey was the first to see the envelope because it was addressed to Jacob Hoffman in care of the Luna House. Beachey knew what it was; he had been one of the signers, along with Hoffman, of the letter soliciting Magruder's political views. Beachey had been waiting for Magruder's response, and saw no reason why he shouldn't open it. It had been addressed to Hoffman, Beachey knew, only because Magruder had needed a name for the envelope and any of fifty names, including his own, would have done just as well. But Beachey didn't open it. He put the letter opener back on the desk and went into the bar, where he knew he would find at least one of those fifty people. He asked James Witt to go find Jake and tell him Magruder's letter was here. They could open it themselves, he said, but they probably shouldn't since Jake was the addressee.

Witt found Hoffman two blocks away in his saddle and harness shop and told him of the letter. Then he went to the office of *The Golden Age* on D Street and offered the news to the editor,

Frank Kenyon. Hoffman finished dealing with his customer and then, leaving his assistant in charge of the shop, he put on his hat and walked to the hotel. Kenyon and Witt were already there in the lobby, along with Beachey, who was tapping the envelope on the top of his desk impatiently. Beachey gave Hoffman barely time to take off his hat, and handed him the letter. Hoffman examined the address and started to put the envelope in his vest pocket. Hold on, Witt said, the letter was for all of them. He said Hoffman should read it now, out loud, then Kenyon could have it for the paper. Beachey handed Hoffman the letter opener. Hoffman opened the envelope, took out the six-page letter, and fanned the sheets of paper between calloused fingers. After staring for a moment at Magruder's handwriting, he gave the pages to Witt. That was too much writing for him to try to read, he said, so Witt began.

"Gentlemen," he read, "Your favor of the 18th inst. is before me, and in reply thereto suffer me to thank you kindly for the honor you propose for me. The position referred to is one of the most honorable within the gift of a free people, and one which I will be proud to occupy, if my views on the vital issues of the times correspond with those of my fellow citizens."

By this time, two other signers, John Vickers and Elisha Whitley, were in the audience, having learned of the letter from Jacob Hoffman's assistant. They wanted to know what they had missed, and Witt told them they could read it in the paper. After three pages, Witt handed the letter to Beachey, saying he was all talked out. Beachey finished the letter and gave it to Kenyon.

Kenyon made no sign of his anger over Magruder's slighting references to Mr. Lincoln. Instead, he put the letter carefully back in its envelope, shook hands with all present, and left for his office at *The Golden Age.* Two days later, Beachey, Witt and the others were shocked to find that Kenyon had not only printed Magruder's letter in full but had responded to it in a seething editorial.

Kenyon denounced Magruder for the "fanatical bigotry writhing to the surface through every pore of his skin" and contended he would be supported only by "mobocratic ruffians" and "those who have sloughed off into the filthy den of secessionists and Copperheads." [30]

After reading the editorial, Beachey grabbed his hat and stormed out the door of the Luna House, heading for Kenyon's office. He arrived at *The Golden Age* in a boiling fury, but instead of going in he kept walking to the end of the block. Then he turned around and walked back, passing *The Golden Age* again, and strode on toward the Luna House. He pushed through the door into the lobby, threw his hat on his desk and kept going, into the bar. There he ordered a shot of whiskey and told his bartender, Dave Strait, what had happened. Strait said he should have beat up the son of a bitch, and Beachey said he probably should have. He wanted to, all right, but in his state of mind he might have killed the bastard, and that would have done no good.

10 It was not as easy now to find grass. So many whites and Indians had traveled this trail that by the end of summer they had left the best camping places overgrazed. Now, although Magruder was across the pass and out of the snow, he had to keep traveling longer than he liked, looking for food for the stock. It was dusk before he could bring an end to another day's travel. One of the crew started a cooking fire while Magruder and the others took care of the mules and the horses. After supper, as was his custom, Magruder took the first watch, along with Lou Holt. They would be relieved at 11 o'clock by Renton and Creely. Now that he had left Elk City, carrying gold, and was camping in isolated places, Magruder kept a two-man watch. It was a pleasant night, several degrees warmer on this side of the mountain, and it passed uneventfully.

In the morning, men and animals were on the trail early. Magruder's map, hand-drawn for him by another packer, indicated he could reach the North Fork of the Big Hole River at Butler Creek that day if he hurried. The spot was well known as a sort of rendezvous point for travelers, a place where gossip and goods could be traded and where there was plenty of good grass and water. It was one of the Nez Perce Indians' traditional camping grounds, not yet sullied by the blood that would be spilled there fourteen years later in the so-called Chief Joseph War.

Once out of the mountains, Magruder and crew traveled down the Big Hole Valley through scattered timber to a broad prairie covered with grass. In late afternoon they reached the Big Hole

River. It was a modest, clear stream bordered by thick willows that ran through a slight depression between the prairie and a gently rounded hill. There they found twenty-odd Nez Perces already camped, probably heading for winter quarters on the Clearwater. Also in camp was a party of a half dozen white men who had been prospecting on tributaries of the Big Hole River to the south. They joined Magruder and his crew for supper, bringing their own grub and some of the latest news. They had given up on the Big Hole and were heading for a place to the northeast called Alder Gulch. They had heard of new strikes there—strikes so promising, one of them said, that people were bailing out of Bannack by the hundreds.

To Magruder, this was not good news. The last he'd heard, Bannack was still the liveliest mining camp in the Beaverhead country. He had never heard of Alder Gulch, or another camp nearby that these men called Virginia City. But he had to believe them, because that was the way towns came and went on the frontier. If Bannack was as dead as they said it was, he would have no choice but to go on to the new camps farther east. It would mean more time—a couple of weeks more, perhaps—and less profit. The alternative would be to turn around at Bannack, if the place was really empty now, and carry his inventory all the way back to Lewiston. That was not even worth considering. Or he could cross the divide again into the Salmon River country and dispose of his goods in the mining camps of Florence and Warrens. There also was the Boise Basin, which had by now become the region's major center of mining activity. In any case, his schedule would be ruined if Bannack had indeed been abandoned.

Magruder mulled all these things as he, his crew and the visitors sat around the fire, smoking and talking. After a while he realized, with some surprise, that it was the fractured schedule that upset him the most. He did not want to take the time to go to Alder Gulch or to Florence or to the Boise Basin. He wanted to get back to Lewiston, where things were happening that he should be a part of. He should be in Nez Perce County, working for the nomination, and here he was on the opposite side of the mountains, stuck for no telling how long. It was galling.

But he would continue on to Bannack in the morning; he should be there in three days if the country between was as easy as they said it was. He would decide then what he had to do. He bent over the fire to light his pipe and told one of the visitors that he'd heard Henry Plummer was now the sheriff of Bannack.

Yes, the other replied, that's what they say.

Magruder observed again, as he had to Lem Akins, that he was a little surprised to hear Plummer was now in law enforcement.

Well, it seemed the previous sheriff had left town in a hurry and Plummer had some influential friends—and some strange ones, too.

How so?

His deputies, for one. Or maybe they weren't really deputies, just boys who hung around the office a lot. Some people were saying that whenever two men rode out of town and only one man came back, the one who came back was always one of them. Just talk, of course, maybe nothing to it. On the other hand, they didn't seem to do any mining or trading, so you had to wonder. Another of the visitors mentioned that one of those boys, in fact, had passed through here just yesterday going east. Probably had come through the pass ahead of Magruder. A fellow they called Skinner, who owned a saloon in Bannack.

Lower was busy with the animals when that name was dropped and didn't hear it. Renton and Romain did, however, and shared a frightened glance across the fire.

*****

Skinner had not gone far after leaving Elk City. He had followed the main Nez Perce Trail up the Red River for a few miles and then turned off to the south on another trail that climbed up and over the ridge. Near the top of this route was a spring where he could halt for a day or two in good cover and wait for Magruder to pass him on the trail below. He knew only that he was ahead of Magruder and that Magruder probably would spend some time in Elk City. Skinner made himself comfortable, and settled down to wait.

He had concluded that Renton, Lower and Romain must have gone to Portland after all. If so, it meant that they were backing out of the holdup that he had so carefully planned; if not, it must mean they were changing the plan in ways that he and Plummer would not like. According to his plan, the three were to follow Magruder to Bannack, at a distance, and get acquainted with him there one at a time. Each was then to arrange to return to Lewiston with Magruder. At the right time they were to rob him, silence the rest of the crew in any way they chose, and carry the gold back to Bannack. It was a good plan, Skinner thought, and Plummer had approved it. Now what should he do?

First, he wanted to see how many people Magruder had with him as he left Elk City, and how many mules. Then he planned to cross this ridge, hurry down the other side and reach the main Nez Perce Trail ahead of the mule train. He would beat Magruder to Bannack and he and Plummer could decide what to do next.

The mule train passed below him on the morning of the third day. Skinner had counted the mules that passed by the shebang at the culdesac, and now he counted again. The string was shorter by a dozen animals. This meant that Magruder had left a good share of his inventory in Elk City, and that meant that he would have less to sell in Bannack.

Skinner doused his cooking fire, filled his canteens from the spring and broke camp. He crossed a wide, bare hogback, nudged his horse down a steep hill, and was back on the old Nez Perce Trail before noon, a good hour ahead of Magruder. The traveling was easy for the next few days as the route wound down to the Selway River and back up again, although Skinner did not welcome the snow that was falling heavily as he approached the pass. He had been able to check on Magruder's progress without being seen himself, and he had met no one going west who might have betrayed his presence.

He did not linger at the Big Hole. He was in a hurry to get to Bannack and confer with Plummer, but when he arrived there he learned that Plummer was in Virginia City. Skinner thought he had better not wait for Plummer's return to fill him in, and started for Virginia City himself. He got only as far as Beaverhead Rock, where he encountered friends from Bannack who were camping and partying. They told him the saloon was getting along fine without him. They plied him with liquor and he wasted two days there, unable to ride.[31] When he finally reached Virginia City he was told that the sheriff was out in the countryside somewhere checking claims in which he had an interest. There was no use trying to track him down in that confusing tangle of creeks and washes, and so he decided that after a night's rest he would start back to Bannack. He did, and this time managed to pass Beaverhead Rock without mishap. He told the people in Skinner's Saloon[32] what he had told his partying friends: that he had been prospecting on the Big Hole River, without any luck.

Skinner put out word that he had information for Plummer and wanted to see him. Within days, the word reached Plummer in Virginia City, but for some reason the sheriff did not act on it immediately. Instead, he spent a week or so examining claims in Alder Gulch and at one point rode to a place called Rattlesnake Station, a stage stop, to make an arrest. By the time Skinner returned to his saloon in Bannack, he had changed his mind. He had decided it would be better not to bother the sheriff with his trivial difficulties just now—at least better for him.

But where could Renton, Lower and Romain have gone? If they hadn't left for the coast they must be planning a double-cross. On the other hand, maybe they and he had simply missed connections. Until he talked to Plummer there wasn't much Skinner could do and so there was little point in worrying about it. He gave the bar a wipe with a wet towel and went to tap another keg of whiskey.

11 Three days after leaving the Big Hole, Magruder reached Bannack, fearful of what he might find. The town's main street ran up a dry gully between bare, sandy hills beside a meandering stream called Grasshopper Creek. There were people and horses on the street, he noticed, as he led his men and mules through town. But there should have been more. His friend Lou Holt, who had come along to Bannack with him only because he had to get over the mountains from Elk City, had a ranch and corral here, and that is where Magruder took his string. After unpacking and feeding the animals, most of the crew rode into town. Magruder remained at the ranch overnight, and the next morning he went into Bannack to check the place out.

It was a grubby, thrown-together burg whose rough buildings had sprouted like weeds after the discovery of gold the year before on Grasshopper Creek. The camp itself was first called Grasshopper. When it began filling up with miners, some with their wives and children, the residents decided to name it Bannack City in reference to the nearby Bannock tribe of Indians. The miners spelled both the city and tribe both ways. On the town's main street were three hotels, three bakeries, three blacksmith shops, two meat markets, two stables, a brewery, a billiard parlor, a grocery store, a restaurant and four saloons.[33]

From the main street, a footbridge crossed Grasshopper Creek to the town's chief residential area, a place called Yankee Flat. Here the typical home was a one-room cabin built of unpeeled logs and chinked with mud, with a roof of willow poles covered with mud, grass and rocks. There would be a packed dirt floor, often covered with dry grass and buffalo hides, fur side up and held down by wooden pegs. There was a fireplace for cooking. Maybe there would be a window and maybe not; if not, the light in daytime came through the open door.[34]

John White, Charlie Reville and William Still discovered gold in Grasshopper Creek in May 1862, and by winter the town had a population of some five hundred, including at least 36 white women. It grew in the spring of 1863 to nearly a thousand as prospectors flooded in from western Idaho or came north from the Oregon Trail. The placer claims had proved surprisingly rich. By some estimates, the district produced between forty and fifty million dollars in gold in its first four years. According to one tale, a man walked into the camp on a rainy day in the fall of 1862 with mud on his shoes. In the saloon, just for fun, some of the boys scraped the mud off his boots and washed five dollars worth of gold out of it.[35]

It had never been a peaceful place. The miners who founded the town in 1862 built an eight-sided log fort for protection against the Bannock and Snake Indians, who had become furious over white intrusion into some of their best hunting grounds. As the town grew it became wilder, and the Indians became less dangerous to the citizens than their fellow whites.

One of the white women who lived in Bannack through the winter of 1862-63 wrote later that she didn't know how many had died violently during those months, "but that there have not been twice as many is entirely owing to the fact that drunken men do not shoot well." This was Emily Meredith, who wrote in the same letter home that she had seen thirty-six dollars in gold weighed out of one wheelbarrow full of dirt.[36]

If the rewards were great, so were the costs. A hundred-pound sack of flour that cost a dollar and a half "back in the states" was worth twenty-five dollars in Bannack, and other prices were comparable. Although freight wagons arrived frequently from Salt Lake City, some 350 miles away, there was no regular transport to serve the swelling population and the price of everything soared almost out of sight.[37]

This was the Bannack that Magruder had been thinking of when he planned his 300-mile pack trip through the Bitterroots. But that summer, Emily Meredith's husband had driven two yoke of oxen to Salt Lake City, thinking to make a handsome profit on a wagonload of flour. When he brought the flour to Bannack, some weeks later, the price had fallen from twenty-five dollars a sack to ten. Magruder was unaware of this state of affairs when he left Lewiston in August. He discovered on the main street of Bannack that day in September that the usual had happened. A party of prospectors had accidentally come across an even richer yield of surface gold that summer in a place called Alder Gulch, some seventy miles to the east. The happy miners had come to Bannack to buy provisions, hoping to keep their discovery a secret, but they spent so much gold dust so frivolously that they gave the game away. When they returned to Alder Gulch, they were followed by a great horde of prospectors, and Bannack was no longer the boom town it had been.

It was clear to Magruder that he would have to travel on to the new camps that had sprung up around Alder Gulch, mainly Virginia City. And the sooner the better. He returned to the ranch and told Charlie Allen to take charge of everything here. He wanted to spend the rest of the day in Bannack and then he and Newburgh would go to Virginia City, and if the prospects were better there he would send word back with Jules. Then Charlie and Jules, and any of the crew they could round up, would take the mules and the merchandise to Virginia City.

Magruder was determined to salvage what he could from the town of Bannack—or what was left of it. So he spent a busy afternoon politicking there. He introduced himself in the saloons and other places of business, saying he was giving serious consideration to running for congress in November from Idaho Territory. He would be glad to share his political views with any who might be interested. He described himself as a southerner, but not "secesh," or secessionist. He was a Democrat to the core, he said, realizing that in most parts of the territory that would put him in good company. As for the Mormons, who recently had been accused of murdering "gentiles" who strayed off the Oregon Trail into Utah, Magruder could speak to that issue as well. He had nothing against Mormons but he thought one wife should be enough for any sensible man. He thought they should have the right to go where they pleased but only as long as they granted the same right to Baptists and Methodists. He said the Mormons should stick to their own religion and leave politics to others. Magruder was pleased to find that these views met with general agreement in Bannack.

Wherever he went, he asked who might be running for the first territorial legislature from this area. He was surprised to find little interest here in territorial politics, and did not meet a soul who was planning to run (although several eventually did). Some of the men told him they wouldn't waste time on Idaho politics because the Beaverhead was probably going to be a part of Montana before long. He also was told that only a damn fool would wish to serve in a legislature that met in Lewiston, on the other side of the Bitterroots, in the wintertime. He was not surprised to learn that most of the residents of the town had no idea where they would be a year from now. Bannack was only a temporary address. Home was somewhere "back in the states."

Magruder ate a saloon supper and rode back to the ranch. There he learned that several of his crew had gone prospecting and might or might not be back. He would let Charlie Allen work on that problem later. Tonight he would see that Bud was cared for and go to bed.

*****

Three days later Magruder and Newburgh arrived in Virginia City and found the place to be everything that Bannack had been, and more. It was teeming with miners and hangers-on, full of noise and hustle and excitement. It was clear to Magruder that this was the place to be, and he sent Newburgh back to Bannack for the mule train. While waiting for his goods to arrive he would find a place to put up his tent, mail a letter to Caroline, and make himself acquainted in the town.

As Magruder walked through Virginia City, visiting the stores, the saloons, the hotels, the blacksmiths and the livery stables, he felt the town pumping new vigor into him. This was still Idaho Territory, there were potential voters here, and Magruder was, if anything, a politician. The MacGregor blood was surging in him, filling him with excitement and high hopes.

Gone was the disappointment he had suffered in Bannack. He realized now that events were moving in his favor. He would have at least a week to spend in one of the most populous parts of the territory, among men who could be of great help to him politically. This merchandising venture far from his home county was not the bit of bad timing that it had seemed at first but a stroke of good fortune, and he would make the most of it. When he was through, the Magruder name would be known from the far western edge of the territory to the eastern border—from Washington to Dakota. And it would be remembered.

*****

Feeling not so lucky were Renton, Lower and Romain. They had spent the first morning in Holt's corral, hiding among the animals, fearing that they might be recognized at any moment by some casual visitor to the ranch. The minute one of Plummer's boys spotted them they were doomed, for Skinner must know by now that he and Plummer had been double-crossed. And Skinner had got to Bannack ahead of them.

Renton decided that they couldn't stay here and shouldn't be seen together anywhere, especially in Bannack. That afternoon he told Lower and Romain to saddle up and leave the ranch separately, as quickly as possible, heading west. They were to go to a rendezvous point just off the trail that had brought them into Bannack and he would follow them there. They would pretend they were going prospecting for a day or two—gold fever, everyone knew, was very catching.

Lower went first. He rode uneasily out of the relative security of the corral onto the open road to Bannack, then dodged around the town itself and caught the road again on the other side. After a mile or two he reached Sagebrush Creek, now dry, and rode up the creek bed until he was out of sight of the trail. Romain left the corral not long after Lower. Then came Renton, after telling Holt he was going to take a look around the country and would rejoin the crew tomorrow. Lower, arriving first at the rendezvous, dismounted and walked toward the shade of an upthrust of rock. With every step he took he stirred up hordes of 'hoppers that bounced ahead of him out of the dry grass. When he heard another horse coming, he led his own behind the rock and waited with it there until he had recognized Romain. Within a few minutes, Renton joined them and the three had to decide what to do next. They were in a pretty fix now. They could not remain with the pack train, either in Bannack or Virginia City, because sooner or later they would be seen. If they stayed away for as much as a week or ten days, Magruder would no doubt replace them, and the plan required that they be part of the crew on Magruder's return trip. Besides, if they weren't around, how would they know when Magruder planned to start for Lewiston?

Renton thought he had the answer. One of them would go back to the ranch and tell Magruder that the three would like to do some prospecting out here but would return to Lewiston with him when he was ready to go. They would meet him when it was time for him to leave Bannack. This plan assumed that Magruder would set up his tent store in Bannack, but Magruder had made it plain to all that he was disappointed in Bannack and might go instead to Virginia City. If he went to Virginia City, which seemed likely, they would have to go there too, and that would be dangerous; Plummer surely would have someone watching Magruder.

They could wait in the hills until Magruder came back through Bannack on his way west and join him there. But what if he found all the crew he needed in Virginia City?

Lower suggested they could drop the plan altogether and find some other victim, hiding in the mountains in the meantime. Renton reminded him that there was no place to hide. Renton and Romain both said they meant to have that gold and they didn't mean to share it with Plummer or Skinner or anyone else.

Then Renton, suddenly inspired, suggested an audacious plan. Why hide from Plummer, when that would only make them targets for Plummer's assassins? Better to go directly to Plummer and explain to him that they had been forced to alter the plan and had not been able to meet with Skinner in Lewiston. Renton would figure out some way to explain all this. They would tell Plummer that they had been following Magruder through the Bitterroots to Bannack as planned, but that Magruder had then gone on to Virginia City. They had therefore left "to go prospecting," and had come to Plummer for new instructions.

Romain was doubtful; for too long he had been thinking of Plummer as his enemy, which assumed that Plummer was thinking the same about him. The thought of walking deliberately into Plummer's presence was frightening to him. Lower put himself in Plummer's boots and asked himself if he would believe that story. Yes, he thought he would. He told Renton he was willing to risk it. Romain would come along, he said; he just needed convincing.

The three rode back down to the main trail and turned east toward Virginia City, again bypassing Bannack. Renton was pleased with himself, Lower was glad they would not be hiding from Plummer's cutthroats, and Romain was finding virtue in the plan. They would salvage this venture yet.

12 Jules Newburgh, returning alone from Virginia City to the ranch at Bannack, made good time in dry, cool weather, spending only one night on the road—at Beaverhead Rock. He met some people he knew there, and was tempted to linger, but he pressed on, reaching Holt's ranch in the early evening of the second day. He told Charlie Allen that Magruder was waiting for him in Virginia City, and offered to round up as many of the crew as he could find. Allen told him to go ahead, and Newburgh rode on into Bannack. He found three of the men in the Bank Exchange Saloon and one in Skinner's, and told them that if they wanted to keep their jobs they'd better get back to the ranch before morning. Three of them did, in good enough shape to work, and Allen had the pack string loaded and under way by first light.

Even short-handed, it was an easy three days on that road. It ran northeastward from Bannack through an area called the Stinking Water and around the Ruby Range of mountains to the east.

Part way between Bannack and the northern end of the range, it passed under the massive rock bluff that had become known as the Beaverhead. It was dry country with gravelly soil and low, white hills dotted here and there with solitary pines. The brush-lined creeks running down from the Ruby Range had begun to tantalize, reward and disappoint the miners who by now were all over the place.

Allen had been Magruder's chief packer since the first days of the business, and he couldn't wish for a better job. He liked what he did, he liked Magruder and Magruder liked him. It was Magruder's pack string, but Allen thought of it as his own and treated the animals accordingly, with care and patience. As he rode into Virginia City at the head of the string that day in early September, Allen felt some of the same pride that he knew Magruder must feel when leading the string into Bannack or Florence or Elk City.

Virginia City was even newer and rawer than Bannack. Younger by a year but richer, and bustling with the feverish intensity that marked the birth of every promising gold camp. Riding up the street in the late afternoon with the men and mules behind him, Allen felt himself awash in the excitement of it all. Surely, he thought, this was the best of all possible times.

*****

The stampede of miners to Alder Gulch—the greatest placer rush in the history of what was to become Montana—spawned not only Virginia City but Nevada City and a half dozen others. And the gold that attracted these hordes of miners and hangers-on was, as usual, discovered quite by accident. A group of prospectors that included Bill Fairweather, Henry Edgar and Barney Hughes had left Bannack in the spring of 1863 to look for gold in the Yellowstone country. They were to join a larger party led by James Stuart at a rendezvous, but somehow failed to connect. After some terrifying run-ins with hostile Crows, the Fairweather party gave up and started back to Bannack. On the evening of May 26, the travelers made camp on the divide between the Madison and Jefferson rivers and while there Fairweather and Edgar decided to prospect for tobacco money. Their first pan produced $2.40 worth of gold, and they knew they had a strike. These were the people who went to Bannack for supplies and found on their return to Alder Gulch that they had been followed by several hundred hopeful miners. Within the next eighteen months some ten thousand people streamed into the district, as Virginia City became the hub of a rich and turbulent mining region.[38] Magruder had come to the right place.

Allen found his boss at the California Hotel, where Newburgh had told him he'd be, and Magruder, riding Bud, led the pack train to a vacant lot on the outskirts of town where he would set up his tent. There was a corral nearby, and packing sheds, and the crew soon had the animals unloaded and fed. The crew hung around for another day, until the tent was up and stocked with merchandise, then all four—Newburgh, Creely, James Spencer and Moran—took their gold pans and disappeared. They might be back and they might not. For now Magruder and Allen were on their own, and Magruder had other things than business on his mind.

While waiting for Allen, Magruder had made the most of his time. He had visited the livery stables, the blacksmith shop, the saloons, the provisioning stores and the hotels. He had taken orders for whiskey, tobacco, flour, sugar, axe handles, shovels, nails, boots, winter underwear, flannel shirts, playing cards, gold scales, pots and pans and kerosene. He had made certain those he talked with knew his name, that he was an anti-war Democrat, and hoped to represent the territory in congress. But here, as in Bannack, he had found little interest in the politics of Idaho Territory. This had been Dakota only a year ago and next year it could be Montana. Sidney Edgerton, whose daughter Martha had been so taken with Henry Plummer, was now in Virginia City serving as an Idaho district judge even while seeking to split up the territory. He would succeed, and become the governor of Montana in the following year.

Magruder was not discouraged. Once the white canvas tent was up and his combination store and warehouse was stocked with goods carried all the way from Lewiston, he hired a wagon and team and began making deliveries to the town's merchants and saloonkeepers. He and Charlie Allen took turns minding the store, delivering goods and repairing broken pack saddles. They looked after the feeding of the animals and they slept in the store at night with the merchandise. Business was so good that within five days they had sold everything except a few pairs of boots and some pots and pans.

Magruder was not actively seeking an excuse to stay a few more days, but he found one anyhow. A freighter arrived one afternoon from Salt Lake City with three wagon loads of goods. Like Magruder before him, the freighter had set out for Bannack only to find on getting there that much of Bannack had moved to Alder Gulch. So he had plodded on to Virginia City just as Magruder was running out of things to sell. Magruder met him before he had set up his store, and told him he would buy one wagon load plus the wagon and team if they could agree on a price. They could, and did. Magruder drove the wagon to his own store, unloaded it, and stocked his tent with flour, whiskey, shirts, pants and mining tools. He would have to charge more for this merchandise than he had for his own, but the Virginia City market, in the late summer of 1863, was virtually bottomless. He was back in business again, and he had no trouble selling the wagon and team.

Magruder had been abandoned by all of his crew except Allen, and the two of them had worked themselves to exhaustion. Magruder was thinking of closing the store for a few days so they could get a little rest when Lou Holt showed up. He had ridden over from Bannack, he said, on the chance that Magruder would like to buy some mules. If he would, Holt knew where to find them. If not, Holt would stick around anyhow and help out in the store. The ranch had got along without him since early summer, and it would get along without him for a few more days. Yes, Magruder said, he would like to buy some mules here and take them back with him to Lewiston. In that case, Holt said, he had a few good ones on a friend's ranch out of Bannack and knew of some others that he would be glad to pick up for an old friend. Holt knew as much about mules and horses as anybody in the territory, and Magruder knew he could be trusted to bring him only good stock. He also understood that Holt would get his cut, taking the difference between the buying and the selling price. But he would be fair.

Magruder was spending his evenings this week in the hotels and saloons of Virginia City and nearby Nevada City, meeting as many potential voters as possible. He frequently found it hard to steer the conversation toward territorial politics, however. Even if the gold fever had not distracted most of the town's residents, there was a war going on. It didn't matter that the news of Vicksburg and Cemetery Ridge reached the gold camps weeks after the smoke had cleared, coming by mail wagon over the Oregon Trail and then north on horseback on the Bozeman Road. Interest in the war was so great, and emotional commitments so strong that innkeepers demanded the subject not even be mentioned as long as anyone in the place was armed. Virginia City was not the only camp whose main street served as the dividing line between the sympathizers of one side and those of the other. People who had strong pro-slavery views did not express them on the northern side of the street; those who favored the abolitionist cause didn't do so on the southern side. Fortunately, the business houses, as well as the prostitutes' quarters, were about equally divided between North and South.

Magruder tactfully played both sides of the street. North of the middle of Main, he could honestly say that he believed in the Union and hoped Mr. Lincoln could hold it together. South of that imaginary line in the dust, he could state with equal honesty that as a Marylander he could see only trouble ahead should the slaves remain in the country as free men. And when the opportunity arose, on either side of the street, Magruder quickly brought up the matter of the coming territorial elections. One evening to his surprise and pleasure, the subject was mentioned by somebody else. He walked into the California Hotel's bar, which also served as the lobby, post office and stage terminal, to find two men asking about the political sentiments in this part of the territory. They had just come in from Boise City, they said, and they wondered who was being mentioned here as a possible candidate for congress.

Magruder said nothing. And sure enough, as he had hoped, he heard his own name mentioned by a blacksmith with whom he had just done some business. The man, who bought a box of horseshoe nails at Magruder's store, told the two men from Boise City that he understood Lloyd Magruder of Lewiston was running for the Democratic nomination. Although Magruder was no novice to politics, it did not diminish his pleasure at hearing this exchange. He stepped up and introduced himself. And, having observed that there were only eight people in the room, he ordered drinks for all.

John Cannady and R.P. Campbell seemed genuinely pleased to meet Magruder. They said they had heard his name mentioned in Lewiston also, but they did not say what their own interest might be in the election. They appeared to Magruder to be people of consequence, so he described his views to them in detail. They and the others listened with interest. Somebody said that the governor, Wallace, could have the Republican nomination if he wanted it, and Cannady said he probably did want it. And he would be hard to beat, everyone agreed. Should Wallace become the territory's first delegate to congress, President Lincoln would have to appoint a new governor. Was there any chance he might appoint somebody already here who knew the country and its problems? No chance, no chance at all. And too bad, because these appointed governors, in most of the territories of the West, were a pretty sorry lot, wishing all the time they were out here that they were still back East, still back in the states. As one of the men from Boise pointed out, most of them accepted the appointment only because it was a quick way to get into congress, as Wallace seemed likely to do.

The evening of good political talk ended too soon to suit Magruder. He walked back up the street to his tent, where Allen was on guard, and told him he had to be up in four hours. Then he rolled his blankets out on the straw and went to bed, only slightly drunk and very happy.[39]

*****

Renton, Romain and Lower found the sheriff's office, in the back half of a building in Bannack that also housed Chrisman's general store, and learned there that the sheriff was in Virginia City. The three bought provisions and set out through country that was partially wooded with large expanses of buffalo grass and creased by streambeds, now mostly dry. Through the grass and the trees ran a confusion of trails that had been worked into the ground by Indians and indelibly preserved by trappers and prospectors. Renton, who claimed a special talent for finding his way around, led the way in a northeasterly direction under a bright blue September sky.

They were in no great hurry, they told one another, and so there was no reason not to stop when they wished to and pan for gold. They didn't stop, however. All any of them wished to do now was get through this meeting with Plummer as quickly as possible. But first: where was he?

Plummer was staying with friends on a ranch some ten miles farther along the trail that Renton, Romain and Lower were now following, but he would not be there long. He had an appointment in Virginia City and would be on the trail within the hour. Plummer had made it a rule never to travel alone, and he was accompanied by two of his boys when he met Renton, Romain and Lower in a little swale where the trail crossed a dry streambed.

At first, he did not recognize any of the three, nor did the three recognize the two men with him, one riding in front and one behind. Lower sidled his horse off the trail and up the creek bed a few steps in deference both to the badge and to the man wearing it, who at any moment could have the three of them killed. Romain and Renton followed Lower's lead, and when the sheriff pulled abreast of him, Renton touched his hat brim and addressed Plummer by name. The sheriff responded after a moment's confusion, calling Renton by his other name, Doc Howard. He said hello to Lower, whom he had known as Lowry when they were in San Quentin together. But he had never met Romain, and he asked now who the kid might be. Renton introduced him and told Plummer that Romain was older than he looked. He said also that Romain was a good hand with stock and would do as he was told. But could he keep his mouth shut? the sheriff wanted to know. Both Renton and Lower assured him that Romain could.

Plummer was plainly doubtful. He also was surprised to see them here, he told them. Where was Magruder, and why weren't they following him? It now occurred to both Renton and Lower that Skinner had said nothing to Plummer about the missed connection at Lewiston. If he had, Plummer would be looking more than a bit puzzled; he would be furious. They both assumed that Skinner knew they were in the Bitterroots since Skinner had been there at the same time. And since they had failed to meet Skinner in Lewiston, as planned, they had to believe that Skinner suspected a double-cross. If Skinner had shared his suspicions with Plummer, would the sheriff be this civil, if not cordial, toward them now? The plan had been that they would follow Magruder to Bannack, get friendly with him there, then worm their way onto his crew for the trip back to Lewiston. At the right time, they would get the gold, and return with it to Bannack. But Plummer must have realized that they could as easily take the gold elsewhere, possibly to Portland, and that is why he had Skinner keeping track of them.

The sheriff gave no sign that he suspected anything. He just wanted to know what was going on. So Renton told him that everything was fine, that Magruder would be in Virginia City for another week or so. They had come looking for the sheriff, he said, because they wanted to explain to him why they had failed to meet Skinner in Lewiston. The sheriff seemed more concerned about Romain, and why he was now part of the plan. Renton, who was speaking for the three of them as though by mutual consent, told Plummer that he and Lower needed a third man to carry the thing off. If just two of Plummer's boys were with Magruder on the return to Lewiston, Magruder would need at least one more "loyal" hand, and that would make the job harder. Three men could handle anything that came up. They and Skinner had agreed on this, Renton said, and he apologized again for the missed connection in Lewiston. Again, Plummer ignored the failure to meet Skinner and instead complained about Romain's youth. He didn't like taking a punk kid into his confidence, he said. Renton acknowledged that Romain was young, but he said the kid was no dummy. He was strong and knew how to shoot and would be handy in a scrape.

Plummer seemed unconvinced, but he said it was too late now to do anything about it. And he added that if Romain should prove him wrong, and give a good account of himself, Plummer might find other things for him to do. To Renton, Lower and Romain, this had the sense of a blessing. Apparently, they had pulled it off. Plummer went over the plan again briefly, set a tentative date and place for the meeting in Bannack, and told the three that he should not be seen with any of them. Then the sheriff and his two silent companions rode on toward Virginia City.

Renton, Lower and Romain watched them go, then rode up out of the dry creek bed and away in the opposite direction, scattering grasshoppers as they went.

The first to speak was Romain, who said he was pleased to have met Henry Plummer and was proud to be working for him. The kid was dumber than he thought, Renton told himself. Aloud, he said he was much relieved that the meeting went as well as it did. They could stop worrying, now that Plummer understood they were still on his side. He also reminded the other two that this meeting had been his idea. Lower, who felt equally relieved, noted that Plummer had not asked them why they had failed to meet Skinner in Lewiston. Just forgot about it, probably. Renton said he did not know Henry Plummer to be a forgetful man. If he didn't ask, it meant he didn't care. The three rode on in silence, but Renton now was full of doubt and wonder. If Plummer didn't care, what could that mean?

After a mile or two they reached a place where another trail crossed, and Renton called for a conference. The other two stopped in the trail when he did. Were they going anywhere in particular? he wanted to know. Well, no, they said, unless he wanted to go back to Bannack. And Lower said he didn't want to do that; the place made him nervous. Renton then suggested that they turn east here and further explore the region that the Indians called the Stinking Water. They could look over the country and do a little prospecting, he said, just for a few days. Then they could rejoin Magruder in Virginia City. That was agreeable to Lower and Romain, and the three turned onto the new road and headed east toward the Ruby River.

13 William "Billy" Page, a grizzled old rancher, muleteer and wagon driver, was fed up with the Stinking Water and wondering what to do next. He and his two mules—one for riding and one for packing—had spent half a month wandering up one creek and down the other and he had found that too many people had been there before him. Claims had been staked everywhere. There was no use wasting more time here, but he was undecided whether to turn north toward the Deer Lodge region or head back across the Bitterroots to a warmer climate. Winter came early in this high country and it was now well into September.

Page had about decided to head for Deer Lodge when he ran into three young fellows who were also just knocking around. Renton, Lower and Romain were camping beside a pitifully small spring late one afternoon when Page came by, riding one mule and leading the other. Page stopped and passed the time of day, with a trace of a Cockney accent, and mentioned that he had run out of tobacco. Lower stood up from where he was sitting, dug into a saddlebag that was lying on the ground and pulled out a small cloth sack. He asked Page if he had kept his empty one. Page had, and Lower poured some of his tobacco into it. Page dismounted in order to express his gratitude and Renton said he was welcome to camp that night with them if he wished. Page accepted the invitation and introduced himself.

He said he had come over the Bitterroots alone earlier in the summer, looking for a fellow who owed him some money. A gentleman named Townsend. He didn't suppose the others had heard of him; they hadn't. Anyway, he'd spent the summer prospecting without much luck, and was thinking of going north.

Page's new companions introduced themselves as Doc Howard, Chris Lowry and Jim Romain. They had been more or less killing time with their gold pans, Renton said, and would soon be going back to Lewiston for the winter, helping out on a pack string. Meanwhile, they were just looking around the country and enjoying themselves. Lower had shot an antelope that morning and they would have fresh meat for a while. Page hadn't eaten fresh meat for two weeks. He stuffed a pinch of Lower's tobacco into his cheek and happily went to tend to his mules.

After supper, Renton told Page that if the old man had traveled alone from Elk City to the Stinking Water he must know those Bitterroot mountains pretty well. Pretty well, Page replied, poking at the embers of the cooking fire. Too many Indians trails going off in different directions, Renton said; it was confusing. Not so confusing, Page said, once you knew where they went. Renton took Page's remark as the understatement of a savvy old hand. Actually, Page had no idea where those other routes went; he was bragging.

Billy Page was born in England and had come to the United States in 1848. He had been roaming about in the western U.S. since 1856 and in the Idaho mountains for the past couple of years. He had been a wagon driver for General Green in Washington Territory, had worked as a freighter, cattle rancher, gold miner and livestock dealer before wandering out to Virginia City in search of his friend Townsend.[40] Page was in his sixties, a short, wiry man with red-rimmed, bright blue eyes and thinning red hair that didn't quite cover the bald spot at the back of his head. He had found that he could do anything he set out to do that didn't require schooling, but an appetite for strong drink had kept him close to broke for most of his life.

As he lay in his blankets that evening, he began to think that going north was not a good idea. He would rather not spend the winter on this side of the mountains and unless he wanted to cross the mountains alone in bad weather, he had better find someone going west to hitch up with, and pretty soon.

In the morning, Page told the others that he probably would not go north to the Deer Lodge country after all. He wouldn't have any better luck there than he'd had here, and winter was coming. This suited the other three, who had decided—at Renton's urging—that they would invite Page to go with them to Virginia City. Renton thought Magruder would be willing to take Page along and it would be nice to have someone with them who knew his way through those mountains. After a breakfast of antelope meat, bread and coffee, the four men broke camp and turned their backs on the Stinking Water. After two more days they were on the outskirts of Virginia City, and here Page said he would leave them temporarily. He knew of a stable nearby where he thought he could sell one of his mules. He would spend the night there and meet them the next day in town.

At Herndon's stable, Page sold his pack mule, a handsome black animal, for less than he had expected to get, but that did not surprise him. His expectations always outran reality. He asked to sleep that night in the stable and turned in early, just at dusk.

He was awakened later by a loud voice. Someone was shouting for the stableman, who came out of a nearby cabin carrying a lantern. Page rolled out of his blankets, wondering what this was all about, and went to the stable door. He saw two men dismount from their horses, and he could tell from the conversation that the two had come to buy mules. The stableman addressed one of them as Lou, and Page heard Lou say that his friend might be interested in buying a couple of good mules if the price was right. All three came into the stable, near where Page was standing, and Page met Lloyd Magruder for the first time.[41]

Magruder and Holt stayed long enough to pick out two mules, which they examined by lantern light, and then left, each leading one. Page had learned that Magruder had a store in town and would be packing over the mountains soon to Lewiston. This could be what he was looking for, Page thought, and he went back to bed.

By noon the next day, Page found Magruder's store, made himself useful with the animals, and repaired two damaged pack saddles. Also, Romain had spoken to Magruder on his behalf, saying that Page would be a good hand with the stock if Magruder needed more help on the trip home. Magruder made no promises, but he was clearly short-handed. Renton and Romain were there now but Lower had not arrived with them and Newburgh and the others were out prospecting. After Renton and Romain arrived, followed by Page, Allen had left with his gold pan, telling Magruder he would meet him later in Bannack. Maybe and maybe not, Magruder told the others; if Allen had luck, they might never see him again, and he hated to lose his chief packer. He would hope for the best. Counting Allen, Renton, Romain and himself, he had only four men to wrangle fifty-odd mules over nearly four hundred miles of mountain and plain. Holt was helping out in Virginia City but Magruder had not been able to talk him into crossing the mountains again. Holt planned to spend the winter at the ranch just outside of Bannack.

Magruder told Romain that if some of his crew didn't come back, and if Lower didn't show up, he probably could use Page. Renton said he had no idea where Lower had gone; probably drinking himself silly in some saloon. The truth was that Renton didn't want Lower around just now. Renton had told him that Magruder was more likely to hire Page if Lower made himself scarce for a few days. Once Page was securely on board, then Lower could show up, maybe when the pack string reached Bannack. Renton had even suggested that Lower return now to Bannack and wait for them there, but Lower had only said he'd think about it.

At about this time, Lower met a young fellow in a Virginia City saloon named Bill Rhodes, a miner who, like many others, had acquired an Indian wife. Rhodes told Lower he would like to take his wife to Elk City, where he had an interest in a horse ranch, if he could find a pack string to ride along with. Rhodes' wife was a Blackfoot, young and attractive, and when Lower took Romain out to Rhodes' place one day for a visit, Romain took a liking to the woman. After a few passes of the whiskey jug, Romain stood up from the bench he was sitting on and went outside looking for her.

He found her before anyone inside knew what was happening, and the woman's shrieks brought both Lower and Rhodes hurtling out of the cabin. Rhodes smashed Romain across the face, Romain pulled a knife, and Lower threw himself on Romain, pinning his arms. Lower apologized to Rhodes for his friend's bad behavior, and got Romain out of there. Later, Lower told him that was a dumb thing to do to a man who might be riding with them over the mountains to Elk City. Romain said he dearly wished that Rhodes would come along so he could kill the son of a bitch. Well, Lower told him, if he was lucky maybe he'd get the chance.

Page spent the next few days hanging around the store, helping where he could and trusting that Magruder would not abandon him when he left for home. Page found himself looking forward to the trek back to Lewiston, over mountains he had crossed before, among people that he knew—assuming that Renton and Romain were along.

Finally, with Lower still out of sight and Newburgh and the rest off prospecting somewhere, Magruder invited Page to join the crew. He told Billy that he would furnish him with a good horse to ride, and he would buy his mule. Page, still with money in his pocket, said that if Magruder didn't mind, he'd rather ride the mule. The mule, he said, had spoiled him with its easy gait.

Page noticed that quite a few men came into Magruder's store during that last week—not to buy but to talk politics. He told Romain it was a good thing Magruder was about sold out because his politicking didn't leave him much time for selling picks and shovels. Page had never paid much attention to politics, English or American, and he couldn't understand Magruder's joy in it. Magruder had come into the store a couple of mornings ago, hung over but happy as Hooligan because he had found some people to talk politics with. Well, Page thought, whatever makes the bear dance . . .

*****

By the last week in September, Magruder had sold out and was ready to return to Lewiston with his pack string and newly-purchased mules. Once back in his home county, among his political supporters, he would pursue that seat in congress. He had done all he could do here, and he was satisfied with it.

His plan was to knock down the tent, gather such crew as he could and go to Bannack, where he would pick up a few more mules. He would then leave for Lewiston by the way he had come, over the southern Nez Perce Trail.

He would be carrying about eighteen thousand dollars, some in legal tender but most of it in gold dust—a tempting treasure to be transporting through mountains where there was no law. Magruder would choose his crew with care, and he would have given a lot now to have Moran and Newburgh with him.

He had Billy Page, who would be competent in everything except defense of the gold, and even in this Page might surprise him. He was pleased to discover that he also would have Renton and Romain with him again. They were handy and good company, and they had found nothing to keep them here, they told Magruder. Two brothers from Missouri, Horace and Robert Chalmers, had stopped at the corral with a small pack string en route to Oregon. They wanted to attach their string to Magruder's, they said, since they were unfamiliar with the country and preferred the safety of numbers. They were carrying some sixteen hundred dollars and didn't want to lose it. Magruder was glad to have them. And Magruder also had Bill Phillips, a disillusioned miner who had turned up looking for work. Phillips and Romain had become friendly, and that was why Page was somewhat surprised to overhear Romain telling Phillips one day that it would be better for him not to come. Page mentioned the conversation to Renton, who assumed that Romain was making sure there would be room for Page. What he told Page was that he didn't have any idea why Romain would say that. What Romain probably meant, Renton said, was that Phillips could make a lot more money mining out here than coaxing mules over the mountains.

Magruder could be sure of a crew of seven men altogether; not enough, but perhaps he could recruit a couple of hands in Bannack. He was sorry Holt wasn't going, but Holt would help Magruder get packed and on his way. Among the things to be packed was the gold. (Holt remembered later that what he assumed to be a good part of the gold dust was stored in a box some eighteen inches square. He lifted it off the shelf and set it on the ground, and estimated the weight to be about ten pounds. Magruder put the box in a canvas bag, sewed the bag closed, and covered the closure with sealing wax. This bag, he said, would ride on one mule, and another bag of gold dust would ride on a second mule. Only Magruder would know which mules those were. The legal tender, in coins and government notes, or "continentals," would ride in a purse inside a saddlebag on Magruder's horse, Bud.)[42]

The pack string was assembled in the corral at dawn on September 29. It was an easy piece of work this time, since most of the mules were carrying empty pack saddles; all Magruder was taking to Lewiston, besides his money, were his equipment and provisions for the trip. Magruder bade goodbye to Virginia City before sunrise, and was well on the road to Bannack by noon, in good weather.

The travelers proceeded as far as Beaverhead Rock, some twenty miles, the first day and put up that night at a tavern. The next morning on the trail they met Charlie Allen, and Allen joined the team. On the third day at noon, at a place called Rattlesnake, they stopped for lunch and Lower showed up.[43] He had been traveling with some friends, he said, just for something to do, and figured that Magruder could use him on the trip west.

Magruder reached Bannack that afternoon. Renton and Romain left, saying they had to see about some horses, and would be back. Magruder made arrangements to buy some government mules, not knowing that in his absence the bottom had dropped out of the market for mules in Lewiston. The mining camps at Pierce City, Oro Fino and Elk City were being depopulated as prospectors hurried to new strikes in the Salmon River country to the south. There would be less business for packers in the Clearwater country and less need of mules. While in Bannack, Magruder also mailed a letter to Caroline, telling her he would be leaving in twelve more days for Lewiston. It was a bit of insurance, a ruse designed to confuse anyone who might intercept that letter. Caroline would understand that it meant he was leaving immediately.

After a full day in Bannack, buying mules, provisions and newspapers, Magruder and Page stopped together at Skinner's Saloon. There, over brandies, Magruder described to Page in some detail what would be expected of him on the trek through the Bitterroots. Page said he would be happy to help with the cooking and the guard duty as well as tend to the animals. Magruder told Page he was glad to have him along and was especially glad to be traveling again with Lower, Renton and Romain. It was this conversation, apparently, that gave Page the impression Magruder had no better friends in the world than those three.[44]

The party made an early start on October 3 for the Bitterroots. Magruder's crew, as he moved toward Big Hole Pass with some fifty mules, included the Chalmers brothers, Bill Phillips, Billy Page, Charlie Allen, Renton, Lower, Romain and himself. Nine men ought to be plenty, Magruder told Page. If they didn't run into bad weather, this would be an easy ride.

14 On the first day out of Bannack, Magruder and company traveled some twenty miles and camped beside a creek in a small meadow. Charlie Allen and Horace Chalmers took the first watch and Renton and William Chalmers took the second. It was a quiet night under a cloudless sky.[45]

Next day, traveling through the easy terrain of the Big Hole country, the string made thirty miles and camped in a stream bottom among lodgepole pines. Magruder and Lower took the first watch, Page and Romain the second.

On the next day, October 5, the travelers logged another thirty miles to the Bitterroot River and camped in a wide valley. Allen and Horace Chalmers took the first watch, Renton and William Chalmers the second. It was another quiet, uneventful night.

On October 6 they were out of the Bitterroot Valley and climbing the divide toward the Clearwater drainage, retracing the route by which they had come. Early on that day they met a party of Frenchmen, some of whom knew Magruder, and there was a pause for talk. Despite this delay, the men and animals managed to reach the pass by evening, and camped in heavy timber. Magruder and Lower took the first watch, Page and Romain the second.

The next morning, after breaking camp and moving out, they met two men riding in the opposite direction who said they were on their way to the Beaverhead. They wanted to know whether any in Magruder's party had seen their friends there. Nobody knew these friends or recognized their descriptions, and the two men rode on. Shortly thereafter, Magruder and party dropped down to the Selway, forded the river, and started up the other side. It was here, as the pack string climbed toward the high ridge, that Lower rode up to Page and asked him to drop to the back of the line of mules. Renton and Romain wished to speak to him there. Page did so. Renton then reminded Page that Magruder was carrying a great deal of money, and that he, Romain and Lower meant to have it.

"We want you to sleep tonight with Phillips," Romain said.

"Very well," Page replied.

"And don't be frightened," Renton told him, "we'll do all the dirty work."

"Yes."

"If you hear any noise in the night, pay no attention to it," Romain said, and he repeated: "This is the night we mean to have the money."

"Yes."

"You sleep with a revolver," Renton said. "If Phillips wakes up, shoot him through the head."

"No, no," said Romain, "Billy can't shoot that good. Shoot him in the gut."

"Yes."

The two then dismissed Page and he rode back to his place in the line, hardly able to believe what he had heard or what he had said in reply. He didn't know what to think. Up to now, he had thought that Renton, Lower and Romain were the best friends Magruder had in the world. Were they joking with him? They didn't seem to be joking. Should he tell Magruder? Magruder would probably not believe him. And if he told Magruder, and the other three found out, they would kill him. Must he be a party to this gruesome business? Dazed and frightened, Page found himself unable to do anything but tremble.

Magruder camped that night high in the Bitterroots beside a fair spring, where there was good feed and big timber. The night was clear. Charlie Allen and Horace Chalmers drew the first watch and Renton and William Chalmers the second. Page rolled his blankets out beside Phillips and lay down with his revolver at his head. All that night he lay in his blankets listening and trembling, unable to sleep. He heard nothing unusual, and the next morning was just like every other morning. Page was more confused than ever.

On the trail that morning, October 8, Lower again approached Page and told him that Renton and Romain wanted to talk to him. Again, Page rode back down the line and again, the other two told him not to be frightened. This would be the night without fail. Neither mentioned what had gone awry the night before, if anything had.

Several times that day, Lower, Renton and Romain in turn rode up to Page and urged him not to be frightened but to do as he'd been told.

Magruder made camp that evening in a clearing with a black rock cliff on one side and a deep ravine on the other. The weather had been clear all day but by nightfall the sky was clouding over, leaving only a few stars winking in the black. Allen, saying he expected snow by morning, put up a tent. The others scoffed at this and laid their blankets out in the open. Magruder kept the supper fire going and sat smoking his pipe until near dark, when he and Lower were to begin the first watch. Page, frightened in spite of the warnings not to be, sat by the fire watching Magruder and Lower walk up a rise in the clearing to where the animals were grazing, out of sight behind a stand of tall firs. Magruder was carrying a rifle and Lower an axe. Lower had planned to take his rifle also, but Magruder had told him one would be enough. So Lower had picked up one of the camp's two axes, saying he would need to make a fire for the two of them.

Page watched Lower and Magruder walk away from the camp until they were out of sight, then he laid his blankets down beside Phillips, who was already asleep. Page was determined to stay awake even though he hadn't slept the night before. He put his revolver near his head and lay listening to Phillips' breathing and the camp's other night sounds and before long, in spite of himself, he dozed off.

After checking on the animals, Lower and Magruder built a small fire and the two of them sat chatting as darkness fell. They were soon joined by Renton, who said he wasn't tired enough to sleep. He was carrying a coffee pot and three tin cups. They all sat by the fire then, drinking coffee and speculating on the weather as the wind began to sigh among the trees.

Renton said he'd go fetch some more wood, and stood up. Lower said he'd help, and picked up the axe. Magruder bent over the fire to light his pipe, and Lower swung the axe hard, smashing Magruder's skull. Renton rushed up, grabbed the axe from Lower, and brought it down once more on the battered head, which now was lying in the fire.

Near midnight, Page awoke. He heard someone coming down from the hill and thought it was the watch coming to call him. It was Renton and Lower.

They walked to where Page was lying and Renton asked him, "Are you awake?"

Page said yes, and the other two then walked on and lay down on their own blankets next to Romain.

In a few moments Renton and Romain stood up and walked past Page, each with an axe in his hand, in the direction of the Chalmers brothers' beds. Renton and Romain were not wearing boots, coats or hats. Page heard the blows, and several low groans, and knew that the brothers were dead. Renton and Romain then returned and lay down again next to Lower. Phillips was still asleep next to Page, and Allen apparently was still sleeping in his tent nearby.

Renton stood up and walked past Page again, this time carrying a shotgun. He went to the corner of Allen's tent and stood there. At about the same time, Romain walked past Page's head, carrying an axe.

Page started to rise up but Romain told him in a low voice: "Lay still. Now you lay still."

Romain then raised the axe and brought it down on Phillips' head. Phillips screamed and kept screaming as Romain hit him again and again.

Renton, as though in response to Phillips' screams, aimed the shotgun through the tent flap at Allen, and blew the back of his head off.

Page was up by now and pulling on his clothes. He heard Romain yelling at the dead Phillips: "You son of a bitch, you shouldn't have come on this trip. I told you not to come. I wish to Christ Bill Rhodes had come, I've wanted to kill that son of a bitch for a long time."

Romain then turned toward Page. "You're scared," he said. "You're all atremble. Now don't be frightened."

"That's right," Renton called out from the corner of Allen's tent. "Don't be frightened, Uncle Billy. All the dirty work is done."

Renton was proud of his work, and of his tools. He rebuilt the supper fire, getting it to blaze brightly and then called Lower, Romain and Page to Allen's tent. Inside the tent, in the firelight shining on the bloody mess, Renton grasped Allen's hair and turned the head over.

"Look at this," he said to the others. The whole back of the head was missing. "That's a beautiful gun," Renton added. "It does its work well." And he pointed out to the others that he hadn't simply held the gun and blazed away. He had taken careful aim, so as to do the job right.

Renton said they would have to get out of here soon. He told Page to gather the equipment they would no longer need and to throw on the fire anything that would burn. This included canvas bags and leather harness and extra pack saddles. The throw-away kitchen equipment was to go into gunny sacks which he was to hide under rocks and logs. Page set about this work while the other three began packing gear and provisions. They were in a hurrying mood, for Allen had been right: it was beginning to snow.

Renton told Page to go up the hill and see where the animals were. Page found the animals and turned some of them out on the road again. When he came back down, Lower asked him if he had found a fire burning up there and he said he had, and that he had put it out because it was burning among the grass and leaves. He shouldn't have done that, Lower said. Lower had kicked the fire about deliberately to burn the blood.

Page also found when he came down the hill that they had been counting the money. There wasn't as much as they had expected, they told him. They had searched all the bodies and all the packs and the most they could find was about twelve thousand dollars. Page suspected he was being lied to. There surely was more money than that. He had seen more money than that in Virginia City, but of course Magruder had been buying mules with some of it. Anyhow, it didn't matter to him. He expected none of it and wanted none of it. He wished only that they would take the money and go, and leave him here to find his own way back. He knew that was not possible. They couldn't leave him here to tell the tale, and for some reason he didn't yet understand, they didn't want to kill him—at least not yet.

The bodies of Allen and Phillips had been tied together, and Page helped roll them over some logs into the ravine. All four were now wearing moccasins, on Renton's orders, so that this would appear to be the work of Indians. Page himself tied up the Chalmers brothers, and Lower and Romain carried them on a pole to the edge of the ravine and rolled them down. Meanwhile, the big fire Renton had built to light the gore in Allen's tent had burned the bags and harness. The four of them picked the metal harness rings and other nonburnable debris out of the ashes, put them in a sack and hid it behind a log. Page picked out two pack saddles and put these to one side where the riding saddles were. Lower and Renton went up the hill to where Magruder's corpse lay in the ashes of last evening's fire and wrapped it in a blanket. Then they tied the blanket with a picket rope and pushed it into the ravine.

It was decided that they would take two pack mules. Page went looking for Magruder's favorite, a big gray, but couldn't find it in the dark. Nor could he find his own riding mule, a large, reddish animal he called Rust. He thought he would take Magruder's horse, Bud, but Romain was taking that one, and he wound up finally with Allen's horse, a sorrel. They saddled and packed the horses and two mules, then they changed from moccasins into boots. Romain had some blood on his pants so he threw them away and put on a pair of Allen's. Romain took a six-shooter that had belonged to one of the Chalmers brothers and Page took a five-shot that Allen had carried. Lower told Page to pack the shotguns and rifles; they would have no need of them.

They mounted their horses in the first light of morning and moved out onto the main trail, leading the two mules. Then they discovered that the rest of the animals were following them. They stopped. They would have to shoot the extra mules and horses, but they couldn't do it here on the main trail. They decided to continue on, and halted again at the bottom of a ravine. Renton, Lower and Romain herded the animals up the ravine until they were out of sight of the trail, and then began shooting them. This caused the mules to start to scatter and hide. Page had been loading pistols for the other three, who were able to kill only a couple of dozen. The rest had bolted into the woods. The only thing to do, they decided, was to continue on, and shoot any of the animals that followed.

In this way, shooting one or a few at a time in places where the animals could be hidden, they finally killed all but eight of the mules. When Page's mule, Rust, came along behind the group, Renton turned his horse aside and pulled out his pistol.

"I'd ruther you didn't shoot him," Page called to Renton. "He's a good mule."

"He has to be killed," Renton shouted back, "or it's a rope around the necks of all of us." And he shot it.

Farther down the trail they met a party of miners, one of whom knew Page, and they stopped to talk. Page's friend said he had lost a gray horse, and if his party found it would they take it with them and leave it at Brown's feed yard in Lewiston? It had a white "A" on the left shoulder. Page said they would.

The snow had stopped falling at midday, and the weather by afternoon was not bad. Lower, Renton, Romain and Page camped that evening in a small meadow and overhauled everything. Renton threw away Magruder's pocket watch and compass lest it be recognized. He and Romain took out all the purses and checked to see if there were names on any of them. They found none. Intending to travel light, they discarded two pairs of leggings. Renton took out the axe he had used to kill the Chalmers brothers and put the handle in the fire to dry the blood. Then, somewhat to Page's surprise, the others divided the money into four purses rather than three, and gave one to Page.

Page did not understand any of this, least of all why he was still alive. But he was beginning to suspect that he might be worth more to them than he had thought. They were going to have to thread their way around populated places on unfamiliar trails, and they assumed he knew the country better than any of them. It occurred to him, with something of a shock, that if he hadn't bragged to them about his knowledge of these Indian trails he probably would be dead now. He had no idea what they planned to do after leaving these mountains, but he now believed he'd live to see the day. And he was canny enough to understand that by giving him part of the loot they had implicated him in the crime. His fate was now bound up with theirs, for better or for worse.

15 Renton had decided they must hereafter steer clear of others on the trail. If somebody should pass them going the other way, and then stumble upon the dead horses and mules, they

could be in trouble. He told Page that wherever possible he should find alternate, untraveled routes for them.

Even if Page had known the country as well as he claimed, this would not have been easy. Within two days of leaving Magruder's last camp there was a foot of snow on the ground, and the snow piling on the trees changed appearances and made reconnoitering difficult. The Nez Perce Trail, like most Indian roads, followed the easiest route, staying mainly on the high ridges and avoiding as much as possible the steep sidehills and narrow valleys. The Nez Perces were a nomadic people who lived by the seasons rather than the clock, and they had time to take the long and easy way around. But for Renton and his companions, this was no time to travel in leisurely comfort. Page did the best he could to find the less-traveled shortcuts, but here he did less well than Renton. And on the sixth day after the murders it was Renton who found a route that took the party around and out of sight of Elk City.

The town sat in a broad valley at about four thousand feet of elevation. Getting around it meant staying on the higher ground to the east and north and rejoining the main Nez Perce Trail where it began to climb the first ridge between the South Fork and the Clearwater. The route took them across that mountain, down again to Newsome Creek, then up to the high country of the main ridge. At five thousand feet they were in snow again.

Since leaving the valley of the South Fork it had become difficult to avoid chance encounters on the trail. There were too many prospectors traveling to and from the mining claims on the creeks flowing down from the heights. At a resting place called Mountain House, at around six thousand feet, Renton's cautionary advice blew away on the wind. All four were cold and tired. Lower wanted to stop for whiskey, and Romain and Page both agreed they needed that. Renton was dubious; he had noticed a couple of men hanging around outside the tavern and suspected there were several others inside who might recognize one or more of them. But Renton was thirsty too. He said they'd ride on a little way and send Lower back alone for whiskey and tobacco. This satisfied the rest. They rode on until they were well out of sight of the place and halted, and Lower rode back down the trail to the tavern. The others dismounted, led their animals off the trail, and waited. And waited. Lower was taking a long time, Romain said, and Renton, worried now, had to decide what to do. He didn't want to leave Lower in there, but he wanted to be on his way. He finally told Romain to go back and fetch Lower out; they couldn't hang around here any longer. Romain had mounted and was starting back down the trail when Lower appeared and handed Renton a bottle of whiskey and a sack of tobacco. If he'd kept them waiting, he said, he was real sorry. He'd had a couple of quick ones to steady his nerves. Renton was angry enough to shoot him on the spot, but controlled himself and said nothing. He took a drag on the bottle and passed it to Romain, and said they'd better get going. He said Lower had had enough, and took the bottle back after Page had his turn. They would continue on a little ways from here, Renton said, and make camp.[46] They spent that night in a canyon some two miles from the Mountain House and next day they crossed that mountain and made their way down to the South Fork again near Cottonwood Creek.

Here they paused to consider Lower's suggestion that they not cross the South Fork quite yet. There was a ferry not far from here, Lower said; he had used it on the way east, not realizing there was an easy ford only a half mile upstream. The ferryman should have collected a good cache of gold over the summer, and he couldn't think of any reason why they shouldn't have it. Renton said he could think of one: they had no time to waste and it would take time to find that gold, which no doubt was well hidden. Romain liked Lower's idea. The ferryman could be made to tell them where the gold was, he said, and they would all be that much richer. Renton said Lower and Romain were both damn fools. They had to get out of this country and get out fast, and there would be no more talk of hidden gold. The worst thing anybody could do in these mountains, Renton reminded the others, was rob or kill a ferryman. It was the unforgivable crime. They would cross the South Fork here, Renton said; it was shallow enough. All crossed behind Renton, and the worst of the traveling was over. From here the route ascended to the Camas Prairie, and from there all the way to Washington Territory, the going would be easy.[47]

They were carrying more equipment than they needed, including extra pack saddles and ropes. Renton said they ought to get rid of the stuff, and he and Page unloaded it and hid it in some dense brush above Cottonwood Creek.[48] Once on the prairie, Renton told the others that they must not be seen in Lewiston or at Fort Lapwai. And to pass by the shebang at the culdesac was now out of the question. He suggested that they leave the Camas Prairie west of the usual route, and ford the Snake River south of Lewiston by the way they had come. Once in Washington Territory they could all relax.

Page, however, said he knew an easy ford where they could cross the main Clearwater east of Lewiston. They could then travel down the north side to the Snake River and into Washington Territory and never go into town. Renton did not care for that plan. There was no place there to ford the Snake River, he pointed out. They would have to take the same ferry at Silcott that they had taken before, and they might be recognized. He reminded the others that they had told the ferryman they were going to Portland; what would he think if he saw them crossing again so soon in the same direction?

Lower did not see that as a problem. They would be dressed differently this late in the season, he said, and even if they encountered the same ferryman, why should he remember them?

Renton gave in and told Page to lead them to the main Clearwater. He did, and got them there after another day's travel. But when they arrived at the ford, at a warmer, lower elevation, they found the Clearwater running high with snow melt. It looked dangerous, and Renton said it would be foolish to try to cross and risk losing everything. Romain wanted to try it and Lower said it didn't look too difficult to him. There was a small island in the river some sixty feet from shore. Renton told Lower and Romain to go that far and then let him know how it looked from there. But as quickly as he said it he changed his mind and told the others it was not a good idea. Romain wanted to know why not, and Renton reminded him that they had two mules. To cross the Clearwater here would mean abandoning those mules since the mules were not dumb enough to try this crossing even if they were. They didn't need the mules, Romain said; they were only a couple of days out of Lewiston and could carry everything they needed on the horses. With great patience, Renton told Romain that the only point in crossing the river here was so they wouldn't have to go to Lewiston. And if they managed to get past Lewiston unnoticed, they would have some long days of travel ahead of them. Romain, humiliated, turned red in the face and Lower feared a fight was about to break out. He moved his horse in between the other two and told Renton that he would explain everything to Jimmie and that Jimmie would understand.

For a moment, Romain appeared to be calming down. Then, in a burst of temper, he wheeled his horse and clattered down the bank to the river's edge. He prodded the horse into the dark, swift-running water. It was slow going but Romain's horse, after some long pauses and much slipping and sliding, managed to reach the rocky, brushy hump of land. Beyond the island the water was faster and deeper still, and Romain sat looking at it for a long time. Renton, Page and Lower looked on from horseback, saying nothing until Lower finally muttered that the kid might actually be crazy enough to try it if someone didn't stop him. Romain turned and looked toward the three on the shore, then again across the roaring river. He may be dumb, Renton said, but not that dumb, and turned his horse. Renton said no more and rode away from the riverbank. Page cast a look back at Romain, and followed. So did Lower. The three of them returned to high ground the way they had come, and were leading the two mules along the south bank of the Clearwater when Romain joined them. He could have made it across, he said, but had decided not to. Probably, Renton said, and dropped the subject.[49]

If the Clearwater was now too high to ford, the Snake would be also, and the Snake was wider. Page said that if they could not cross the Clearwater here, there was nowhere they could cross it. Renton said they would have to go to Lewiston after all. Perhaps they could find a boat there and get across the Snake that way. Page found an Indian trail that would take them out of the deep valley of the Clearwater onto the Camas Prairie again, and they pressed on.

They had lost precious time and they were low on food. Furthermore, the snow had turned to rain when they reached lower ground and some parts of the trail were deep in mud. There was no pleasure in this journey now, and there was still Lewiston to get through. But at least they would find food and dry clothes there.

*****

They reached Lewiston at about 9 o'clock on the wet and windy night of October 18, ten days after leaving the scene of the crime. They took the animals to a packing yard that had once been owned by an acquaintance of Page named James Hays, and Page and Lower stayed there, in the packing shed out of the rain, while Renton and Romain went looking for a boat. They had no luck. When they returned to the yard, Renton reported that the stage was leaving early the next morning for Walla Walla and they would all go down on it. Renton told Lower to go and engage four seats on the stage, but Lower said he had no coin. Page gave him fifty dollars, and Lower left for the Luna House.

Reaching the hotel, Lower stepped into the lobby and went quickly to the desk. Hill Beachey, who normally left his post around 8, had remained late that night to work on his accounts. He looked up when Lower came in but took no particular notice of him, and returned to his books. Beachey's clerk was behind the counter preparing the waybill for that night's coach and it was he who answered Lower's request for tickets. Lower asked for four. The clerk explained to Lower that the stage line did not sell tickets. Instead, he would take the money and add the passengers' names to the waybill.

This caught Lower by surprise. He was not prepared to supply names, and he fumbled about for a moment before blurting out four of them. The passengers, he said, would be Wm. Johnson, G. Clark, D. Smith and F. Perkins. Aware of the confusion, Beachey looked up from his books and this time took some notice of the man at the desk. Although he was wearing his coat collar turned up high around his face he looked vaguely familiar. Still, Beachey could not place him and assumed he was just some fellow he'd seen hanging around the hotel bar. Lower paid for four seats in the coach and left.

When he returned to the shed, he told the others which names they would henceforth be carrying, adding that the transaction had given him a bad case of nerves. Was there anything left in the bottle? he asked Renton. What they all needed now, Renton said, was some sleep. He suggested that they get two rooms at the French hotel and turn in. Page could find a more permanent place to leave the animals and join them later at the De France.

The three left, taking all the gold with them, and Page went looking for a rancher he knew named Bishop Goodrich. Goodrich had a place out in Tammany Hollow where they could leave the animals until spring. Page visited several saloons but could find Goodrich in none of them and wandered over to the Luna House. There, at about 11 o'clock, he ran across the watchman, whom he knew as Leo and who greeted him as Billy Page, shining a lantern in his face. Page said he was looking for Goodrich, and Leo told him he could find him in the bar of the Luna House. Page had no desire to go in there and asked Leo to go and call Goodrich out. Leo did so, after calling his rounds, and Page told Goodrich what he needed. Goodrich considered this for a moment, then told Page he would soon be leaving for the winter; however, there would be someone at the ranch, and he would see that the animals were cared for until spring. Page and Goodrich then led the animals to a different corral that Goodrich preferred, and they parted.[50]

At the Hotel De France, Page found the bar empty and the desk clerk sitting alone and half asleep. He had been told to wait up for a late guest, he said, and presumed that must be Page. That was correct, Page said, but he would like a brandy before going upstairs and would be pleased to have the clerk join him. The clerk accepted the offer and poured two brandies in the bar. He and Page, exchanging pleasantries, emptied their glasses and Page trudged up the stairs, undressed to his underwear, and went to bed with Lower.

Beachey, meanwhile, stared long and hard at those four names on the waybill. He had been in the hotel business long enough to get a feel for these things, and the longer he looked the more convinced he became that these four passengers were traveling under false identities. Finally, he went outside and walked around the hotel to the Luna stables and found Chester Coburn, the man in charge. He knew that two of Coburn's friends were planning to leave for Portland and San Francisco on that same stage. Beachey advised Coburn to tell his friends not to take that stage because he sensed danger in the air.

As Coburn later recalled the conversation, Beachey told him, "Try to keep your friends here until the next stage. Have they any money?"

"Yes, one of them has twenty-five thousand dollars I know of and the other may have some. But they won't stay because the boat leaves Portland for San Francisco only every two weeks and if they miss this stage they will have to lay over."

"Well then, warn them to be sure to take the back seat and keep their guns handy. And tell them to keep a close watch all the time."

Shortly after midnight, Coburn went to his friends' room and woke them. At Coburn's suggestion they got into the stagecoach in the stables, taking the back seat, and Beachey and Coburn rode the brake blocks to the front of the hotel.[51]

The night was cold, and there was a hint of rain on the wind. Judge John Berry, who had been dozing in the lobby, came out on the veranda to watch the departure and so did Leo Guion, the hotel's night watchman. Beachey joined the others and was standing on the edge of the veranda when the four passengers arrived, dressed in heavy clothing and wearing scarves high around their faces. They climbed silently into the coach and sat staring straight ahead, avoiding eye contact as though they had never met. Something about the scene confirmed Beachey's suspicions, and the innkeeper picked a lantern up off the veranda and thrust it inside the coach. In the dim light, Beachey could see on each man's lap a cantina, a small metal and leather case often used in the territories for carrying gold.

Beachey turned to Judge Berry and demanded that he hold the stage. The judge, surprised, asked why. Beachey said he wanted to find out who those men were. Go inside and look at the waybill, the judge advised, but Beachey had done that. Realizing he had no real grounds for action, Beachey gave up and watched in frustration as the driver emerged from the hotel, stuffing papers into an inside pocket, and mounted the high seat. He released the brake, snapped the reins, and gave the team a shout. The stagecoach pulled away from the hotel, moved down D Street toward the ferry, and disappeared in the dark.

Beachey turned to Coburn and told him his friends were probably in no danger of being robbed. The four other passengers all seemed to have money. That relieved Coburn, who returned to the stables. Beachey, whose stomach was now churning in anger and fear, went back inside the hotel, sat down at his desk and closed his account books. He put them in a small safe behind the registration counter and locked it with a key. Then he took his coat and hat off the rack beside the safe, put them on and walked slowly out into the night. A cold rain was falling as Beachey stepped off the veranda onto a wooden sidewalk and then into the muddy street. Halfway across, he stopped and turned, staring in the direction the stage had taken. The coach and six by now would be on Silcott's ferry, heading for the north bank of the Clearwater en route to Walla Walla.

Who are those men? Beachey asked himself. For a while he stood in the middle of the street in the dark, a stocky figure in a long black coat, listening to the rain on his hat. Suddenly it came to him where he had seen Lower before, and the rain was forgotten.

Now he knew what had to be done, and who would have to do it.

16 Hill Beachey had seen enough of Chris Lower's face to understand now why it filled him with such horror. It was the face of the man in his dream, the man swinging the axe.

Some would later scoff at the notion that Beachey could have seen the murder committed in a dream well before Magruder ever left Lewiston for Bannack. But others, including Chester Coburn and James Witt, later said that Beachey had indeed had such a dream and after the murder he had described it to them.

Beachey had told his wife the morning after the dream that he had seen Magruder bending over a campfire to light his pipe; and in the firelight another man rise up behind him and bring an axe down on his head.[52] Beachey wanted to describe the dream to Magruder as a warning that he must not go to Bannack. Margaret urged her husband to say nothing because Magruder wouldn't believe him. She also told him that if he mentioned the dream to anyone else he would quickly become the laughingstock of the town.[53]

Beachey thought that maybe if he just told Magruder's wife, Caroline, then she might be able to talk her husband out of this recklessness. For God's sake, Margaret had said, he mustn't tell

Caroline. She didn't need anything more to worry about while Lloyd was away in those mountains.

So Beachey, who respected Maggie's advice in most matters, had mentioned the dream to no one else. He had kept it locked up inside himself, afraid to ignore it but wishing it would go away. Of course it wouldn't go away. It would surface suddenly when he was doing his accounts or registering a guest or reaching for a glass, and torment him with a series of silent images like the pictures in a magic lantern show: a picture of nighttime and a small fire and his friend Magruder kneeling beside the fire; a picture of Magruder lighting his pipe from a burning twig; a picture of a face, a fiend's face, standing behind Magruder with an axe; the axe raised; the axe falling . . .

And Beachey would blink and shake his head and try to re-member what he was doing. It was what came of keeping a thing like this to yourself. Maggie probably wouldn't understand it, but Maggie no doubt was right. Magruder would laugh and think the dream was quite a joke, and Caroline would drive herself crazy with fear.

Convinced that it would do no good, Beachey had agreed not to say anything about the dream to Magruder. Instead, he would give his friend the prized Kentucky rifle as a warning of danger.

Now, hurrying back to the Luna House in the rain, Beachey had to fight the urge to gather some men and go after the stage. That would be foolish, he realized, for what would they do when they caught it? He had no evidence that any of those four passen-gers had done anything wrong. The four were not fugitives, yet. Beachey would first find some evidence that Magruder was dead— since only he was now convinced of it—and that those heavily scarved men were in some way responsible.

To the people still lounging in the Luna House lobby, Beachey expressed his concern. He was convinced, he said, that the four had been up to no good, and he pointed out that at least two well-known packers had still not returned from the mining camps. Beachey's concern was contagious. At daybreak, October 19, Mose Druillard rode out to seek news of Capt. A. P. Ankeny, a merchant packer who was thought to be somewhere in the Oro Fino area. Another volunteer, Shull Kenney, left for Elk City in search of news about Magruder.

After sunup that day, Beachey and some others began to check the livery stables on the assumption that four men riding into town from the east would have left their animals at one of them. For some reason, no one thought to ask Chester Coburn, the manager of Beachey's own Luna Stables, about this. Only later did Beachey learn that the four travelers had left their horses and mules in the care of Bishop Goodrich, and that Goodrich had moved them from the Luna Stables to his own place in Tammany Hollow. Beachey rode out to Tammany and identified one mule, a saddle and a shotgun as the property of Lloyd Magruder. Goodrich then agreed to move all the animals and equipment back to the Luna Stables for the time being.

Beachey by now had succeeded in passing his fears along to others even though Magruder himself was not yet overdue. In his letter to Caroline, mailed from Bannack on October 2, Magruder had said he would be leaving there in twelve days or so. It was a kind of code intended to confuse any larcenous characters who might intercept the mail. Caroline understood it to mean that Magruder was leaving immediately. Assuming he took as long coming back as going out, Magruder on the twentieth could still be en route to Lewiston.

As it was, three men came into town with a pack string on October 23 and found it odd that Magruder had not yet arrived; he had left Bannack three days ahead of them, they said, and should have been here by now.[54]

To everybody in Lewiston it was now apparent that Lloyd Magruder had been robbed and killed, along with his crew. The only man known to be with Magruder (because he was a regular on Magruder's crew, and Magruder had mentioned him by name in the letter to Caroline) was Charlie Allen. So when Beachey sought a warrant for the arrest of the four suspects, he claimed they were wanted for the murder of Lloyd Magruder and Charles Allen.

Beachey acquired the warrant, and from Sheriff James Fisk he received an appointment as deputy sheriff. But since the fugitives by now were well on their way, it would not be enough simply for Beachey to arrest them and bring them back. He would have to get requisitions authorizing their return by the governor of the state or province where they might be found. The Governor of Idaho Territory would have to sign the requisitions addressed to the governors of British Columbia, California, Oregon and Washington. But Idaho was without a governor since William H. Wallace had resigned to campaign for election as the territory's delegate to congress. Beachey thus had to deal with the acting governor, William B. Daniels, and Daniels proved to be difficult. The acting governor was unsure of his authority, for one thing. For another, he was without a precedent, since Idaho Territory was so newly organized that it had no criminal code. It had a court system of sorts, but as Supreme Court Justice Alleck Smith noted apologetically in one of the affidavits in the case, he could not affix a seal because "as yet no Seal has been adopted for said Courts."[55]

Beachey finally was able to persuade Daniels to sign the necessary documents, insisting that time was short and he would take personal responsibility for any expenses that might be involved. He further told Daniels that he would accept full blame if it turned out that no crime had been committed or that these fugitives were innocent. In order to convince Daniels of the urgency of his mission, Beachey had drawn upon the testimony of several other citizens who assured Daniels that Beachey's concerns were widely shared. One of these was Wesley Wickersham, a peace officer and Magruder's partner in the Elk City store. Another was Thomas Farrell, also known as Thomas Pike, who had offered to accompany Beachey on the chase.

Finally, Daniels agreed to give Beachey the document he needed, and he wrote it out himself, addressing it to the two governors most likely to see it:

"Be it known, that on this the 23d day of October AD 1863 Personally appeared before me W. H. Wickersham who presented to me an affidavit by him made, which is in due form of Law, and which discloses that a murder and highway robery has been committed in this Territory, and that Wm. Johnson, G. Clark, D. Smith and F. Perkins committed the same, and that they the aforesaid Wm. Johnson, G. Clark, D. Smith and F. Perkins have fled from this Territory to British Columbia, or to the State of California. Therefore I request that the said fugitives be delivered up to Hill Beachy and Thomas Farrell, citizens of the United States and of Idaho Territory, whom I hereby appoint and constitute the proper authorities to return the aforesaid fugitives under the treaty between the United States and Great Britain bearing date of August

the 9th 1842, so that the aforesaid fugitives may be tried in this
Territory in acordance with the Laws of this Territory and of the
United States."[56]

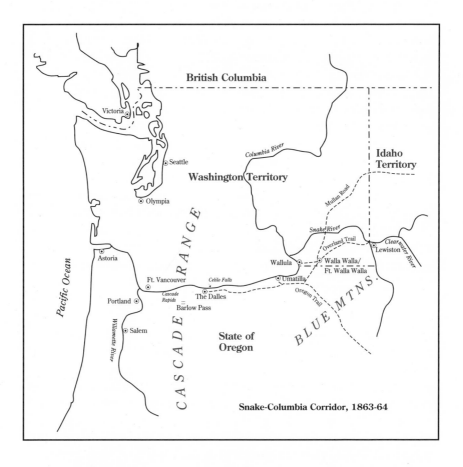

Snake-Columbia Corridor, 1863-64

Daniels signed it once as acting governor and again as secretary of the territory, which he still was.

Armed at last with the papers, Beachey and Farrell set out for Walla Walla by private coach. Beachey's own stage line would not get the pair to Walla Walla quickly enough.

Once there, Beachey and Farrell learned that the fugitives had lingered only long enough to catch a stage for Wallula, a small settlement on the Columbia River, and they did the same. From Wallula they took a steamboat down the Columbia as far as The Dalles, where river navigation was blocked by Celilo Falls. They made inquiries at The Dalles and learned that four men answering the fugitives' descriptions—but now using different names—had spent a night there with friends. One of these men, it was said, had shown some gold and talked about a fight over a mine that had led to a killing. After one night, the four had left for the coast.

Beachey and Farrell took a rail coach around Celilo Falls to the so-called "middle river" of the Columbia where they could board a second steamer. This one took them as far as the Cascade Rapids, another Columbia River barrier, and there they boarded a rail car which carried them to the head of navigation on the "lower river." It was an easy steamboat ride from there to Portland, a great relief after the complications of switching boats and portaging.

But for Beachey and Farrell, Portland was an excruciating disappointment. Their prey had spent several days there, partying and losing money at the faro tables, and only two hours before their arrival had sailed on the *Sierra Nevada* for San Francisco.

At about this time, Beachey and Farrell encountered another friend, Captain A. P. Ankeny, the packer whom Mose Druillard had gone to seek word of. Ankeny had arrived in Lewiston on the day of Beachey's departure and followed him to the coast. The merchant-packer, who later would become one of Idaho's first millionaires, was a man of action and imagination. He told Beachey that even if the *Sierra Nevada* had departed for San Francisco, he should not despair. The boat had to cross the Columbia River bar before reaching the open ocean, and it could do that only when the weather and the tide were right. Ankeny proposed that he and Farrell hire a tug and go after the steamer. If it was still waiting to cross the bar, they could board the vessel, show Beachey's papers to the captain, and arrest the fugitives on the spot.

Well, why not? Beachey agreed that it was worth a try, but they would have to hurry. Beachey would remain on shore, making arrangements to travel by coach to California should Ankeny and Farrell return empty-handed.

The two of them rushed down to the waterfront on the Willamette River, found a tug with steam up, and told the pilot they would pay him well to take them out to the bar. The pilot was willing, and he cast off immediately. The tug carried the three of them down the Willamette into the Columbia and out into the estuary against a west wind that was pushing a cold, late-October rain ahead of it. The two men stood in the wheelhouse on either side of the pilot, staring into the gray mist, barely speaking as they searched the dark waters ahead of them for the darker figure of a coastal steamer. The visibility was so poor that they could not be sure until they reached the bar that the *Sierra Nevada* was not there. She had crossed over and was already out of sight.[57]

The tug turned about in the choppy waters and brought them back to the pier, both despondent and slightly ill. Ankeny paid the skipper, and he and Farrell left in search of Beachey. They found him at one of the waterfront hotels, preparing to board a stage south; there would be no sleep for him that night. Ankeny would stay over a few days in Portland, he said, and return home, where his business awaited him. Beachey said he would go alone by stage to San Francisco, and told Farrell that he might as well return to Lewiston with Ankeny. Farrell, however, said that if Beachey didn't mind, he would rather go with him to San Francisco since his help might be useful in bringing the fugitives back. Beachey admitted that he would be glad of the help and the company on the long journey south. Ankeny saw Beachey and Farrell off on the stage, then he signed the hotel register and headed for the dining room.[58]

Together, Beachey and Farrell bounced over primitive roads from one tiny settlement to another through the Willamette Valley, the fertile plow land at the end of the Oregon Trail. Within three days they were in northern California. At Yreka, the first town with a telegraph office, Beachey sent a wire to the San Francisco police department describing the fugitives and asking for their arrest. When he and Farrell reached San Francisco a few days later, they discovered that the telegram had arrived too late. The *Sierra Nevada* had docked and the fugitives had disappeared into the city.

For Beachey, weary and sleepless after days on the road, this was another bitter disappointment. But the police chief had good news also: the police had tracked the four down somehow and they were all behind bars.

Hearing this, Beachey's spirits revived. He felt suddenly newborn, fresh, and eager to get on with it. He and Farrell went to see the prisoners, to assure themselves that they were indeed confined, and found them surly and unrepentant. Renton told Beachey he had wasted his time coming all this way, because there was no chance of his ever taking them back to Lewiston. The four had retained a lawyer, Alexander Campbell, who was preparing a petition for habeas corpus. Once that was filed, Renton said, the four of them would be free, no question about it.

Beachey had not counted on this. As they left the jail, he told Farrell he must have been dreaming again. He had thought he could go to San Francisco, find the fugitives and then, after presenting his papers of authorization, take custody of them. Now it looked as though he faced a drawn-out legal battle. And how long would that take? Worst of all, did he really have enough evidence to overcome a petition of habeas corpus? Renton, Lower and Romain appeared confident of their ultimate release. As for Page, it was hard to tell what he was thinking; he didn't say much and appeared confused.

Also facing Beachey and Farrell now was another long journey. They would have to go to the state capital at Sacramento and present their requisition to the governor. Beachey had thought that this, too, would be only a formality. Now he was not so sure that Governor Leland Stanford would see it that way.

California
Autumn 1863

Part Two

17 As the *Sierra Nevada*, under steam and sail, puffed its way down the coast to San Francisco Bay, and as Beachey and Farrell pursued the vessel by land, the four fugitives prepared to step ashore with new identities. They would have to separate, Renton told the others, just in case they came under suspicion. He agreed with Lower and Romain that they probably were safe, but he didn't believe in taking chances.

They would go to different hotels, he said, and get some new clothes. They would pretend to be miners in town to recuperate from the rigors of a long, hard summer. They would take their gold dust to the San Francisco Mint and exchange it for legal tender after which, as far as he was concerned, they would never see one another again.

Separating did not come naturally, however. Two of the four, Page and Lower, went together to a rooming house on Dupont Street and the other two rented rooms at a comfortable hotel called the Lick House. They gambled and drank so much of their money away that by the time they got to the mint, the four together could cash in only seventeen thousand dollars in gold out of the twenty-five thousand or so they had collected from the corpses in the Bitterroots.

Meanwhile, Captain J.W. Lees of the San Francisco police department was busy tracking down the passengers who had got off the *Sierra Nevada*, hoping for the one sliver of luck that would put him on the trail of the fugitives. It was a frustrating task. The passengers had been swallowed up by the city and the police had no record of one of the fugitives, Page. Yet Lees and his men managed to locate the travelers, one by one, and one by one eliminated them.

As the *San Francisco Bulletin* reported:

"After having drummed up and examined many of the passengers who came by the steamer, and found that they were not entitled to a return to Idaho at the expense of the young territory, their attention was attracted by two rough looking strangers who had taken lodgings at an obscure house on Dupont Street, near Market, pretending that they had come from Oregon to recuperate broken constitutions and desired a quiet and secluded room."[59]

These two were Lower and Page. Captain Lees put a detective on their tail, and continued searching for the other two. The detective reported that a genteel-looking young man (probably Renton) had visited the two "invalids" and Lees found that the same young man and a companion were staying at the Lick House and associating with people of wealth and position. Renton and Romain had clothed themselves in expensive suits. They were dining in the best restaurants and spending time in the city's many clubs and music halls. Lees' men began tailing them also.

One day when Lower and Page left the house on Dupont Street for a walk around the Mission district, followed by the detective, Lees searched their room. As he later reported, for a couple of sick men they carried a pretty heavy armament. They obviously were prepared to defend themselves against someone, and Lees assumed that someone was the law. He left a loaded shotgun behind the door and departed. When the two returned to the room, Lees and Officer Levatt followed them inside. Before Lower and Page realized they were there, Lees had the shotgun aimed at them and was demanding they put their hands up. Page complied immediately; Lower wanted to know what the hell was going on and didn't raise his hands until Lees had barked the order a second time. The officers quickly handcuffed the two, confiscated their weapons, and hurried them downstairs to a waiting buggy.

While they were en route to the station, Officer Clarke was sitting in the lobby of the hotel where Romain was staying. He watched Romain come in from the street and go up the stairs. He waited for a few moments, then showed his badge to the desk clerk and said he had to get into room 223. The clerk sent a bellhop along to unlock the door, and Officer Clarke walked inside, pistol drawn. Romain was lying quietly on the bed. Near the bed, on a small table, were two revolvers. Clarke told Romain he was under arrest and picked up the revolvers. Romain sat up on the edge of the bed, looking surprised but saying nothing, and slowly raised his hands.

Renton was arrested a few moments later by Officer Greer as he walked out of a nearby music hall.[60]

Lees now had all four of the fugitives in custody and Chief Burke could hardly wait to give the news to Beachey, who was still on his way down from the north.

The four prisoners were placed at first in separate cells but later, to save space, Burke ordered them put in one cell together. All claimed to be innocent of any crime, and Lower loudly threatened to sue for false arrest. For at least three of them, trouble with the law was not a new experience. Renton had been imprisoned for bank robbery in Missouri and both he and Lower had spent time in California prisons. If Page had ever before been jailed for anything more serious than drunkenness, it was not recorded. He told the court later "I never had a sheriff take hold of me before."

Their confinement in the same cell gave the four a chance to agree on a strategy and an alibi. As their first move, they would retain a lawyer who should be able to get them out on a writ of habeas corpus. After all, as Renton put it, how much evidence could the Idaho authorities possibly have against them? But even as he said it, Renton, an intelligent man, must have known better. Bishop Goodrich had some of Magruder's stock and equipment, and he could tell the authorities where it came from. There were those in Bannack and Virginia City who might remember that the dead men weren't the only people in Magruder's crew. And Renton's decision not to try to ford the flooding Clearwater above Lewiston had forced them to spend a night and a day in the one town where all four were known. Renton also was aware that the ferryman had a look at them when the stage pulled onto his boat after leaving the Luna House. Would he recognize three of them as the same men who had made that crossing in August en route to the coast? Probably not, but it could be one more twist of the rope. Renton kept his fears to himself; he didn't want anyone to panic and talk out of turn.

All Renton and the others had learned from the police was that they were wanted in Idaho Territory for questioning in connection with a double homicide. They knew they had been seen together passing through Lewiston. People could testify to having seen them at the Hotel De France, the Luna House, in the stage, and on Silcott's ferry. They needed a story that would explain their passing through Lewiston, and Renton, with Lower's help, concocted one.

Page was to be their witness and mistaken identity was to be their claim: they were not the three men who had left Lewiston with Page that night in the coach to Walla Walla. Page was to say that Magruder's party had met five men with ten mules on the second day out of Bannack and that these men had made several trades with Magruder. At one of the camps, according to this tale, Magruder had sent Page out to look for some lost mules and three of these men had caught up with him and told him Magruder didn't want him along any more; he was to come with them. One of them put a revolver to Page's head, called him a son of a bitch, and ordered him to show them the trail west. These were the men who passed through Lewiston that night with Page, he would say. Meanwhile, Renton, Lower and Romain were traveling on the Mullan Road toward Walla Walla, and somewhere en route they ran into a friend who told them that a purse had been found in the Beaverhead country with Magruder's name on it. Page would say that when he and the three men with him reached Wallula they had met the other two. If anyone asked who these five men were, he was to say they called themselves the "Willamette Webfeet."[61]

This story, Renton said, would suggest to the authorities that the "Willamette Webfeet" had murdered Magruder while Page was looking for the lost mules, and that two of them had taken Magruder's purse back to the Beaverhead country. If a crime had been committed in the Bitterroots, Renton, Lower and Romain could not have been responsible because they were far to the north at the time, on the Mullan Road. (The Mullan Road, a military route built by Captain John Mullan a few years earlier, ran from Fort Benton on the Missouri River over the Continental Divide well north of Bannack, and down to Walla Walla.) No one traveling that road would come even close to the Nez Perce Trail on which Magruder had met his end. Renton apparently did not explain how the two

"Webfeet" managed to travel to Beaverhead then back over the mountains to Walla Walla and reach Wallula at the same time Page's party did. And Page, apparently, didn't ask.

It was a fragile alibi, but it was agreed upon by Renton, Lower and Romain as the best they could invent. They would use Page as their witness, Renton said, and if he stuck to this story it would set them free. To clinch it, Lower made Page hold up his hand and swear ten times that he would never flinch from that tale.[62]

If the state of California approved, they would be turned over to Idaho authorities and taken to Lewiston. They had no idea who those authorities might be until Beachey and Farrell walked into the San Francisco jail. They knew Beachey. All four had drunk in his bar and Lower had been thrown out of it a couple of times. Lower also remembered that Beachey had been sitting in the Luna House lobby when he went in to buy tickets for the stage. Did the innkeeper see enough of Lower's face that night to recognize him? He must have. Otherwise, why would Beachey be staring at him now so fixedly, with that strange and frightening look in his eye?

To Page, Beachey was the very figure of doom, in his long black overcoat damp with rain, clutching a crumpled black hat in one hand, a grim look on his round, brown-bearded face. This short, stout man filled Page's field of vision so utterly that the old fellow didn't notice there was another man with him. It didn't matter. It was Beachey, an avenging angel from his recent past, who had come to fetch him to judgment. For the first time, Page knew without question that the game was up.

He would not share this knowledge, Page decided, for fear it would anger the others against him. Nor would he flinch from the tale he had sworn to tell. So he said nothing as Renton scoffed and bragged, assuring Beachey that he would have done better to stay in Lewiston minding his own business than canter off on this wild goose chase.

Romain for a change was letting Renton do the talking, joining in now and then with a wisecracking sally of his own. Page thought Romain might be the only one of the four who actually believed what Renton was saying. Renton surely couldn't, now that the terrible sword of justice was standing in front of him. Lower, as if to add some weight to Renton's bluster, declared that the San Francisco police were beginning to realize they had nabbed the wrong people. He said they already were scrambling to dodge a suit for false arrest and would soon be turning them loose with apologies.

Lower was still talking when Beachey and Farrell turned without a word and walked quickly away.

* * * * *

The rain had stopped, but a cold breeze was blowing off the bay when Beachey and Farrell emerged from the jail. It was a gray late afternoon and both were weary. Beachey was not only tired but troubled, and he told Farrell he had no desire just now for food. He wanted to get his clothes off and get into bed, where he could think in comfort. The two found a hotel a short walk from the jail and took rooms there. Beachey told Farrell to go eat some supper and wake him in the morning, then he washed his face at the water basin, folded his clothes with care, and gratefully climbed into bed.

He lay between the muslin sheets watching the daylight fade on the ceiling and listening to city sounds through the slightly opened window. He could hear boat horns and ship bells on the bay, the clatter of wagons, the shouts of drivers, and from some nearby saloon the sound of a violin. After these past frantic days of fear and desperate pursuit he should have found some comfort in the rational music of normal life, but it all seemed unreal to him and out of joint. The world was going about its business as if nothing had happened while the law in running its normal course might be about to set four killers free.

He and he alone could prevent that, and he must. He had to admit that Lower's threat of false arrest had unnerved him, perhaps unnecessarily. There was no doubt that these four were the same men listed in the warrants, and the warrants were in order. The four surely knew he could identify them. So there should be no danger of false arrest here. Lower was clutching at straws.

The writ of habeas corpus was something else again. "Produce the body," it said in Latin; in other words, show why this person must be held or let him go. But what did Beachey have to show that Magruder was even dead, except his dream? And he daren't mention that for fear of being laughed out of court. There was Magruder's saddle, and the two animals, that had been turned over to Bishop Goodrich. They didn't show that Magruder was dead, only that he might have been robbed. And there was nothing at all to connect these four men definitely with the homicide of Charles Allen.

Beachey himself had no doubt that Magruder and Allen were dead and that three of the men in that cell had killed them. He wasn't so sure about Page, who didn't seem the type. To Beachey, Page looked more like an old muleteer than a desperado, yet here he was. There had to be some connection, if only Beachey could sort it out.

There was one thing, Beachey told himself, that the fugitives must not be told, at least not yet. They knew that Magruder was dead and assumed that the authorities in Idaho knew it too. In fact, the authorities did not, and had simply taken Beachey's word for it on the flimsiest of evidence. Magruder was not even overdue on the trail from Bannack when Beachey and Farrell dashed out of Lewiston in pursuit of the suspects. The more Beachey mulled all this, as the violin played on somewhere below, the more troubled he became. Was Renton right? Had he hurried all this way for nothing? Sleep came at last, but fretfully, and Beachey was awake and dressed next morning before he heard Farrell's knock on the door.

18

Hill Beachey was now in his forties, a robust, overweight, temperamental man of firm convictions and strong loyalties. He was also dogged, ambitious and restless.

He had left his home in Warren County, Ohio, at the age of thirteen to go steamboating on the Mississippi River. During the Mexican War, when he was about twenty, he was on the Rio Grande baking and selling bread to the soldiers. Then he was back on the Mississippi, where he earned his pilot's license.[63]

In 1848, he and three friends traveled across Mexico to the coastal town of Guaymas, planning to sail from there to the Sandwich Islands, later called Hawaii. While they were waiting for their ship, they heard about the gold strike at Sutter's Mill on the American River in California. All thought of the islands vanished, and the four took the next ship for San Francisco, arriving there in the spring of 1849.[64] If Beachey made any money mining gold, there is no record of it. By 1858, he had settled in Marysville on the Feather River, and in that year he married Margaret Anne Early and the two became friends of Lloyd and Caroline Magruder. Hill and Margaret moved from Marysville to Red Bluff, California, and assumed the operation of a hotel called the Luna House. A couple of years later he and Margaret were running another hotel, the Empire House, in a mining town known as Shasta. In the spring of 1862, hoping to take advantage of a new gold rush, he moved his family to Lewiston and built another Luna House.[65]

Beachey had been drawn to Lewiston not by the gold but the opportunities for commerce that the gold represented. He had learned in California that it was better to serve the miners than to work the mines. Lewiston in 1862 was the fastest growing city in the western United States. Already it held more people than Seattle and Portland combined, and they needed to be fed and housed. Buildings could not be put up fast enough to accommodate the masses of people surging into town from the west en route to the placer fields of Elk City, Pierce City and Oro Fino. The hotel that Beachey hastily erected on arrival at the forks in 1862 was made of cotton cloth stretched over a wood frame. Within a few months, he had replaced the original tent-like structure with a building of square-hewn logs—but still with a cloth roof, to partially comply with a law restricting permanent buildings on Indian land.

Beachey had arrived at the best of times. The Lewiston country was teeming with new population, there was great excitement up and down the Clearwater, and the mining towns were about to get a government of their own. The whole Washington Territory could no longer be governed from Olympia. If Olympia was to remain the capital, the territory would have to be divided. Otherwise, political control would move to the eastern end where most of the voters were now. It meant new opportunities for those inclined toward politics. To Beachey, the prospects were exhilarating and in almost no time he found himself a member of the Lewiston City Council.

Beachey wanted to send for Magruder, but Margaret urged him to wait. Nobody could tell about the future here, she said; the place was too new. It would be a shame if Magruder brought his family all this distance for nothing. But the way things were going for him in California, Beachey said, Magruder had nothing to lose.

He overruled Margaret and wrote to the Magruders, urging them to come north.

His friend Magruder, shortly after arriving, set up a store in Elk City and divided his time between that place and Lewiston. Magruder was nominated to the Elk City Council but declined because he felt he could not spend as much time there as a councilman should.

The most exciting prospect of all, to Beachey and Magruder, was that they might be living in the first capital of the new territory, whatever it was to be called. Lewiston was the largest town in the region in 1862 and the logical place from which to administer its affairs. Nobody knew then where the boundaries would be drawn, but wherever they were, the city between the forks was sure to be the heart and hub of a new territory and eventually a state. There could hardly be a better place to build a hotel.

There was a downside to all this, as Beachey was soon to discover. The nearest law was in far off Olympia, which meant that as a practical matter there was no law at all. This was the frontier, beyond the reach of any effective government. Gangs of road agents roamed the trails, killing and robbing without much hindrance. In the absence of regular courts and juries, people were forming vigilante committees to keep the peace. But it was a catch-as-catch-can kind of justice.

Beachey witnessed a good example of this in his second summer in Lewiston. While he was putting a wood roof on the Luna House, and Madame Bonhore was building the much more sumptuous De France, two brothers were accosted on the road from Walla Walla to Lewiston. The brothers were armed, but they had no time to draw their weapons. Three men on horseback appeared suddenly on the trail in front of them, pointing double-barreled shotguns. The robbers demanded their money and took it: twelve hundred dollars. They evidently were not well masked, for their victims recognized them as Nelson Scott, David English and William Peoples. The brothers followed them toward Walla Walla and near that town, with the help of some of the locals, captured them. They caught a stage outside Walla Walla, brought their prisoners to Lewiston, and turned them over to a citizens committee. The committee met in a room of the Luna House, where the prisoners also were kept, and decided to give the robbers a trial.

They did so, in a vacant saloon, with twenty-four jurors whose names had been drawn from a hat. The jury retired after the first day's proceedings without having reached a verdict and during that night some impatient citizens overwhelmed the guards, dragged the prisoners from their makeshift cell and hanged them practically on the spot.

That was followed a few days later by another example of frontier justice. A man was found hanging from a tree near the forks of the Clearwater on the way to Florence. He was identified as Charles Harper, a well-known horse thief.[66]

Almost never, on the frontier, was a man executed by gunshot. To die by the gun was too dignified for horse thieves and murderers. The rope was the symbol of justice. A man hanging from a cottonwood tree on a well-traveled route was thought to be the most effective possible warning to others, for it signified the presence of the law. Not the official law of lawyers and judges but the hurry-up law of citizens acting in self-defense.

Henry Plummer, who arrived in Lewiston from California at about the same time Magruder did, was not the only gang leader to prey upon the miners, but he was almost certainly the worst. It was one of the great ironies of Beachey's life that this well-dressed scoundrel, who ordered the killing of Beachey's best friend, had been a welcome guest in Beachey's hotel. That was because the innkeeper knew him only as a fancy gambler and man-about-town who attracted admirers wherever he went.

In late October 1863, as Beachey sat in his hotel room in San Francisco awaiting Farrell's knock on the door, Plummer was still riding high as the sheriff of Bannack. He had by this time eliminated his rival, Jack Cleveland, had married a respectable woman, and become a partner in a Bannack bakery. From his office in the back of a log building on Bannack's main street, Plummer continued to direct a band of cutthroats in the murderous business of highway robbery. Whether he knew he had been double-crossed by Renton, Lower and Romain, he never said. Perhaps he never cared; one more crime out of the hundred-plus he is said to have ordered could hardly have meant much to Plummer. His agent in the affair, Cyrus Skinner, must have known, but one can think of a couple of reasons why Skinner might have preferred to say nothing about it.

The fear that pressed hardest upon Renton, Lower and Romain as they fled the scene of the crime had been of Plummer. Now, in a cell in the San Francisco jail two thousand miles from Bannack, it was Beachey who concerned them. There was no thought of Plummer or Skinner here. Lower's arrogant bluster could not hide from Renton and Page the danger they were in. Romain, childlike, clung to everything Lower said and prayed that it was so.

*****

On the morning of their second day in San Francisco, Beachey and Farrell were back at the jail. As Beachey told Farrell when they left the hotel, he wanted the prisoners to get a good look at him when he was refreshed and in full command of himself. He was afraid he had left an impression of weariness and doubt when he stood before them the day before. He still was not sure he could take the prisoners back with him, but a night's sleep had put some iron in his spine and he wanted them to know that he was feeling new vigor. Farrell replied that if Beachey impressed the prisoners the way he was now impressing him, this psychological battle was won.

Beachey had little chance to display his intimidating new confidence, for the visit that day was a short one. The jailer who escorted the pair to the front of the cell had barely departed when Lower called him back. Lower demanded that Beachey and Farrell be removed or that their own lawyer be summoned. It occurred to Beachey that the prisoners had expected this visit and had agreed on Lower's tactic. He told the jailer he did not plan to ask the prisoners any questions; he intended only to explain to them what their situation was as he saw it. The jailer told Lower he had no authority to remove Beachey and Farrell from the corridor. But by a sudden inspiration he advised the four of them that if they did not wish to communicate with their visitors they could turn their faces to the wall.

Lower got the idea immediately and sharply turned his back on Beachey and Farrell. Renton followed, then Romain, then Page. Beachey began to address the backs of their heads. The evidence against them was so compelling, he said, that there was no point in fighting his requisitions. The sheriff had custody of Magruder's horse, his shotgun and other items known to be his. There were witnesses who would identify . . . Then, feeling suddenly embarrassed, he stopped talking. He turned to Farrell, who was looking at him with a puzzled stare. Then he turned to the jailer, but the jailer had left. Let's go, he said to Farrell, and the two of them strode down the corridor, past the officers' desks out front, and into the street.

Once on the sidewalk, Beachey exploded. Farrell had never seen him so angry, and Beachey had found plenty to be angry about since leaving Lewiston. Sputtering and swearing incoherently, Beachey tore the hat from his head and dashed it on the boards. Then he turned and without a word to Farrell ran back into the building. Farrell picked the hat up off the sidewalk and followed. Inside, Beachey was demanding to see the jailer who had accompanied him on his visit to the prisoners. One of the officers, seated at a desk behind a low railing, asked Beachey what the man's name might be. Beachey replied that he had no way of knowing since the two were never introduced. The officer asked if Beachey needed the jailer for any particular reason, or whether he could help. Beachey said he doubted it. He wanted to know why the jailer had told his prisoners to turn their backs on him. The officer said he didn't understand. Beachey, calmer now, described what had happened. The officer then introduced himself as Sergeant Ames. He said he couldn't speak for the jailer and couldn't condone what the jailer had done, but he had some idea what might have gone through his mind. As far as the jailer knew, Ames said, he might never see Beachey or Farrell again. But he could have these prisoners on his hands for days and weeks. If he'd had the authority to escort Beachey and Farrell out of the corridor, he probably would have. Since he didn't, he may have figured that he needed to find another way to show the prisoners that he was on their side.

It was just a guess, Sergeant Ames said, but that could have been why the jailer had told the prisoners they could face the wall if they didn't want to face their accuser.

That didn't satisfy Beachey, but he could hardly direct his anger at Ames, so he demanded that Ames make sure the jailer was disciplined. Ames said he would find out which jailer was guilty and see to it that the fellow never did that again.

Ames' manner had a soothing effect. Beachey thanked the sergeant, put on the hat Farrell handed him, and the two men walked out of the building for the second time. Back on the sidewalk, Beachey headed for the hotel. That jailer was going to be in for a big surprise, he told Farrell, if he thought he would never see him again. If he thought those prisoners could cause him problems, he ought to see what this citizen could do.

Farrell walked along beside Beachey, hurrying to keep up. He recalled the scene in the jail house corridor as Beachey lectured the backs of four heads, and to his surprise suddenly found the whole thing rather funny. But he kept that thought to himself.

19 Madame Melaine Bonhore, although she considered the Beacheys her friends, nevertheless hoped to capitalize on her prime competitor's sudden departure for the coast. Hill and Margaret Beachey had been preparing the Luna House for important guests in anticipation of the opening of the first territorial legislature in December 1863. By the middle of October they had made improvements in the kitchen and the bar and had installed new furniture in the lobby. Everyone expected that the Luna House would be the principal dining and watering place for the legislators. It was across the street from the territorial capitol, a bare wooden building which also was undergoing renovation, and it had the advantage of Hill Beachey's reputation and political connections.

The Hotel De France, however, had some advantages also. It had more rooms, and Madame's French chef, Baptiste Escude, was known and admired throughout the region. Besides, Madame had taken pains during construction to furnish the De France with touches of elegance that the Luna House lacked—for example, the richly polished balustrade leading from the lobby to the second floor and the gilt-framed mirrors in the sleeping rooms.

When Beachey left for Portland with Tom Farrell, she assumed he would be back within a few days. In early November, after two weeks had passed, she went to see Margaret. She intended not only to offer Mrs. Beachey what help she and her staff could provide in Hill's absence, but to gauge the state of preparation at the

Luna House. She found Margaret managing quite well with the help of some of the Beacheys' friends, and she also found that preparations for the legislative session had virtually halted. Margaret did not invite Madame upstairs, so she had no way of knowing what had been done in the sleeping rooms. Downstairs, she noticed fresh oilcloth covers on the tables and two new kerosene heaters in corners away from the central wood stove. She returned to the De France and ordered a bolt of white linen, which she would make into tablecloths and napkins.

She reminded Escude that things would not be the same now that Lewiston had become a territorial capital, and that he would have to run the kitchen accordingly. In the first week of December, lawmakers would start arriving from Boise City in the south, from Florence and Warrens on the Salmon and from Bannack and Virginia City to the east as well as from points near at hand. They would be here for at least a month. And between sessions of the legislature the town would be occupied by territorial officials and even, from time to time, representatives of the federal government in Washington, D.C.

Madame wished no ill upon the Beacheys, but business required that she take every advantage of Hill's absence. She bought a carriage in which her guests would ride to and from the stage stop at the Luna House, and a uniform for the driver. By mail, she placed ads in newspapers in the Boise Basin and the Beaverhead region offering the services of the De France. From Frank Kenyon, the publisher of *The Golden Age*, she ordered posters to be tacked up in the towns which had no newspapers. She assumed that Margaret would not think of this; she didn't know that Beachey, back in August, had given Luna House posters to Magruder for distribution in the Beaverhead country.

To Madame, who had never voted, the political maneuvering involved in the creation of a new territory was a complicated bore. She paid little attention to any of it and barely noticed that the Democrats, in their convention at John Welch's cabin in west-central Idaho, had nominated for congress a man named John Cannady. Her chef had to remind her that this was one of the two men who had so impressed her when they visited her dining room in August. Well, she said, he would probably make a fine delegate to congress.

That news had a far greater impact at the Luna House, where friends of Lloyd Magruder gathered to exchange sad reminders of what might have been. Had he lived, all agreed, Magruder would have given a good account of himself at that convention. Jacob Hoffman expressed some resentment toward Cannady, suggesting that Fate had allowed a lesser man to win the contest that Magruder should have won. Others, including James Witt, reminded Hoffman that with Magruder presumably dead, someone else had to win or the Democrats would have lacked a candidate. What they all had to do now, Witt said, was get behind Cannady. And that should be easy enough, he added, since Cannady had freely expressed his views to them on the night they had written that letter to Magruder. Both Cannady and his friend, R.P. Campbell, had been present that night, and Hoffman admitted that if he hadn't been so fond of Magruder he would have been attracted to Cannady.

The Republicans, or the Union Party, as they now called themselves, had met in Brown's Hotel at Mount Idaho and nominated William H. Wallace, the first and short-time Governor of Idaho Territory. A damned carpetbagger, the Democrats called him. He had gained the governorship only because he was a personal friend of President Lincoln and had used it as a stepping stone to congress. Because of Wallace's political ambitions, Idaho was now without a governor. Who cares? was bartender Dave Strait's attitude. No governor at all was as good as one of those appointed political hacks who didn't give a damn about the people they were sent out here to govern. Strait got no argument on that. Hoffman started back to his harness shop but paused at the door and returned to the bar. He was not used to drinking in the afternoon, and the liquor together with the day's reminder of his friend Magruder had put him in a sentimental mood. He told Strait to set up drinks for all and he would offer a toast. To Lloyd Magruder, he said, the man who should have won the nomination. Before Hoffman could get his glass to his lips, someone quickly added, And to John Cannady, who did. Hoffman flushed, but regained his composure and joined in the toast. By now another name was hanging in the air and Jim Haygood plucked it out. Here's to the man, he said, who will fetch back the sons of bitches that did the dirty deed—Mister Hill Beachey. That capped the ceremony. As the group applauded, Hoffman made his way out into the October sunshine and headed unsteadily for the harness shop.

*****

One evening during this busy period, Madame stepped into the dining room of the Hotel De France as she often did to ensure that all was well. Everything seemed in order. The guests were eating, talking and laughing as usual; the boy who waited the tables was hurrying about as always. The setting sun, shining through the windows on the western side of the room, gave everything a typical early November glow. Only one thing struck Madame as out of the ordinary: it was the figure of a tall, neatly dressed man dining alone at a table near one of the windows. He was clean-shaven except for a small mustache. In his dark hair, even at a distance of some twenty feet, Madame could detect the glint of silver in the sunlight. He was eating slowly and appreciatively, sipping occasionally from a glass of red wine. Clearly he was enjoying his meal. Suddenly aware that she was staring, Madame pulled her gaze from the figure at the window and stepped through the room toward the kitchen to have a word with Escude. As she passed the gentleman's table, the serving boy arrived there and she heard the man speak to him, in a low voice, with a French accent.

Madame Bonhore could not help herself. She stopped and turned, and when the boy left the table she approached it, smiling. She intended it to be a smile of professional welcome, the kind she knew how to put on and take off at will regardless of her mood. But as Captain Charles LaFrancois described it jokingly to friends later, it was not that kind of smile at all. Madame would have been humiliated had she known it at the time.

She introduced herself as the proprietress of the De France, welcomed him to her dining room, and asked if the service and the food were satisfactory. Indeed they were, he said, pushing his chair back and rising to his feet. He was amused and pleased that they were conversing in French—and not the ungainly Breton French or the syrupy language of the south of France but the lilting French of Paris and Marseilles. He invited her to sit down, and offered to order wine, but Madame had a rule against sitting with gentlemen dining alone. If he planned to stay over for a few days, she said, they might have a chance to chat later. He assured her that he would be in town for at least a week and would not consider staying anywhere but here. Well then, she said, perhaps they would have time for a visit. Meanwhile, there was work to be done, and she sailed off toward the kitchen.

Nothing in the kitchen needed her attention. Escude was too busy to talk, and Madame was here only because she had started in this direction so as to have some place to go. But she looked into the pots and pans, suggested to Escude that there was a customer out there he might want to meet, and laid out a clean apron for the chef to wear later—just in case. Then she left the kitchen, marched through the dining room without a glance to right or left, and crossed the lobby into the bar. She asked the bartender for a glass of sherry and carried it back across the lobby into her private sitting room. She settled into a silk-padded rocker facing the north window and sipped her sherry as she watched the lengthening shadows carve new shapes on the gold and purple hills across the river.

$$* * * * *$$

Captain Charles LaFrancois had finished his meal and was nursing a snifter of brandy when the chef, Escude, emerged from the kitchen in a spotless white apron and approached the table with a look of quiet expectation on his face. Escude, who considered himself the only decent cook in the territory, was used to compliments and expected another. To the chef, each meal was a performance, and after dinner he liked to appear in the dining room to accept the applause, as it were. He was not disappointed this evening. He recognized the captain immediately as a worthy audience and was pleased to hear LaFrancois say that the *Feuilletons de Veau en Croute* was as good as any he had eaten anywhere outside of France. Escude was delighted to hear this because he himself considered his stuffed roast veal, baked in a pastry crust, one of his supreme achievements. He gratefully accepted the captain's invitation to join him and for the next thirty minutes the captain and the chef visited cheerfully in melodious French as the dining room emptied and the brandy disappeared.

Later, as Escude was preparing the kitchen for breakfast, Madame came in, wondering whether he had found the time to meet the French gentleman. Indeed he had, and he told his employer everything he knew about Captain LaFrancois. He was a former officer in the French Army who had decided to trade the military life in Europe for a sojourn in the United States. As it turned out, both LaFrancois and Escude had abandoned France for the same reason: LaFrancois, like Escude, was an anti-royalist who supported the republic that had been formed after the abdication of King Louis Philippe. He had watched helplessly as the republic disintegrated under the presidency of Napoleon Bonaparte's nephew, and when the president dissolved the assembly and had himself elected Emperor Napoleon III, LaFrancois had decided to leave the country rather than remain and get caught in a political purge of the army. The captain had sailed directly to San Francisco, around the Horn, and had done some prospecting on the Feather River in California and then wandered north to the Willamette Valley, thinking to buy some farmland there. But he hadn't. Instead, hearing of gold strikes in the Clearwater Mountains, he had embarked on a steamer in Portland and by stages had come up the Columbia and Snake rivers to Lewiston. Once in the mountains, he had found the best claims already taken. He had tried innkeeping for a while on the road to Florence, operating a wayside hotel known as the Frenchman's. The hotel had not done well and he was back in town now, undecided what to do next. He was thinking, according to Escude, that cattle might be a good investment. There was plenty of good range in the area, and as long as there were miners to feed there would be a market for beef.[67]

Escude, casting a sly wink at Madame, also added that the captain had said nothing about a wife.

Coming from anyone else, the remark would have been impertinent. Coming from Escude, Madame didn't mind. Although she had been widowed only for a little more than a year, she did not intend to remain that way. She would like to find out, she had once told her chef, what it would be like to have a man around the house who was of some use. Her husband, Bonhore, was a decent, kind sort, but he had been sickly through most of the marriage and she had built the hotel and then ran it virtually alone. He had died in the previous year, shortly after the family's arrival here. Their son, Eugene, now twelve years old, didn't show much promise either. Among the miners, the merchants and the gamblers who passed through the Hotel De France, Madame had seen none that interested her. Until today. And she had no idea what sort of person this French Army captain might be. But my, he was charming. And rather handsome, too. From what Escude had told her, she suspected that he might be a drifter, one of those men who knocked about the country aimlessly, sticking to nothing and dying poor. She had seen plenty of those since leaving France.

But he was a countryman of hers. That counted for something out here on the American frontier. They had common roots in another place, another culture. They spoke the same language in more than words. As for his politics, that simply didn't interest her. She had left Paris only because her husband had thought there was more money to be made in America than he would ever make in France. It hadn't worked out that way, but here she was and here she planned to stay. The people she knew had come here for all sorts of reasons and as far as she was concerned, all were equally valid. The captain was here because the political tide had shifted against him in France. Escude had escaped a country that could not govern itself in the hope of finding one that could. Now here they all were, and Madame was satisfied that things were turning out well. She would find out for herself much more about this captain, and if she didn't like what she found, then good riddance.

The captain came down for an early breakfast the next morning and then left, returning in mid-afternoon. Madame Bonhore, who was standing at the registration desk when he came in, invited him into her sitting room for a glass of wine. She sat in the rocker, he in a straight chair, facing each other with a small table between them. For propriety's sake, she had left the door open between the sitting room and the lobby. They shared a lively, comfortable conversation about Parisian life, the California mining camps (where Madame also had lived), the coming legislative session, and, inevitably, the apparent murder of Lloyd Magruder.

They agreed that Hill Beachey had done the right thing in going after the suspects, although the captain doubted he would find them. The country is too big, he said. And he said the talk in the bar, where he had spent some time the night before, was that even if Beachey could find the suspects and bring them back, he might not have enough evidence to hold them.

The captain also had heard talk of a lynching if Beachey brought them back, but he didn't mention this to his hostess. He knew about the hanging of Scott, English and Peoples the year before and thought she would not care to be reminded of that. She was trying to civilize this place, after all.

It was the first of a number of visits by the captain to Madame's sitting room. And the night before had been the first of many visits to the bar of the De France, where the dashing Frenchman became the center of admiring attention. Madame noticed this. She also was aware that when the captain stopped in at the Luna House bar, as he sometimes did, he usually brought several Luna House patrons back to the De France with him.

Before the week was out, Captain LaFrancois had become a fixture at the De France and the most talked-about, sought-after *bon vivant* since Henry Plummer's departure for points east.

20 Beachey had no stomach for another long stagecoach ride, but it couldn't be avoided. He would have to go to Sacramento, the California state capital, and present to Governor Leland Stanford his papers of requisition. Things were getting complicated.

He had thought the capture of the fugitives would be the hard part of his expedition. He had never dreamed he'd have this much trouble getting them out of California. Lower's attorney, Alexander Campbell, was now representing all four and he was like a terrier on the case. He had invented a dozen reasons why Beachey should not get custody of the prisoners, and because of him Beachey now had to go bumping and rattling all the way to Sacramento and back, a total of some two hundred miles. It was that damned habeas corpus petition that was gumming the works. Had it not been for that, and for Campbell's tenacity, he could have had everything settled in San Francisco.

He could see no reason why Tom should have to share the misery. Chief Burke had told Beachey that the department would be glad to send a guard along as far as Portland to help with the prisoners, once Beachey got them released to his custody. As a courtesy to the new territory, Burke had said. The chief was moved mainly by his respect for Beachey, whom he admired tremendously for undertaking this mission. Beachey, advising Farrell that he should return to Lewiston now, was thinking not only of poor Tom. He wanted the people of Lewiston to know what was going on, and Tom was the ideal messenger. Beachey told Farrell to catch the next boat north and wrote several letters for Farrell to deliver in Lewiston—one to Margaret explaining why he was being delayed even further, one to Sheriff Fisk saying much the same thing, and one to Caroline Magruder assuring her that she would see justice done as soon as the law and the bureaucracy permitted.

Farrell was glad to get out of the cold and damp of San Franciso even though he did not relish the prospect of an ocean trip in this bleak autumn weather. But he was in luck; his boat would leave in two days and he would soon be breathing the softer, warmer air of Idaho. Holding that thought, he bade Beachey farewell as Beachey departed by stage for the California interior.

The journey was fully as bad as Beachey had expected. During most of it he was wedged between two equally miserable creatures, knees and hips touching and unable to move, except by occasionally shifting a leg slightly to ease the pain of extended immobility. The road was no rougher than most, but poor enough, and when the wheels of the coach slipped into a rut the passengers were rudely jounced together. They made occasional attempts at conversation and tried to nap, but managed neither with much success. The only relief came when the coach stopped at some way station to change horses, giving the passengers a few moments to get out, walk around a bit and visit the privies.

The Luna House weighed on Beachey's mind as the stage bounced along the rutted road between station stops. Maggie was a competent, energetic woman and she knew the hotel business— this was, after all, their third. But it was a terrible time for him to be away. Within a month the territorial legislature would be in town and he hadn't had time to get the hotel ready. He knew Madame Bonhore and her staff would be working hard at the De France, and he suspected that she might even be taking deliberate advantage of his absence. He must remember to tell Maggie in his next letter that if Madame came around she should not be taken upstairs. If she wanted to know the state of the bedding, let her find it out from the guests. The De France was the only real competition he had. The Alta was tiny and crude, the Oriental was changing hands again and the Globe was temporarily closed for repairs to its sewage disposal system.

The journey to Sacramento took a day and a night. The coach arrived just at dawn at a hotel in the center of town, and Beachey checked in at once. He carried his bag upstairs, doused his face in cold water from a pitcher on the dresser, and went to bed in his underwear. He slept until noon. Then he arose, trimmed his beard with a straight razor, combed his hair and dressed. He had intended to make an appointment first thing with the governor, but realized he was too hungry to think of anything but food. So he put all else out of mind and went downstairs for lunch.

After lunch he went out to the lobby, found some stationery, and wrote a note to the statehouse asking for an appointment. When he mailed it at the desk, the clerk assured him that he should have an answer the following morning. He didn't. Nor was there an answer that afternoon. When nothing arrived on the morning of the second day, Beachey's patience ran out. He took a horse cab to the capitol and presented himself in the governor's outer office. One of the clerks found his note in a tray of unopened mail but was unable to arrange an appointment. That would have to be done by the appointments clerk, who had gone home with a bad cold. Beachey would have to try again the next day.

After three days in Sacramento, Beachey arranged an appointment and two days later was able to see an aide to Governor Stanford. The governor had been advised that he should not sign the necessary documents, the aide told him. Alexander Campbell had raised serious questions about the legality of it, and those questions would have to be answered before Beachey could get custody of the prisoners.

What legal questions? Beachey wanted to know. Well, for one thing, the law was clear on the extradition of prisoners from one state to another, but it was fuzzy as to extradition from a state to a territory. Alexander Campbell, not satisfied with his habeas corpus petition to the court, had made that point in a brief mailed a few days ago to the governor. In it, he argued that congress had no power to pass any law relating to the extradition of fugitives because the U.S. Constitution had not granted that power to congress. The constitution, Campbell said, made it clear that extradition applied to fugitives escaping from one "State" to another "State" and said nothing about fugitives fleeing from a "Territory." He acknowledged that the State of California had passed a law providing for the delivery of a fugitive to the state or territory from which he fled, but he claimed that neither congress nor the state legislature had the power under the U.S. Constitution to pass such a law.

Campbell also questioned the validity of the arrest warrant the governor had given to Captain Lees of the San Francisco police. He said the law established certain conditions for issuing an arrest warrant and that this case did not meet all those conditions. For instance, he said, this warrant was defective because it failed to state that these fugitives had fled from justice or that they could be found in California. Further, Campbell argued that the courts were more competent to handle matters of extradition than governors.

Aside from Campbell's petition, the governor's staff was not entirely satisfied that the evidence against the prisoners was strong enough to support a requisition for custody. Beachey was prepared to present arguments of his own, but the aide advised him to do nothing for the time being. Beachey was told, politely, to wait until he was sent for.

He was more angry than disappointed as he left the capitol, and he decided to walk back to the hotel in order to work some of that rage out of his system. The distance wasn't far enough so Beachey was still fuming when he walked into the hotel lobby. His first impulse was to go directly to the bar for a drink. Instead, he picked up one of the San Francisco newspapers that had been thrown off the stagecoach that morning and dumped himself into a chair. When he opened the paper he realized he should have gone to the bar after all. There on the front page was a story reprinted from the Portland *Oregonian* that was going to make this dreary task even drearier.

The *Oregonian* apparently had been following Beachey's case ever since the arrest of the four fugitives in San Francisco. In fact, Beachey was surprised to learn, the alleged murder of Lloyd Magruder and Beachey's pursuit of the suspects had been making news up and down the coast. Now the *Oregonian* was suggesting that when Beachey returned the suspects to Idaho Territory—if he did—there would be a memorable "necktie party" in Lewiston. The *Oregonian*'s writer recalled what had happened in the same town just a little over a year ago to English, Peoples and Scott.

Putting down the paper, Beachey walked into the bar and ordered whiskey straight. After two drinks he felt better and went for a stroll in the dusk, to think. It was better to be outdoors in Sacramento than in San Francisco at this time of day and time of year. He didn't care for the damp and drizzle of the bay area and he didn't find the sound of fog horns particularly romantic. Sacramento was better. Lewiston would be better yet, and he wanted desperately to be there. With every day of his absence the Luna House and the needs of his family pressed more heavily upon him. He fretted helplessly over his tiny son, Early, the sickly one whose latest illness had worsened before he left.[68] Now, because of this latest jolt, getting home to Lewiston would take even longer, and there was nothing he could do about it. Or was there?

The possibility of a "necktie party" would give Alexander Campbell one more argument to raise against him. The governor would not feel disposed to deliver four men, still presumed to be innocent, into the hands of a lynch mob. Beachey would have to convince the governor that the prisoners would be treated in every respect according to law. Could he do that? He could try.

The summons to the governor's office came the next afternoon, somewhat to Beachey's surprise. He had prepared himself for a longer wait. When he arrived at the capitol he found himself face-to-face for the first time with Alexander Campbell, a thin, short, bald-headed man with a large black mustache and dense, black eyebrows. An aide introduced the two of them in an anteroom, then quickly ushered them into the governor's office.

Stanford was a large, slow-moving and deliberate man with thinning white hair, a somber mien and heavy-lidded eyes.[69] He was standing at the front of his desk in a black suit speaking with somebody, apparently another aide. He turned to shake hands with Beachey and Campbell, and after introductions were over he moved around the desk to his chair and sat down. The man he had been talking with left the room and the governor motioned Beachey, Campbell and the remaining aide to chairs. As he settled into his,

Beachey noticed the newspaper lying on Stanford's desk was the same one he had seen the day before. He knew then what was coming.

Stanford told the two visitors that he had been briefed on the extradition matter but wanted to hear from them before making a decision. He asked Campbell if it really mattered, for the purpose at hand, whether Idaho was a territory or a state. Campbell said he thought it did, even though the law was unclear. Territories were more loosely governed than states, he pointed out, and their legal systems tended to be less scrupulous. Therefore, you could not turn a suspected felon over to a territory with the same confidence of fair treatment that you might enjoy in turning him over to a state.

Campbell spoke in a strong, resonant baritone that Beachey found surprising in such a small man. His own voice, he feared, would seem ragged and weak by comparison.

The lawyer, who also read the papers, then mentioned the lynching the year before of English, Peoples and Scott, saying it demonstrated a certain lack of gumption and professionalism typical of frontier law. Who could ensure that these four prisoners, his clients, would not be treated the same?

How did Beachey respond to that? the governor asked. Beachey reminded Stanford that when those three were lynched, Lewiston was still a part of Washington Territory and without any effective law. Lewiston was now the capital city of Idaho Territory, he said, and the law was firmly enforced and close at hand.

Stanford noted that the law could not be so firmly in place as Beachey suggested if the supreme court of the territory didn't even have a seal to attach to its documents. And he referred Beachey to the affidavit signed by Judge Alleck Smith.

Beachey agreed that the territorial courts were brand shiny new, and untested. It was true that they had not yet conducted a murder trial. But he said that was all the more reason for confidence in the safety of these prisoners. This case would give the courts a chance to prove themselves, to establish justice securely in a place where it was badly needed. He pointed out that the first session of the territorial legislature would convene in Lewiston within a few weeks and that the County of Nez Perce would be in all respects on its best behavior.

If that weren't enough, Beachey said, his own honor was at stake. He would be personally responsible. The governor had his word that these prisoners would get a fair trial, and his word was respected by all who knew him. Beachey felt himself rising to the occasion, but Stanford waved a hand for silence and turned to Campbell.

The lawyer found Beachey's reasoning interesting, he said, for its novelty. He had never before heard it argued that a law enforcement system could be trusted because it had never been used. His black eyebrows flew up as he turned and gave Beachey an incredulous stare.

Stanford picked up the newspaper, leaned forward with his elbows on the desk, and read aloud part of the story that had been reprinted from the *Oregonian*. Then he slumped back into his chair and told Beachey that apparently there were some who didn't agree with him concerning the quality of justice in the new territory.

Beachey replied that he had just come from Lewiston and could judge the quality of justice there far better than someone in Portland who had probably never been farther inland than Umatilla. He respected Campbell's concern for his clients, he added, but justice required that they face their accusers in court.

That was fine, Stanford said, but he wasn't sure there was enough evidence against the prisoners even to have arrested them, much less turn them over to a territorial court. This was the basis, after all, of Campbell's petititon for habeas corpus, was it not?

Oh, there was evidence aplenty, Beachey replied, and he began reciting some of it—Magruder's saddle, his horse, his rifle, the phony names, the dream . . .

It was too late. Maggie would have told him not to mention the dream, but Maggie wasn't here. The words were out, and Beachey couldn't get them back.

The lawyer turned to him quickly, the eyebrows this time descending in a puzzled frown.

The dream? Stanford was asking. Beachey sighed and gazed at the floor. Then out the window. Then he turned to the governor and said, yes, there had been a dream. It was before the murder, before Magruder had left Lewiston for Bannack. He would have told Magruder, but his wife had talked him out of it. Anyway, in the dream he had seen one of Campbell's clients kill Magruder with an axe.

Which one?

Christopher Lower. And he had recognized Lower as the killer when he and the three others boarded the stage at Lewiston that night that now seemed so long ago.

The lawyer was dumbfounded by this strange confession, but Stanford seemed not so much startled as fascinated.

Did this mean, he asked, that if it hadn't been for the dream, Beachey never would have pursued that stagecoach, the four men would never have been arrested, and the three of them would not be discussing this case in his office now?

It seemed to Beachey that Stanford's question answered itself, and so he said nothing.

21 Tom Farrell boarded the *Shasta Queen* on a cold, damp November morning, fearful of what he was about to endure but glad he was not making this journey by stage. Most of his fellow passengers, he noticed, were prospectors from the worn-out placers of the Feather River, heading for better diggings on the Clearwater and the Salmon. They planned to reach Idaho Territory before winter so they could be on the scene when spring came. Despite the disappointments of the past, they were a cheerful lot. Hope kept them going; hope gave them the gumption to fall on their faces time after time and then get up again. Farrell didn't envy them. They were heading into a cold northern winter with no guarantee of shelter. And what would they find, come spring? The gold rush on the Clearwater by now was nearly spent. Even in the newer camps of the Salmon, miners were abandoning their claims and heading south.

Word had reached California of the new gold strikes east of the Bitterroots and several of these miners were going there, not realizing the faster route was overland through Salt Lake City. They had heard of Bannack and, more recently, of Virginia City, and California couldn't hold them now.

It was not only miners who were heading for Idaho on this boat. Farrell met a couple of lawyers, a dentist, a portrait photographer, and an elderly man traveling with seven young women. The old fellow was not a pimp, Farrell learned, but a marriage broker bringing brides to the mining camps. After finding husbands for these he would return to San Francisco for more, and he was sure to find more waiting. He was doing well, he told Farrell, by serving the needs of both the women and the men while at the same time helping to civilize the frontier.

Also aboard the *Shasta Queen* as it plowed through the long offshore swells toward Portland was a newly elected member of the Idaho Territorial Legislature. William Rheems was on his way to Lewiston from Virginia City to attend the opening session, and he was still only half way to his destination. He had traveled overland from Bannack down the Bozeman Road to Corinne, Utah, then a vigorous little settlement on the Oregon Trail, south to Salt Lake City, and from there by stage across northern Nevada to the Truckee River and over Donner Pass into California. He had worked his way down the west slope of the Sierras along the Ruby River to Marysville in the central plain, from there down the Feather River to Sacramento and into San Francisco. He told Farrell that by the time he reached Lewiston he figured he would have been on the road for three weeks. But that wasn't the worst of it, he said; when the session ended, in January, he would have to return to Bannack in even worse conditions. He had no idea how long that would take; he might not get home until spring.

He said he could have done what the delegate from Deer Lodge was planning to do: travel north along the Jefferson to Fort Benton and go west from there on the Mullan Road over the Bitterroots, down the Coeur d'Alene River and south across the Palouse prairie to Lewiston. He would cover the distance riding one horse and leading another. That would be a shorter trip by far but there was the danger of getting trapped by deep snow in those high northern mountains. The most direct route from the Beaverhead country, of course, was over the southern Nez Perce Trail along the high ridge between the Clearwater and Salmon rivers, but nobody used that route after October, not even the Indians.

The man's sad tale gave Farrell quite a shock. He hadn't realized until now how vast this new territory was. He wondered whether this lawmaker, having labored so hard to get to and from the first session, would find the grit and the time to attend another.

There wouldn't be another, the delegate said, at least for him. Everybody on the Beaverhead expected that in another year they would be a part of a new territory and either Bannack or Virginia

City would be the capital. And a good thing, too. The territory the way it was laid out now was just too damn big.

Farrell had suffered some squeamishness on the first day out of San Francisco, but he found his sea legs on the second and began to enjoy life aboard ship. There had been a change in the weather and he was able to sit in the sunshine on the starboard deck and watch the northern California coast slide by in the distance. Fair weather continued on the third day as the vessel pushed northward along the rugged coast of Oregon, and at dawn the next morning the *Shasta Queen* arrived off the broad mouth of the Columbia River. There it joined two other vessels that were standing by, waiting for the morning tide to lift them over the bar.

By midnight, Farrell was ashore in Portland and a day later he was moving up the lower Columbia on a stern-wheel steamer. Some forty miles above Portland the vessel reached Cascade Rapids and its passengers proceeded around the falls on rail cars and boarded another stern-wheeler. This one carried them as far as Celilo Falls at The Dalles. After still another portage they carried their bags aboard the *Colonel Wright*, which transported them through the upper Columbia to the Snake and finally to the boat landing at Lewiston.

Five days after arriving in Portland, Farrell was sitting in the lobby of the Luna House, ready to report on events in San Francisco.

Word spread that he was back, and the bar emptied its customers into the lobby. Captain Charles LaFrancois, hearing of Farrell's return, hurried over from the DeFrance. The publisher of *The Golden Age*, Frank Kenyon, locked the door of his office on D Street and joined his fellow townsmen at the Luna House. Margaret Beachey, the most concerned of all, sent Mose Druillard down the street to gather more people and urged Farrell to delay reporting until they had arrived. Farrell was not accustomed to such prominence. He had never before addressed an audience, for any reason on any subject. He had thought the letters he carried from Beachey would suffice to keep the city posted. Yet here he was and here were all these people, waiting to find out how Beachey was faring in California.

Somewhere inside himself Farrell found the courage to stand and do his duty, and he did it commendably while repeatedly shoving his hands into his pants pockets and pulling them out again.

Farrell had no way of knowing what had been happening in Sacramento the past few days, and on that score he had nothing to report. But he said that Beachey was confident his mission would go well there, and that he would have everything wrapped up soon. Farrell could tell his listeners that the prisoners were in custody, that he and Beachey had seen them, and that Beachey by now would have had his conference with the governor. He said that Beachey had no intention of returning to Lewiston without his prisoners, and that drew a cheer.

Margaret had hoped for better news. The Luna House needed Beachey, and so did she. The first of the out-of-town legislators had arrived that day from Virginia City and the hotel would soon be full. She could handle the business of running the Luna House; Margaret was as experienced as her husband and at least as clever. But the guests needed a host, and she had neither the time nor the gift for camaraderie and she knew nothing about politics.

She turned to speak to Farrell, but he had become the center of a tight knot of men all talking at once, so she went upstairs to check again on the sleeping rooms. Everything was in order. She went back downstairs to the bedroom she shared with Hill, and sat in the rocker. She took his letter out of a pocket of her long, gray dress, and opened it. She read it for the second time, just in case there was something there she hadn't noticed earlier. There wasn't. Her husband had never been much for sentiment, especially in his letters, and she was neither surprised nor chagrined that this one was all business: what he was doing in California, suggestions for stocking the Luna House bar in preparation for the legislature, his best to the children and his hope that Early's cough was clearing up.

Margaret got out of the chair, put the letter in a dresser drawer, and stood at the north window for a moment watching the smoke curling out of Vic Trevitt's chimney and floating toward the hills across the river. Then, chiding herself for wasting time this way, she hurried out to the front desk to meet the stage from Walla Walla.

*****

A nervous quiet had settled on the office of Governor Leland Stanford. The governor sat behind his desk studying Beachey with a quizzical eye, as though sizing him up. Beachey, saying nothing, sat looking first at Stanford, then at the books in a tall, glass book-case behind the governor's head. Alexander Campbell, the lawyer, sat keeping his own counsel, his eyes darting from Beachey to Stanford and back again. The image of Beachey's dream, blurted out inadvertently, hung in the air so vividly the governor felt he could almost reach out and touch it. One man bringing an axe down on the head of another, by firelight.

Finally the governor expressed the opinion, to no one in particular, that dreams could sometimes be significant and sometimes not. He wondered if Beachey had ever had so portentous a dream before. Beachey said he hadn't. That was why this one caused him such alarm, he said. Campbell, sensing a sudden, subtle rapport between the other two men, decided that his own cause could best be served by his silence. When the governor glanced at him, clearly expecting a comment, Campbell merely raised and lowered his eyebrows, his way of saying he had nothing to say.

The governor then made the point that Campbell would have made. There was still the matter of the habeas corpus petition, he reminded Beachey. He was not satisfied that Beachey's evidence was sufficient to warrant holding these prisoners in jail. And if he couldn't justify holding them, he could hardly in good conscience turn them over to another jurisdiction for trial and possible punishment. That was really the only problem he had. He was no longer worried about a "necktie party" in Lewiston; he was now convinced of Beachey's honesty and his determination to see justice done.

Beachey felt great relief at hearing this. He was even more pleased when Stanford remarked that he respected Beachey's dream and understood his reliance on it. The governor, it seems, became rich in the railroad business partly because of a dream of his own. Now, more at ease and confident, Beachey gave the governor another accounting of his evidence, reminding Stanford that both Renton and Lower had prison records in California and that Romain had been in trouble here before.

Campbell remained mute. At Beachey's offhand mention of a dream, Campbell had considered his case won; the governor surely would find this piece of "evidence" as ridiculous as he did. But the governor didn't, and the lawyer's bright hope of quick victory was suddenly dimmed.

Stanford heard Beachey out with great patience, all the while fingering a button on his coat. Finally he held his hand up and said he was satisfied. He would sign the necessary papers, he told Beachey and Campbell, and give Beachey custody of the prisoners.

But the court had yet to act on the habeas corpus petition, Campbell objected. That was true, Stanford said, but the court had control in this matter only while the prisoners were in California. Once they were turned over to Idaho Territory they were out of the jurisdiction of this court. And Stanford reminded Campbell that governors, not courts, have the authority to grant extradition.

If Beachey would return in the morning, Stanford told him, he could have his papers. Meanwhile, he had better arrange passage on a boat north. His prisoners could be transferred that way more safely than by coach.

It had happened so quickly that Beachey was momentarily stunned. At one moment he had been on the defensive and then, after making an embarrassing blunder, he suddenly had what he'd come for. He felt an impulse to fall on his knees and kiss the governor's hand, but he controlled himself and simply thanked the great man for his time and attention.

In the anteroom, where he and Campbell paused to put on their coats and hats, Beachey turned to the lawyer and put out his hand. The lawyer took it and gave it a firm shake. Then, with a broad smile, Campbell wished Beachey well on the long voyage home. Beachey had his prisoners now, he said warmly, and he was welcome to them.

The two walked together out of the anteroom, down the corridor and into the street, and parted there. Beachey hurried to his hotel, composing in his mind the letters he would mail tomorrow to Margaret and the sheriff. For the first time since glimpsing Lower in the coach that night in front of the Luna House, Beachey felt sure of himself. There still were many miles to go, but they would be easy miles, for he could feel it in his bones now that he was going to win.

He stepped briskly into the lobby of his hotel, went directly to the desk and booked a seat on the next stage to San Francisco. It was now November 4. Beachey had in his pocket the executive warrant signed by Governor Stanford giving him custody of the four fugitives. When he got back to San Francisco he would arrange passage on the next steamer north. The governor was right, but his advice was unnecessary. Beachey had planned all along to take the prisoners home by boat. He hoped there would be one leaving in the next few days. As he considered this, Beachey felt a sudden tightening in his chest and a new fear washed over him. While he waited for the steamer, his prisoners would be sitting in Chief Burke's jail, still in California, still subject to whatever the court decided to do about the motion for habeas corpus.

This was incredible. No wonder Alexander Campbell had parted from him so cheerfully less than an hour ago. The lawyer understood what he had only now come to realize. While the prisoners remained in California with that motion still to be acted on, Beachey's warrant of extradition was worthless. What if the boat did not leave for another week? Two weeks?

He raced up the stairs to his room and began throwing things into his bag. He knew he didn't have to hurry this way, since the stagecoach wouldn't leave until morning, but he couldn't help himself. An uncontrollable panic had seized him and was driving him toward certain madness. But the seizure passed, leaving Beachey damp and drained. He took off his overcoat and hat and threw them over a chair. He took off his suit coat and his tie. He unbuttoned his shirt and fell down on the bed, still frightened and still furious but sane once more. He lay on his back, his arms across his face, and breathed deeply. Think, he told himself. Think.

What was the worst that could happen? The answer to that one was easy: the court could free the prisoners, they could drop out of sight, and Beachey would be back where he and Tom Farrell had started. But even if freed, would they really be able to disappear? Beachey had developed a huge respect for Chief Burke and Captain Lees. It did not seem likely to him that these two professionals would simply let the four melt into the population and drop into limbo. Burke and Lees were almost as convinced of their guilt as he was. They also understood that at least three of the four would have a hard time staying on the right side of the law.

So even the worst that could happen was not calamitous. And it might not happen. Yet Beachey knew that Lower's attorney was even now working to free his clients, and Beachey had to do something about that. Perhaps he should abandon the boat and take his prisoners out of California immediately by coach. Why had he sent Farrell back to Lewiston? He needed help now. When he got to San Francisco he would ask Chief Burke's advice. Maybe he ought to have a lawyer. Well of course; that was it.

Beachey, suddenly clear-minded, sat up on the edge of the bed and buttoned his shirt. He stood up and splashed some water on his head. He combed his hair, put his clothes back on, and went downstairs in search of a lawyer. At the desk in the lobby, he consulted a *Directory of Professional Persons* and by evening he had retained the services of J.W. Coffroth, attorney at law.

22 Alexander Campbell knew he had no time to waste. He assumed that Beachey would take his prisoners out of California on the next boat to Portland, and once out of the jurisdiction of this court it would be impossible to free his clients on a writ of habeas corpus. The governor had the authority to extradite fugitives but the court held the power to free them first. And the court needed time. Campbell telegraphed San Francisco for the departure date of the next boat north. Then he pressed Judge E.B. Crocker, who was hearing this matter, for a quick decision. He declared that if the prisoners were not freed soon, they would be on their way to Idaho and an almost certain lynching. Crocker wanted first to hear from the other side, and then he would make his decision.

Beachey's attorney, J.W. Coffroth, also was concerned about time. If he had too much of it, Campbell might win freedom for his clients before the next boat sailed. The next steamer for the north was due to leave in five days—too much time, Coffroth feared. Since he could not hope to stall the proceedings for that long, he would have to win the case by argument.

In his motion for a writ of habeas corpus, Campbell had used all the arguments he had given to Governor Stanford—the lack of evidence against the prisoners, the deficiencies in the arrest warrant, the vagueness of their identifications. But he had put the most force and research into his contention that the U.S. Constitution prohibited the governor from extraditing these men to a relatively lawless territory.

Coffroth dismissed Campbell's arguments as irrelevant. It was clear, he said, that the governor had the authority to issue an arrest warrant, and he had issued one. It was clear that the men in the San Francisco jail were the same ones that Beachey had sought to have arrested. As for the evidence against them, that would be considered in an Idaho court; it did not have to be considered here. And as for the vague language concerning extradition in the U.S. Constitution, that problem had been cured by a California law that made it all perfectly clear.

Judge Crocker agreed with Coffroth. Habeas corpus was denied.[70]

Beachey, jammed between the coach wall and a snoring female passenger, was thinking he would gladly endure even more grinding, swaying and bouncing if that would make the stage go faster. Now in sight of his goal, with the signed requisitions in his bag and his prisoners secure, he was painfully eager to get to San Francisco. While the coach was under way it wasn't quite so bad. It was the station stops, where it took forever to change horses and put the mail aboard, that made Beachey itch with impatience. But San Francisco was reached at length, in roughly the same day and a half it had taken him to get to Sacramento five days earlier. He arrived at mid morning and went directly to the police station. There he showed his papers to Chief Burke and fought back an urge to pay another visit to his prisoners. He wanted to watch the sneer fade from Lower's face when he told them they were going back to Lewiston in irons to stand trial. But that pleasure could wait; he first had to find a boat going north and book passage for himself and his charges.

Captain Lees told him to be sure the boat was equipped with a secure stateroom—one big enough for all four of the prisoners. They could be guarded more easily in one room than in two or more, and Lees added by the way that he would send a guard along as far as Portland, as a courtesy.

At the shipping office, Beachey learned that almost every coastal steamer had a brig aboard since prisoners were commonly transferred by sea. The steamer *Pacific*, he found, would depart in three more days. Beachey reported this to Captain Lees, and then succumbed to the temptation to see his prisoners.

The jailer who accompanied him down the corridor—not the same one who had angered Beachey in his previous visit here—said nothing at all to the four men in the cell but posted himself silently nearby. When the prisoners rose to see whose footsteps these might be, they found themselves facing Hill Beachey and Beachey's alarming smile. Lower uttered an oath and flung himself around to face the wall.

Renton understood immediately what this visit meant, and sat down again. Romain started to follow Lower's example just as Lower turned back to Beachey, his face red and his eyes blazing, and spat at him through the bars. Lower's fury frightened Page, who melted into the background. Beachey brushed at the front of his coat with his cuff, still smiling, and told Lower he would be on the boat to Portland in a few days. Beachey had no particular interest in Renton, Romain or Page; the law would take care of them. His own personal vengeance was focused on Lower, and Lower knew it. Lower knew also, as he stared at Beachey, that the habeas corpus petition was dead and that he and the others were going back to Lewiston—to a lynching, he supposed.

But Lower was more angry than scared. Angry at Beachey, at the law, at Alexander Campbell and at Lloyd Magruder. They would never get him to Portland, he shouted at Beachey and at the jailer standing silently across the hall. He had powerful friends, he said, and no ship's brig could hold him. Furthermore, he was innocent. He had been up north on the Mullan Road when the killing was done, if there really was a killing.

Finally Renton told him to shut up. Lower's voice was giving him a headache.

Neither Page nor Romain had said a word during Beachey's visit, and they said nothing now. Page was sitting on a bench on the far wall and Romain was standing beside Lower staring at Beachey with dull eyes. Beachey, still smiling, looked again at each of them, then fastened his gaze briefly once more on Lower. He turned to the jailer and nodded, and the two of them walked off down the corridor.

Back at the hotel, Beachey learned that a reporter from the *San Francisco Bulletin* had been asking for him, and would be back. And indeed he was, that very evening. He sent a note up to Beachey's room, asking whether Beachey could join him for dinner. The note was signed by Gregory Schwartz. Beachey was both surprised and chagrined. Although he had seen the news item the *Bulletin* had reprinted from the *Oregonian*, predicting a "necktie party" in Lewiston, it had not occurred to him that he was anyone a reporter would be interested in. He did not like the notion of being interviewed, and he had been looking forward to a quiet drink in the hotel bar and then a leisurely meal alone with his thoughts. Now he felt trapped.

He sent a note back down by the bellboy saying he would meet the reporter at the front desk in a few moments; he wanted some time to freshen up. He combed his hair and washed his face, and went downstairs to meet this man Schwartz and find out what he wanted from him.

To Beachey's surprise, it was a pleasant dinner. Schwartz was an engaging fellow in his middle forties, a bit paunchy now and balding, much as Beachey was. He had covered the Mexican War for *Leslie's Weekly*, an east coast magazine, and knew his way around all the important mining camps. The gold strikes on the Clearwater in 1860 and 1861 had made headlines in California, and now it seemed everyone was fascinated by the murders in the Bitterroots. Schwartz wanted an exclusive interview with the man who had traveled all this way in pursuit of the killers—if indeed they were the killers. Schwartz guided Beachey, steering him gently by the elbow, to an out-of-the-way table where they were not likely to be seen by other reporters.

He asked Beachey what he thought of the article from the *Oregonian,* and was not surprised by Beachey's response. It had angered him, he told Schwartz. If the governor had not been so kindly disposed toward his cause, that article could have doomed his mission. Furthermore, he said, there would be no lynching in Lewiston; the idea was preposterous. And he told Schwartz what he had told Governor Stanford: that Idaho Territory, newly minted, would not tolerate mob justice in the capital city on the eve of its first legislative session. The people in the Clearwater country had an effective justice system in place for the first time, and they were going to use it.

Schwartz offered him a sympathetic ear and told him that any damage caused by the *Oregonian* article could be canceled out by Beachey's argument in the *Bulletin*, which was much better read.

After dinner, Schwartz put his notebook away and the two men reminisced over brandy about their experiences in the mining camps of central California. Schwartz had once stayed in the Luna House in Red Bluff, probably during the time when the Beacheys were running it. Beachey told him he would be a welcome guest in the Luna House at Lewiston, should he ever get that far north, and Schwartz assured him that some day he might.

Beachey felt some weariness in his bones as he climbed the stairs to his room but he reflected, as he was getting undressed, that this had been the best day for him since leaving Lewiston. Still ahead was the ocean trip to Portland and the long journey up the Columbia and Snake rivers with four unpredictable men in irons. He was not looking forward to that, but he was ready.

Lying in the dark near an open window, he stared at the reflection of gaslight on the ceiling and listened to the foghorns on the bay. And yes, there was that violin again. He could hear momentary snatches of the music, apparently when the saloon door was opened by someone going in or out. Despite the cold and the damp, he thought, it was good to be back in San Francisco and almost ready for the long journey home.

He realized with some alarm that he was not as confident of a peaceful reception as he pretended. There could be a lynching at Lewiston if something went wrong—if the sheriff lost control of his deputies, or if the deputies were overpowered by a mob, or if the sight of the prisoners should stir a lynching fever too hot to quench. It might be a good idea, he thought, to see whether Major Truax would provide some troops from Fort Lapwai to keep the peace at least until the prisoners were securely in jail. He wondered if there was time to get a letter to Sheriff Fisk to that effect. At any rate, he would send one in the morning.

It probably shouldn't matter to him, Beachey thought, whether these villains died by a judge's decree or at the end of a lynching rope. But he had given his word to the governor that they would get a fair trial, and so he was responsible. It would be up to him to shepherd them safely back to the jurisdiction of this brand new territorial court. He wanted to see them hang eventually, but in the meantime he would do everything in his power to keep them safe and alive and—he hoped—duly frightened.

Beachey was sitting in the hotel lobby the next afternoon when a runner dropped off several copies of the *San Francisco Bulletin*. Beachey bought one immediately and sure enough, there on the first page was Schwartz's story. It occupied a full column and a half, causing Beachey to wonder what the reporter could have found to write about at such length.

The one-column headline read:

IDAHO FUGITIVES
RETURNING HOME
TO FACE TRIAL

This was followed by a deck, or smaller head:

Governor Signs Papers
Turning 4 Prisoners
Over to Hill Beachey

And then a still smaller one-line deck:

Still no sign of missing packer

The story that appeared under that daunting battery of headlines described Beachey's pursuit of the fugitives, their arrest by San Francisco police, and Beachey's assurance that there would be no "necktie party" in Idaho. Schwartz also had interviewed the captain of the *Pacific*, apparently, for he quoted the captain as saying the prisoners would be secure on his ship and describing the stateroom they'd be occupying.

As he finished the story, Beachey was beaming with pleasure. He wrote a note to Gregory Schwartz, thanking him, and mailed it to the *Bulletin*. He then walked down to the police station and conferred with Chief Burke and Captain Lees on the final arrangements for transferring the prisoners from the cell to the ship. They would be moved in pairs in two wagons, heavily guarded, and would be on board a couple of hours before the vessel was due to sail. If he wished, Beachey could ride on one of the wagons. Beachey said he would like that very much. He would be at the police station at 8 a.m. on the day of departure.

There was nothing more for Beachey to do in San Francisco now but wait. He ate a quiet dinner in the hotel dining room. Then, because it was still early, he put on his coat and hat and stepped into the street, planning to take an evening walk. He had hardly left the hotel veranda when he heard again the sound of that violin. Well, he thought, why not find out where it was coming from? And he turned expectantly in that direction.

23 The *Pacific* was a wooden sailing ship converted to steam. She still carried her rigging and a full suit of sails because her owner, like many of the shipping companies of that day, didn't quite trust the steam engine. The captain didn't like it for other reasons: the paddle wheels at the sides were an ugly interruption of the clean lines of the ship, the engine created a fire hazard below decks, and when it was running it had to be fed fuel interminably— fuel that was carried where there ought to be cargo. But to Beachey, that steam engine was a source of great comfort. He didn't want to be responsible for his gang of cutthroats aboard a ship that was becalmed. Get us to Portland as fast as you can, he whispered silently to the engine below and the tall wooden masts as he followed Captain Lees up the gangplank.

They had come from the jail in a police buggy and two patrol wagons, the buggy in the lead carrying Beachey and Captain Lees and the patrol wagons coming along behind with the prisoners and their guards. Renton and Page were in one of the wagons, handcuffed and in leg irons, and Lower and Romain rode in the second. At dockside, Lees and Beachey went aboard first, and after they had inspected the barred stateroom that would serve as the seagoing jail, the guards brought the prisoners up and hurried them into their cell. Two of the guards would remain aboard until the ship reached Portland and return on the next boat south. The cell had a single barred window on the port side of the ship. As the *Pacific* steamed north toward Portland, the prisoners would see only the open ocean; they would not see land again until the boat reached the mouth of the Columbia River. Opposite that window, a narrow steel door opened upon the passageway that ran lengthwise down the center of the main deck. There was no window in this door and therefore no way for the prisoners to harass people using the passageway or be assisted by them. There was a narrow slit at the bottom of the door, covered by a hinged steel flap, through which a guard could push food and retrieve dishes. Inside the cell there were four bunks, two fore and two aft, hinged to the bulkhead, and a toilet connected to a holding tank below that drained directly into the sea. The only other amenity was a wash basin and a tap supplied from a fresh water tank somewhere above.

The prisoners were silent and sullen as they were hustled aboard ship and thrust into their cell. Once the door was closed and double-bolted, Officer Welch posted himself outside the barred window on the port side of the boat, where he would remain until the other guard relieved him. Lees and Beachey, and the officers who were going ashore, returned to the head of the gangplank and paused there while Beachey signed a paper stating that he had assumed custody of the prisoners and would henceforth be responsible for them. He then gave the paper to the police captain, thanked him warmly for all his help, and watched as Lees and his men walked down the gangplank and climbed into their rigs.

It was a little after 9 a.m. The weather was cold and damp and threatening rain. Beachey picked up his bag and found his own stateroom, on the starboard side. In it was a bed, well anchored to the floor, a table and chair, wash basin and toilet plus a small closet. He threw his bag into a corner and returned to the deck, unsure what to do next. The ship wouldn't sail until late afternoon, and Beachey had some time on his hands. He would go ashore for a while, he thought, but first he walked around to the port side, to the officer outside the cell window, and told him he'd be glad to stand guard from time to time. Beachey had been deputized by Sheriff Fisk in Lewiston and he carried a pistol in his bag. It seemed to him that the San Francisco police already had given him more help than he had any right to expect. The four men inside that cabin were his responsibility now.

Officer Welch appreciated the gesture. In fact, he told Beachey, if it was all right he'd like to go ashore for an hour or so and pick up a few things. He had left home on rather short notice. That would be fine, Beachey said. He went to his cabin, got his pistol, loaded it, and returned to the window. Go along, he told Welch, and the officer, with a grateful grin, turned and hurried off the boat.

Beachey felt better now that he had something to do. It seemed to him that he had been forever on this journey and he fairly ached with the need to get home, get his prisoners safely in jail, and do whatever needed doing at the Luna House. He would much rather be here guarding his charges, than wandering ashore with nowhere to go, killing time.

Somewhat to his own surprise, his attitude toward those four had changed. He still considered them scum, and would like to see Lower in hell, but his fierce desire to get the villains had been overcome by his need to protect them. If they were attacked, for example by someone avenging their crimes, he would defend them—to his own death, if necessary. They were no longer objects of the chase but persons dependent upon him for their lives. And they surely were, because only he could save them from the mob once he returned them to Idaho. And he wasn't certain he could do that despite the glib assurances he had given to Governor Stanford. Beachey's chase after the fugitives, and his promise to get them safely into Lewiston, had been well covered in the press. Captain Lees had not publicly announced their departure date for Portland, but he had made no great secret of it, either. Beachey wondered now how many interested people knew where the prisoners were at this moment. And he remembered Lower's boast that he had friends in California. It could be true. As the keeper of this odd menagerie, he had lost sight of his charges as a single enemy and become aware of the four as persons.

Page, he thought, was more stupid than evil; he had known Page at Lewiston as a frequently drunk old panhandler no worse than a hundred others he had known. Romain could be vicious but he had a childish, strangely innocent side, too. Renton was clever and on the make, susceptible to temptation and ever capable of impersonal murder for gain. Lower was something else: nasty, headstrong and downright mean, the kind who kills for pleasure and enjoys the memory. But he had seen panic in Lower's eyes, a humanizing glimpse of the man behind the sneer. Even with Lower now he felt the kinship of people caught up together in some dark and tragic enterprise, sworn enemies clinging to the same raft.

From the covered deck where he was standing, Beachey had a good view of the harbor, a vast sea of masts, still and silent as though waiting for orders. There were some four hundred vessels standing idle in the harbor besides several dozen crawling back and forth across the water under steam and sail. Most of these idle ships weren't going anywhere. They had carried prospectors around the Horn from the East Coast during the height of the gold rush and then had been abandoned by their crews. There was no money in seafaring compared to the wealth of gold in California. Many of these vessels were tied permanently to their piers and were serving now as hotels, brothels and restaurants. They would never go to sea again.

The sun had broken through a bank of clouds and was slanting down across a section of the harbor, dancing on the water and painting the huddled masts with a golden glow. Beachey was standing at the rail, enjoying the sight, when Officer Welch returned to his post at the window and said he would now take over.

Beachey gave Welch a soft salute and walked to the stern of the ship. There he leaned against the taffrail and watched passengers coming aboard, carrying bags and suitcases and pausing at the top of the gangplank where a purser with a clipboard checked them off. There were a few women and children but most of his fellow passengers were men traveling alone—prospectors, by the looks of them. Beachey didn't envy them. If they were heading for Idaho Territory—where else was there to go?—they were too late. They might have some luck in the Boise Basin, but the placer mines of the Clearwater and the Salmon were already nearly worked out. All the claims had been staked and the best a newcomer could do was work for somebody else, shoveling gravel and hauling water.

They didn't seem to know that. They looked cheerful, devil-may-care and full of optimism as they came up the gangplank one by one with their belongings on their backs. They hadn't made it in California, but what the hell, it was a big country.

Only one of these men, a tall, thin fellow, seemed less than enthusiastic as he paused in front of the purser. He was apparently a miner like the rest, for he was dressed the same and carrying the same kind of kit on his shoulder. He wore the same brown broad-brimmed hat, the standard wool jacket over a plaid shirt, black pants and well-worn boots. But he lacked the carefree attitude of the others. He looked down at the deck, or he shifted his gaze rapidly to bow and stern. He appeared to be uncomfortable here, and Beachey wondered why. Then he said to himself, well of course. He's on the run. It was easy to get into trouble in the mining camps, where liquor was plentiful and tempers short. Horse thieves and claim jumpers often had to scamper or wind up dead, and this man could be one with the good sense to skip.

As Beachey watched, the tall man turned from the purser, shifted his bundle on his shoulder, and disappeared into the passageway.

Lunch was being served in the dining salon, and Beachey remembered he had gone without breakfast in order to be at the police station early. He had spent too much time the night before in a saloon on the waterfront nursing a glass of whiskey, watching the people around him and listening to an old man playing violin tunes for drinks. By the time Beachey had left the place the hour was late and the old man's tunes unrecognizable. So he had overslept and missed breakfast. After lunch he went to his cabin and lay down on the bed, thinking to catch a short nap.

When he awoke the cabin was nearly dark and the ship was under way. He could hear and feel the steam engine pulsing somewhere below. He knew the ship was still inside the bay because it was riding smoothly. He stood up and went to the window. He could see part of the waterfront receding into the distance, a few other boats moving in the bay, and long shadows on the hills beyond the water. The sun was going down. He put his coat and hat on and went out on deck. He walked to the stern and put his back to the breeze. The clouds had vanished as he slept and a few stars already were visible in the light blue sky. Around him the water sparkled, and far back, beyond the ship's white wake, a forest of masts and rigging glowed in the setting sun.

Meanwhile, in his cabin on the port side of the main deck, Cy Skinner lay stretched out on a bed too short for his tall frame, staring at the ceiling and thinking to himself that this ocean trip might not be so bad after all. Skinner had never been to sea, but he had heard sad stories from some who had. This ride was pretty smooth, he thought; if it was no worse than this, his assignment might not be as gut-wrenching as he had feared.

He had a hankering to go out on deck and take a look around, but he decided it would be better to wait until dark. He would just lie here for a while longer, he thought, and listen to that steam engine. It had been a long, hard trip, and he could use the rest.

*****

John Cannady had the election results in his hand. The figures were neatly written out, efficiently arranged, and unbelievable. Cannady had been staring at those figures for some time now, and he was as incredulous as ever. So were several other Democrats who were sitting with him in the lobby of the Luna House in Lewiston. The totals showed that Cannady had lost the election and that William H. Wallace, the former governor, would be the first delegate to congress from the new Territory of Idaho. Cannady didn't like to lose but he could accept it. What he could not accept, he told the others, were the returns from the Fort Laramie district in the eastern end of the territory. According to the figures from Fort Laramie, which had been compiled by U. S. Marshal Dolphus Payne, the district had voted 479 for Wallace and zero for Cannady.[71] That was enough to arouse suspicion. But there weren't supposed to be 479 voters in Fort Laramie. Payne himself, after conducting the census prior to the election, had reported only 100 eligible voters there. If there were only 100 voters in September, how could Payne have counted 479 votes in November?

Assuming that Payne must have tampered also with other returns, it was clear that Cannady had been robbed of the election in a most brazen manner. Fortunately, since he had decided to come north after casting his own vote in Boise County, he was well placed to do something about it. He would demand a recount, of course. He also would demand to see the ballots from Fort Laramie. He would remain in the territorial capital until he had satisfaction, he assured his supporters.

Cannady met frustration at every turn. Marshal Payne could not produce the ballots because they had been lost. Shortly after offering that explanation, Payne himself disappeared. The Wallace supporters argued that there was no way to get a recount of the Fort Laramie balloting because there were no ballots to count. The voting population of Idaho, which included only white males, was highly mobile—so mobile that no residency requirements were possible. The white male voted wherever he happened to be at election time. Thus, said the Wallace people, there could have been 479 voters in Fort Laramie that day.

Nobody believed that. But when Cannady appealed to the court, Justice Alleck Smith ruled that the official tally would have to stand. There may well have been fraud, he agreed, but it would be impossible to prove with Payne out of the territory.

Jacob Hoffman and Jim Witt, attempting to cheer Cannady, told him that the scandal would work for him in the next election. For themselves, they found a different source of comfort. Terrible as Magruder's murder was, they agreed, at least it had spared him this nastiness.[72]

24 Skinner could hardly believe his good luck. After sixteen days of travel by horseback and stagecoach, he had reached San Francisco only two days before the departure of his prey for Portland. Had he been late, and missed this boat, he would have had to chase Renton and his gang northward by land, in another series of coaches, and hope to intercept them somewhere on the Columbia. This was much better. He would have some time at sea in which to carry out the assignment given to him by Henry Plummer back in Virginia City.

Plummer's orders, as usual, were not specific. He had told Skinner only that Renton, Lower and Romain were heading for San Francisco and that he wanted them dead. Skinner should be able to figure out what to do, he had told him. To Skinner, this meant going to San Francisco, finding the double-crossers, and killing them, and so he had set out. Skinner had gone from Virginia City to Bannack, across southern Idaho to Salt Lake City, down through Nevada and over to the Sacramento River of California, and on into San Francisco, with no more plan in his head than to get to there. Skinner's mind was unclouded by the complications of scheming, and that was fortunate because he was not good at it. It was Skinner who, at Plummer's request, had developed the plan by which Renton and party were to waylay Lloyd Magruder, pluck him of his gold, and carry the treasure to Bannack. The plan had failed, and Plummer now held Skinner responsible along with the traitors. If Skinner could dispatch the thieves before they had a chance to implicate the sheriff in their crime, Plummer might look with favor again on one of the most loyal of his troops.

It was Skinner's bad luck that he never read the papers. When he reached San Francisco they were carrying the news of Hill Beachey's pursuit of the Renton gang, the capture of the fugitives and Beachey's efforts to get them back to Idaho. His good luck was that he happened to be in the same saloon one day where Gregory Schwartz's story in the *Bulletin* was being read aloud at the bar. On learning that the fugitives were in jail in San Francisco, Skinner had then done the obvious, uncomplicated thing. He found the saloon nearest the jail and hung around there, trusting that this would be a gathering place for off-duty police. Skinner, a saloonkeeper himself, knew how to hold his whiskey, which was fortunate because in three days' time he had to hold a lot. It was an unpleasant three days. Skinner had rented a room in a nearby house but when he went there to sleep, he worried that in his absence from the saloon someone would drop just the information he wanted. He would lie awake, wondering what they were talking about now. He heard lots of police gossip of no use to him but finally he heard what he needed. A policeman came in, ordered a beer, and said to another officer who was standing at the bar that they were losing four of their prisoners. Beachey was taking them to Portland on the next boat north. That would be the *Pacific*, the other officer observed, leaving the day after tomorrow.

Now, stretched out on the bed in his cabin, Skinner wondered how Plummer had found out that the fugitives were heading for California. Somebody must have told him, Skinner thought, but who? Somebody coming into Virginia City who had seen them and talked with them, maybe. That could have been the answer, and that satisfied Skinner because he could not have understood what really had happened.

The fact was that Plummer didn't know where the culprits were heading. He had heard from somebody who had told somebody else who had told one of his boys that they had gone through Lewiston. The sheriff then had asked himself where he would go if he were Renton. Not to Walla Walla or The Dalles or Portland. Those towns were too small to hide in. Not to British Columbia for the same reason. And if he had passed through Lewiston, he clearly could not be going to Salt Lake City. If he were Renton, looking for a place to hide, he would go as fast as he could to the biggest city on the coast, and that was San Francisco. Then who should go after Renton? There were a lot of people smarter than Skinner, but no one had more reason to want Renton and company dead than Skinner, unless it was Plummer himself. And since Plummer's duties tied him down in Bannack and Virginia City, Skinner would have to go.

So here he was, traveling in comfort for a change, on the same boat with Renton, Lower and Romain. Plus a fellow named Page, he understood. Skinner had met Page, and Magruder too, for that matter. Both had come into his saloon in Bannack and Skinner had heard Page agree to go with Magruder across the mountains to Lewiston. Skinner didn't know what Page had to do with the crime or why he was traveling with the other three, but he could only assume that Page must be involved in the double-cross and must be as dangerous to Plummer as the others were. So Page also became a target.

Skinner had not figured out how he would accomplish his task. Plummer had told him merely that the prisoners must be hunted down and killed, preferably while they were still at large; once arrested, any one of them could identify Sheriff Plummer as the brains behind the most fearsome road gang on the Idaho frontier. Skinner had expected he would have to track them down one at a time, maybe spending the whole winter at it. Now he had them all in one place, where they couldn't get away, and he would have plenty of time to get his work done.

There was a possibility, of course, that plans had changed and that the four were not on the boat after all. He hadn't actually seen them come aboard. But Skinner discarded that idea for the most practical of reasons: if they weren't on board there was nothing he could do about it because he was, and the boat was under way.

It was dusk now. Skinner thought he would go out on deck after a while and have a look around, but first he would get a little sleep.

He awoke in pitch dark, with no idea what time it was. Nor did he care. His bed was sinking with him, down, down, and then rising, up, up, pausing tenuously then dropping again, down, down. His stomach was churning and in the back of his mouth he could taste his gorge rising and retreating. All around him there was a great creaking and groaning. His first thought was that he was descending into Hell and then it occurred to him that he was on a ship and the ship was sinking. He had heard about lifeboats; he would have to get to one.

He rolled off the bed onto the floor and tried to stand but he could not. He managed to get to his hands and knees and he remained there, bracing himself beside the bed and clinging to the floor until, with surprising suddenness, his insides turned over and the burning vomit gushed out of him onto his hands and wrists. He tried to crawl away from the slippery, stinking stuff but the boat gave another heave that threw him onto his back. He lay there until he started to choke, then rolled onto his stomach and inched his way toward the faint bar of light that he could see under the door. Once there he pushed against the wall, got his legs under him and lifted himself high enough to get hold of the doorknob. The door came open and he fell again, still clinging to the knob, but managed to squirm through the opening into the passageway. Then, clinging to the railing, he inched his way toward the afterdeck, which he could make out in the distance by the flickering light of hurricane lamps. Once there he lurched crazily across the deck to the outer rail, wrapped his arms around a stanchion, and saw with great relief that the ship was not sinking. While he slept the vessel had steamed out of the bay and was plowing through the long swells of the ocean.

A few stars had appeared but there was no moon, and the water was black and forbidding. In the glow of lamps attached at intervals to the staterooms' outer walls he could see the dark forms of other people at the rail. He could hear the groaning and scraping of the spars and rigging out of sight above the covered deck and the splash and sigh of water rushing past the hull. Now that he could see the water and the stars, he could tell where he was in relation to the world, and the panic subsided. His mouth was hot and his throat ached and his stomach was still in revolt, but he felt better. Somewhere on the ship a child was wailing and for reasons he did not try to understand, that human sound made Skinner feel better still. As long as he stayed where he was, and made no sudden moves, he might yet survive this night.

Behind the barred porthole of the brig, the prisoners were enduring varying degrees of illness. Page, who had made one crossing of the Atlantic, was doing relatively well. He had suffered a momentary intestinal spasm but reached the basin in time and was sitting on a wooden bench with his back hard against the wall and his feet braced solidly on the floor. He was not looking forward to several days and nights of this. Lower and Romain were fighting over the porthole, pushing and shoving and gulping the fresh salty air. Both had been sick and both had contributed to the stench in the cabin that had driven them to the window. Renton sat on a lower bunk, one hand grasping the chain that held it to the wall, eyes closed and rolling with the ship. Although he found the movement unpleasant, he had not been sick. He had not only been on the ocean before, he had spent some time on a prison ship in San Francisco Bay and heard many sea tales from fellow convicts. Renton knew what to expect. He knew, for instance, that these were coastal swells they were experiencing and that once the boat was well offshore, the going would be much better.

Beachey had found that as long as he was moving about and watching the water, he was all right, and he spent the first hour outside the bay walking the deck from port to starboard and back again, holding onto the railing bolted to the wall. Occasionally he would meet another passenger doing the same thing in the opposite direction, and there would be a polite little dance while the two maneuvered around each other.

By morning the worst was over, and the ship was steaming under sail northward in relatively placid waters. Through intermittent sunshine and rain, the people on the starboard side could sometimes make out the coast of northern California and sometimes not.

Stewards with buckets and mops were washing down the decks and those staterooms that needed it. The breeze was fresh and clean except when it caught the gray smoke from the stack and tossed it about the ship. The wind was blowing toward the shore, and the *Pacific* would be sailing on a starboard tack all the way to the Columbia River estuary.

As the sun rose in the sky the weather warmed, the rain clouds vanished, and a holiday air invigorated passengers and crew. It was the first day at sea after a trying night, and there was laughter on the decks and in the salon. Beachey, feeling indestructible, offered to relieve Officer Parker outside the ship's brig. Parker said he'd rather remain on duty and visit since he didn't know anyone else on board the ship but his fellow guard, Officer Welch, who was asleep. So Beachey stayed and engaged Parker in what they both called California talk—talk about the mining camps and what had happened to them, about the way San Francisco was changing under the pressure of a swelling population, about rumors of a railroad coming down the Sacramento Valley.

At one point Lower appeared at the window and complained that no one had come to clean up the mess inside the cell. The stench was making him sick all over again, he said. Romain, joining him at the porthole, said he couldn't eat his breakfast or his lunch because of the odor, and he was getting weak. He did look bad, Beachey thought, but Parker, who had worked for years with prisoners like these, told Lower and Romain to stop their bellyaching and clean the place themselves. What with? Lower wanted to know. All right all right, Beachey said, and he went looking for a steward. He found one and asked him to push a mop through the food passage at the bottom of the cell door. He returned to the porthole and told Lower the mop was on the way and he could use the basin as a bucket.

Beachey had been terribly seasick once himself—on the Mississippi River, of all places—and felt sorry for the poor devils caged in their cell with the odorous refuse of their illness. He understood Parker's insensitivity because Parker no doubt had been much abused in his time by the thieves and murderers who had found their way into his jail. But these were human beings after all, and in his keeping. Besides, the smell was getting out of the brig onto the deck. Parker had noticed it too, and demanded that the porthole be closed. That brought a scream of outrage from Lower together with a plea from Renton, who had come to the window for fresh air. Beachey told Parker he agreed with Renton. Let them leave the window open, he said; he and Parker could step away from it far enough to evade the smell and the passengers didn't have to linger here.

As Beachey and Parker chatted comfortably on the deck, they could hear the water running inside and the swish-swish of the mop. They could hear the prisoners talking purposefully, like busy craftsmen, as they went about their housework. There was even a bit of laughter from Page in response to something Renton was saying, probably a joke. The change of mood pleased Beachey, who was gazing at the sparkling blue ocean, and he was about to mention it to Parker when he felt a damp object pushing against the back of his head. His hat came off and suddenly something heavy and wet and obnoxious was shaking itself against his hair and his face. As he dropped to the deck he put an arm up, grasped the handle of the mop, tore it away from the window and hurled it into the sea.

25 Beachey, in a seething rage, tore around the deck and into his stateroom, trying not to breathe. Once inside, he began throwing off clothes and then, down to his shoes and underwear, he turned on the tap and put his head under it. As the cold water splashed into his hair, he reached for a wash rag, soaked it, and pulled it across his face and neck. He grabbed a piece of bar soap from a tray beside the basin, without looking up, and rubbed it hard against the top of his head. He rinsed his hair and beard again. He took the wash rag once more and thoroughly swabbed his neck and his whole head, and then rubbed his hair roughly with a towel. As he dried himself, he paced back and forth across the small stateroom, boiling with fury, and stopped in front of the mirror that hung above the basin. He was planning to comb his hair, but he found himself gazing at the image in the glass with fascination and fright. The eyes were bloodshot, the hair damp and curly, and the expression on the face malevolent. He had never in his life been so angry, and the mirror showed it.

The man in the mirror, Beachey knew, was capable of murder and that man was him. Thank God he could not get his hands on Lower at this moment, for he would not be able to restrain himself. He would kill him, and regret it for the rest of his life.

It was Lower, all right, who had done this. Beachey didn't doubt that for a moment. But the face in the mirror had shocked him with a warning: he must not go near that brig today. Lower would live long enough to enjoy his little prank, but he would never know how close it had brought Beachey to losing his self-control.

Skinner's problem was different. He had no personal grudge against Lower even though Lower and the others had double-crossed him. It wasn't Skinner's money that the Renton gang had stolen, it was Plummer's, and what Skinner was here to do he would do on Plummer's behalf. His problem was that he was still too sick to manage the chore.

As Beachey fumed and splashed in his cabin, Skinner sat in his, fearing to lie down because his stomach was still in rebellion, and too weak to walk. He had not eaten since early yesterday but he knew he couldn't hold food down. He had asked a steward to mop his cabin, unaware that the steward would expect a tip, and that had led to some unpleasantness. It hadn't occurred to him that there might be a doctor on board, and so Skinner didn't realize that he was suffering not only from sea sickness but from the flu. Fortunately, perhaps, he didn't know that; he kept thinking that if he could get through another six or eight hours he would probably be all right. Then he would be able to go to the dining salon and eat. He would be able to sleep. He would get his strength back and get about the business he was here for.

He had accomplished one thing. Shortly after daybreak, as he was trying to navigate back to his cabin, he had passed the barred porthole. He had seen the officer standing outside and heard from inside the voice of David Renton. Later, unable to lie down, he had gone out on the starboard deck and seen another barred porthole that was unguarded. That meant to him that all four prisoners were in Renton's cell. Would that make his job easier? Maybe, maybe not. He was too tired to think further about it.

By evening, after two glasses of brandy in the ship's lounge, Beachey was feeling more calm and comfortable. Officer Welch was standing guard and Officer Parker had joined Beachey for dinner and drinks. Although Parker sympathized with Beachey's earlier fury, he could not help finding some humor in his encounter with the mop. Parker had seen the whole thing; he had been facing the porthole when the mop head came thrusting out. But it had all happened so fast, and it was so surprising, that Parker could only stand and gawk until Beachey was roaring away in retreat and the mop was adrift in the sea. There had been a loud guffaw from Lower, after which Parker had cautioned him that he might live to regret this deed. Lower had snickered at that and demanded another mop which, as Parker assured Beachey later, he did not get.

Some of the men at the bar, feeling very brave now, were telling seasick stories. Parker asked if they had heard the one about the flying mop, and described the episode with only minor exaggerations. Everyone agreed it was outrageous, and funny, and Beachey soon joined in the laughter. He was especially pleased to note that even after hearing this tale, his drinking companions had not moved away from him. In gratitude, he ordered another round.

The weather continued fair, and on the third night out of San Francisco the *Pacific* arrived outside the Columbia River estuary. She crossed the bar on the morning tide and steamed into the Columbia. The estuary had the look of a huge bay, dotted here and there with little densely timbered islands. Like most of the other passengers, Beachey was out on deck to watch the approach to Astoria, and like most of the others, he found the prospects gloomy. The hills on both sides of the estuary, like the islands in it, were thick with trees. Astoria itself had been hacked out of the forest, and it looked to Beachey as though the forest might recapture it overnight. The air, under an overcast sky, was heavy with a mist that was almost rain. The dark woods came down to the water's edge on every side, thick as fur and seemingly just as impenetrable. Beachey wondered how people made it from one place to another through this dense and forbidding growth. Was there anywhere for a person even to stand?

The boat was not long at Astoria. Only those who lived or had business here bothered to go ashore since the place clearly had nothing to offer. Every aspect of it—the sodden town, the gray estuary, the gloomy hills—was so depressing that Beachey retired to the lounge and remained there, drinking coffee, while the boat proceeded up the Columbia to the Willamette River and finally, with the help of a harbor tug, nudged up to its Portland pier.

Skinner, still weak and wavering, had no idea what to do next. The luck that had seemed to be his three days ago had turned sour. The best he could do now was try not to let the prisoners be taken away from him. That meant that wherever they went, he would have to go. But what was Beachey's plan?

Beachey's plan, once he got his prisoners this far, was to seek help from Oregon authorities in getting them upriver to Lewiston. That leg of the journey would require three steamboats and two portages—at Cascade Rapids and Celilo Falls—and would entail considerable risk. Welch remained on board while Beachey and Parker disembarked and sought out the chief of police. Parker presented him with a letter from Captain Lees stating that the San Francisco police would appreciate any courtesy that the Portland police could give to Beachey and that whatever help was offered to Beachey would be reciprocated. The Portland police got in touch with the Multnomah County Sheriff, who had been asked by Sheriff Fisk of Nez Perce County to give Beachey whatever help he could.

Beachey was startled to discover how much information had been passing up and down the Columbia by horseback, stagecoach and riverboat. And, he was pleased to learn that the commanding officer at Fort Vancouver had offered a military escort from Portland to Lewiston.

Beachey arranged for his prisoners to remain aboard the *Pacific* until the army was ready. Then he left Welch and Parker with the prisoners, took a launch across the Columbia River to Fort Vancouver and asked for a meeting with the officer in charge. He was welcomed warmly by a colonel and an aide-de-camp, both of whom had read the accounts of Beachey's mission. They understood that feelings were running high against the presumed murderers and that there was a good chance they would all be lynched if stern measures were not taken to protect them. It was important, the colonel said, that the first criminal case in the new Idaho Territory result in a fair trial. He considered himself a peacekeeper as well as a soldier, he added, and felt a strong obligation to do his part in seeing justice done.

It seemed to Beachey that he was rehearing his own argument in Governor Stanford's office for custody of the prisoners. He felt relieved that the responsibility for their safe passage would not be his alone, and he was grateful beyond measure to the Army of the Columbia.

The colonel asked Beachey to give him a day, and to return to Fort Vancouver tomorrow. By that time, he should have transportation arranged. Beachey returned to Portland, boarded the *Pacific*, and told Parker and Welch that their duties here were about done. He spent the night on board and next day took the launch back across the Columbia.

The army did what it had promised. A small sternwheeler, the *Julia*, would depart from Vancouver the next morning with freight for Fort Lapwai. The colonel arranged for a military escort to accompany Beachey and his charges on board the *Julia* and all the way to Lewiston. Furthermore, he ordered troopers to fetch the prisoners from the Portland-docked *Pacific* at dawn and transfer them to the *Julia* before it cast off from Vancouver.

Skinner had remained on board the *Pacific*, determined that he would not leave the ship until the prisoners did. But Skinner was sicker than he thought. When the steam launch arrived from Fort Vancouver to take away the prisoners, Skinner was lying on his cot with his face to the wall. He heard some commotion, and found the strength to get up and stagger to the door, and into the passageway. There he saw Beachey, several soldiers and the two San Francisco police hustling the four prisoners out of the passageway onto the afterdeck. Skinner followed, clutching the handrail, and emerged on deck just as the troopers were putting the prisoners aboard the launch. Skinner could only stand at the rail and look, knowing that he would never catch them now. As he watched Beachey bid farewell to officers Parker and Welch, he thought briefly about his future. First he would pack his bag and disembark, then he would find a room somewhere and go back to bed. There was nothing he could do now about Lower, Renton and Romain and so there was no point in worrying further about them. There was a strong possibility that the whole bunch of them would be strung up as soon as they reached Lewiston. At least he hoped so.

The *Julia* was waiting, with steam up, when the launch arrived on the Vancouver side of the Columbia. The vessel was frequently used for missions like this one, and was designed to carry prisoners. There were several staterooms on the main deck along with half a dozen small cells. Whatever freight it carried, and it was not much, was lashed to the foredeck and afterdeck. The sternwheeler had been under way for about an hour when Beachey, carrying a mug of black coffee, walked out to the foredeck and saw straight ahead of the *Julia* the base of a huge mountain whose peak was lost in the overcast. It was Mount Hood, which he had seen once before, on his first journey to Lewiston. He had not been able to see the top of it then, either, and he wondered now whether anyone ever had. The majestic mountain dominated the horizon, and for several hours, as the *Julia* churned her way upriver, the mountain was there, straight ahead. At length the river took a turn and the mountain disappeared.

The scenery everywhere now was wild and picturesque. The timber that choked the lands around the estuary gave way in places to rocky capes. Miles-long cliffs of smooth rock dropped to the water's edge. Rocky spires thrust up from the river, trees clinging to their crevices. In the afternoon, the steamer approached signs of civilization—a large island with fences, houses and some fruit trees, and nearby, on the Oregon side of the Columbia, a little cluster of piers. For the *Julia*, this was the end of the line; its passengers would disembark here and get into the coaches that carried travelers around Cascade Rapids, from the lower to the middle Columbia.

On the middle river, the prisoners were put aboard another steamer, this one not as well appointed for the task, and carried as far as The Dalles. After another portage, the soldiers, the prisoners and Beachey embarked on still another steamer on the upper river. This one would take them to the big bend of the Columbia, and then into the Snake River and finally the Clearwater.

It was now December 1. Beachey had been some five weeks in pursuit of the fugitives, in getting custody of them, and in bringing them back this far. Since his moment of fury on the *Pacific*, he had wanted nothing to do with them; he felt the sight of Lower's face would make him both sick and murderous. As for the others, he wished only to see them in court. After leaving Vancouver, he had let the soldiers have sole responsibility for getting them on and off the boats, seeing that they were fed and keeping them under guard. He felt a bit guilty about that, since he had sworn to take care of them, but he had to prepare himself in every possible way for the test that was to come on reaching Lewiston. He had no doubt there would be a lynch mob waiting, armed and carrying ropes, and it would be up to him to face the mob down one way or another.

On the morning when the boat turned east into the Snake River, Beachey stood up from his breakfast, put on his coat and hat, and walked forward to the bow. It was a clear, cold day. A light skiff of snow whitened the treeless benches above the river on either side and the sun was still low enough in the east to leave the river canyon in shadow. Beachey gazed at the dark water ahead and the sparkling prairie above and breathed deeply, filling his lungs with the sweet, dry air of the interior. What a tonic this was, he thought, after weeks in the cold and damp of the Pacific coast. He had feared his bag of clothes would never dry out, but he knew better now. Here on the clear and arid side of the Cascade Range the breathing was easier, the spirit was lighter and the gravity of Earth itself seemed to have relaxed under the sun. With a lighter step than he had known in a month, he walked around the deck to the vessel's stern and stood listening to the whooshing of the steam engine and the churning, splashing, gurgling of the water under the big paddle wheel. The vibrations of the engine thrummed pleasurably through the soles of his boots, up his legs and into his ribs, making him feel a part of the machinery of this noble enterprise. What a beautiful boat, Beachey thought. What a glorious country. How good it would be to see Maggie again. He remained there, enjoying the rhythms and basking in the warming sun as the shadows crept down the canyon walls and the dark smoke from the stack curled lazily into the sky.

Lewiston
Winter 1863-1864

Part Three

26 Margaret Beachey was sitting at her husband's desk in the lobby of the Luna House, working on the accounts, when the breathless young man rushed in. The boat was coming, he shouted to the lobby at large. He was crossing on the Silcott ferry, he said, when he saw the steamboat come around the bend from the north, and he had raced his horse all the way to town to bring the news.

Margaret jumped from her chair and reached for her wrap as the young man dashed out the door, heading pell-mell for the De France. As she wriggled into her long coat she could hear the messenger out on the street shouting to the town at large and her spirits soared at the words: Mr. Beachey's coming! Mr. Beachey's coming! It was about two in the afternoon of a blustery day of mixed sunshine and shade. A light snow reached halfway down from the top of the hills across the Clearwater, but the valley floor was bare and dry.

The stage from Walla Walla had brought word two days ago that Beachey and his party had reached The Dalles and would continue to Lewiston on the next boat to climb the riffles of the upper river. Low water made navigation difficult at this time of year and the Oregon Steam Navigation Co. had only a few boats that were both small enough and powerful enough for the Snake in early December. One of them was the *Tenino*, and it was the *Tenino* that young Jeff Grigsby had seen pushing its bow wave around the bend north of Silcott.

The Luna House bar emptied into the lobby and the lobby emptied into the street and Margaret, buttoning her coat with one hand and pushing her hat onto her head with the other, was swept along in the excitement. At the De France, Captain LaFrancois heard the news and went immediately to the kitchen, where Madame Bonhore was discussing cuisine with the chef, Baptiste Escude. Madame told the captain to go along if he wished; she had work to do here. And she reminded Escude that he had work to do also. Escude glanced pitifully at the captain, who told Madame that it was only a little after two, the quiet part of the chef's day. Why shouldn't he come down to the landing for this historic event? Madame not only relented, she decided she would go also, and went to fetch her coat and hat.

Young Grigsby, after leaving the Hotel De France, ran down C Street toward the Snake River, still shouting the news. He pushed his head through the doors of Cassidy's Saloon, Bonner and Jones' Barber Shop and Bath House, the general store of Grostein & Binnard, the Grey Eagle Saloon and James Levitt's blacksmith shop. Tom Cassidy simply said, let's go, boys, locked the saloon and headed for the landing. Frank Kenyon was hand-pegging a stick of type in the office of *The Golden Age* on D Street when he noticed a sudden surge of traffic outside. He put down the type and went to the door to find out what was happening. Then he threw off his apron and his eyeshade and joined the crowd without bothering even to close the door; there was nothing in the office of *The Golden Age* that was nearly as valuable as Tom Cassidy's whiskey.

Among the crowd gathering at the landing was Sheriff Fisk, who had deputized a half-dozen citizens in anticipation of trouble, and the town marshal, W.H. Wickersham. Fisk had planned to ask Major Truax to send some soldiers from Fort Lapwai to help keep order, just in case. But then he had learned that the army was sending a military escort with Beachey from Fort Vancouver. Neither the sheriff nor the marshal wished to appear unable to maintain control without still more military support. So Fisk had decided not to call upon Major Truax after all. He had no way of knowing at the time that Beachey's military escort consisted of only four troopers.

*****

Beachey had returned to the bow of the *Tenino* as the little sternwheeler pushed through the Snake River toward Silcott, and when the boat rounded the bend he could see smoke rising above Lewiston in the distance. His emotions as he approached the crucial moment of his enterprise were intolerably mixed. He would become a mental wreck if he dwelt on them, so he tried to concentrate on the scenery passing by on either side. On his right, near the mouth of Alpowa Creek, where the coach road started up to Walla Walla, was the farm of Indian Reuben, one of the first of the Rev. Spalding's converts. Here was where Romain and friends had bought berries from the old woman. Passing by soon on his left was the Silcott ferry, tied up now on the north shore whence Grigsby had recently spurred his horse toward the town. High overhead, geese were flying in chattering columns in a southeasterly direction. The river was lined on either side by bushy willows, now leafless. As the river level dropped during the summer and fall it had left quiet sloughs of stranded water in shallow cups of land on the boat's starboard side—still water, stagnant but teeming with life even now in December. If Lewiston was lucky, and the coming winter cold enough, there would be ice on these sloughs to be sawed up, hauled to town and stored for summer.

Within a few minutes the bluff rising on Beachey's right fell away, the vista opened up, and there ahead was Lewiston, lying under the smoke of its December fires on a spit of land jutting out into the junction of the Snake and Clearwater rivers. Even from this distance Beachey could see the people and the buggies on First Street, which gave the best view up the river. He had supposed he would be met—all the boats were—but he had not expected such a crowd. He turned in some exasperation and hurried back to where the soldiers were guarding the single stateroom that served on this boat as the brig.

Journey's end was just ahead, he told the troopers. Was everything ready? Everything was, they said, as far as they could tell. The regular passengers would disembark first, and when they were safely off, the prisoners would be taken ashore. They would be put into a coach and driven directly to the Luna House and lodged in two of the sleeping rooms upstairs. Those two rooms had served as the town jail since Beachey had built the hotel two years earlier. He did not look forward to the transfer from ship to shore and thence to the hotel. He could not forget what had happened to Peoples, English and Scott in '62, and they had been guilty, or presumed so, only of a botched armed robbery.

*****

The sight of the *Tenino* steaming toward town sent an excited murmur through the crowd and prompted Sheriff Fisk to deploy his troops. He cleared the dock, which lay parallel to the Clearwater shore and where some boys had been running and jumping. He and the marshal then posted the deputies at intervals on either side of A Street as far as Second. Later, as the coach proceeded, they would move them up Second Street to C and on C Street to the Luna House at the corner of Third. The deputies were to keep the people back of them so the road would be clear and passable. Each man carried both a pistol and a shotgun, and the sheriff advised each to keep his weapons in plain sight. The crowd was in a good mood and offered no trouble. The sheriff saw Margaret, standing on tiptoe and staring toward the steamboat, and told her she must not approach her husband while he was in the road with the prisoners. Fisk apologized for that but said it was necessary to maintain order. Margaret understood and promised to comply.

A coach and four was brought up and parked on A Street at the top of the ramp that connected the street and the dock.

By now the *Tenino* was close enough to whistle its arrival and the throaty blast echoed off the northern hills, causing a cheer to rise up from the waiting throng. The people who had been watching the boat from First now were moving around the corner onto A Street, to be nearer the landing when the vessel docked. The sheriff and the marshal, however, would let no one closer than forty feet to the dock or to the A Street ramp.

It was Hill Beachey's party, but the onlookers had seen Beachey many times before; they were there to get a glimpse of the prisoners and, in some cases, to watch a hanging if there was to be one. So far the sheriff had seen no sign of a disturbance and no evidence that a lynch mob was forming. Despite the cold, it was a holiday atmosphere that prevailed as the *Tenino* eased slowly up to the dock and as two deckhands jumped off with their hawsers to tie her up. The captain, in a visored cap and long gray beard, delighted the youngsters in the crowd with another blast from his whistle, then pushed open the window of the wheelhouse and waved at the people on the shore.

The passengers, carrying bags and satchels, began to descend the stairs from the staterooms to the rear deck, then down a short gangplank onto the dock and up the ramp to A Street. There were buggies there from the Luna House, the Hotel De France and the Globe, each driver with instructions to snare as many of the passengers as he could. Some of the debarking travelers, apparently unaware that they had shared accommodations with a group of murder suspects, seemed surprised at the crowd. One of the first people off, an elderly man in a black suit who could have been a doctor or a preacher, asked one of the deputies what was going on. Just taking precautions, the deputy said, leaving the old man as unenlightened as before.

More people were coming out of the mining country at this time of year than going in, and the *Tenino*'s passenger list was short. Within a few moments, everyone was off the ship but the prisoners, their guardians, and the crew. Beachey came out on deck and signaled to Sheriff Fisk, who was standing at the top of the ramp, that all was ready. Fisk in turn signaled to the driver of the coach and four, who maneuvered his team into the middle of A Street, pulled on the brake, and jumped down. Margaret Beachey, seeing her husband for the first time in five weeks, waved eagerly to him, but she could not catch his eye. Beachey turned and disappeared inside the boat and a moment later two soldiers came out with Romain between them. Romain, pale and frightened, was draped with chains and wearing leg irons that forced him to take short, mincing steps. The troopers half dragged him across the dock and up the ramp to the coach, lifted him onto the step and pushed him inside where Marshal Wickersham was sitting with a shotgun on his lap.

The soldiers returned to the boat and came out again, this time with Page. After putting Page in the coach they went back for Renton, then for Lower. Page looked confused and Renton was

subdued but Lower, as usual, came out of the boat with a defiant air
and once up on A Street, while the troopers were shoving him toward the coach, he turned and spat at the crowd. A man nearby
rushed into the street toward Lower with his fists cocked and was
dragged back, cursing, by one of the deputies. A scuffle ensued as
several men came to the deputy's aid, and suddenly the mood of
the crowd had changed.

Fisk could feel and hear the difference. The sight of the prisoners, Lower's obvious contempt and the anger on the sidelines
had dispelled the holiday atmosphere and stirred up dark passions.
The sheriff called the marshal out of the coach and motioned the
two soldiers to get inside with the prisoners. They did, and the
driver mounted the high seat, waiting for a signal to proceed. It
didn't come quickly. The crowd had surged into the street in front
of the coach and several deputies were trying to move the people
back, pushing with their shotguns and cursing. At this moment
Beachey and a third soldier came off the boat and hurried up the
ramp to help. After coming all this way, Beachey knew, he couldn't
let anything happen now.

Beachey and the soldier joined the sheriff and the marshal
and together with the deputies they managed to clear the street so
the coach could proceed. The driver released his brake, slapped
the horses smartly with the reins, and gave a commanding shout.
The coach and four was moving along A Street toward Second, and
everything now seemed to be under control. Beachey was walking
beside the coach, carrying his pistol, when he spotted Margaret in
the crowd. He put the gun in his pocket and trotted over to her,
smiling broadly. She was standing with Madame Bonhore and Captain LaFrancois but Beachey did not seem to notice. He put one
arm around her shoulder and laid a hand against her cheek, and
quietly told her to leave immediately and go straight home. Now,
he said. Then he turned to the captain and urged him to take Madame home as well. There could be trouble here, he said. Madame
took Margaret's arm and guided her away from the crowd in the
direction of Third Street. She turned and nodded to the captain as
if to say she would handle this, and the two women hurried off
toward the Luna House, neither having said a word.

Captain LaFrancois told Beachey he'd be glad to help in any
way he could, and Beachey accepted the offer. The captain had a

martial look about him in or out of uniform, and Beachey could use a man like that just now. He asked the captain to come with him, and both caught up to the coach, which by now had reached the corner of Second and A. Beachey asked the captain to walk beside the coach on the left hand side and he would walk on the right. Beachey would have his pistol, which he hoped would be half as effective as the captain's air of command.

The coach turned the corner and headed up Second Street away from the river. The crowd now seemed to consist of men and boys only, and it was on the verge of becoming unruly. There were dark mutterings and occasional shouts and jeers. Somebody shot a pistol, apparently into the air. A rock sailed past Beachey's head and bounced off the side of the coach. The coach moved faster now as it passed B Street and both Beachey and the captain trotted alongside. At the intersection with C Street the driver turned the team to the left toward the Luna House and then the coach abruptly stopped. A fight had broken out in the middle of the street, the crowd was moving in, and the horses refused to go forward. Beachey, close to panic and breathing heavily, ran toward the scuffle, brandishing his pistol. He fired one shot into the air and demanded that the people in the street disperse. That brought the deputies into action and within less than a minute order had been restored.

The coach started moving again, slowly, and Beachey noticed with great relief that the crowd at the side of the street had drawn back. Then he saw a rifle barrel extending out the coach window on his side, aimed at the crowd. He assumed that the captain was seeing the same welcome sight on his side and trusted that this would get them safely to the Luna House, now only a half block ahead.

It was the longest seventy-five yards in all of the innkeeper's desperate journey to San Francisco and return, but the distance closed at last. The coach came to a halt and Beachey walked forward to find the sheriff, who presumably was getting his deputies in position to move the prisoners from the coach to the second floor of the Luna House. But Sheriff Fisk was not in sight. Instead, coming toward the coach with determined pace and somber air was a gang of men with four persons in the lead, each one of them carrying a rope.[73]

27 Beachey's heart skipped a beat, then raced. He felt cold panic followed by anger, an anger directed not at the advancing mob as much as at the insane fate that had teased him this far with his prisoners only to bring him face to face at the very last moment with a lynching party. Where was the sheriff? Where was his military escort? Where were the deputies? He felt the hand of Captain LaFrancois on his shoulder and turned to him in momentary bewilderment. Then he saw the sheriff pushing his way through the crowd toward the men with the ropes. LaFrancois strode ahead and planted himself in the street, blocking the gang. Standing there with feet apart, hands on his hips, the captain declared that these prisoners were wards of the territory, were going to stand trial, and would not be turned over to anyone but the sheriff. One of the soldiers, struck by the incongruity of the scene and the captain's French accent, started to smile, then thought better of it, and grasped his rifle more firmly.

By now the sheriff had joined LaFrancois, facing the mob, and motioned with his shotgun that the men should move back. The men did not, but stood their ground saying nothing. The crowd of onlookers had become both silent and motionless. Beachey, standing in front of the lead horse, turned quickly to look back toward the coach, and saw the door on his side open. One of the soldiers stepped down warily, closed the coach door and stood facing the mob with his left hand on the door handle and his right arm balancing a rifle. Another soldier emerged from the coach's left passenger door and stepped down, pointing his rifle straight ahead. The two soldiers who had been walking behind the coach came forward and joined Beachey.

The sheriff announced to the crowd that the prisoners were to be taken into the Luna House, and he ordered that the way be cleared.

Nobody moved. Where were the deputies? Beachey wondered, then spotted two of them. They were trying to urge people away from the veranda of the Luna House so that the team could pull the coach up parallel with the door. The veranda was packed with people who were standing like statues, motionless and immovable. Some of the other bystanders were moving, sullenly, and Beachey signaled the driver to move the team ahead. Once the two deputies had moved on down the line, however, the crowd closed in again and the team stopped.

Beachey could hear the sheriff demanding the ropes and getting nowhere. He noticed that some of the men and boys in the crowd were carrying rocks they had picked up off the ground. The soldiers were maintaining their positions, one on each side of the coach and two in front of the team with Beachey. LaFrancois, saying someone should be with the prisoners, borrowed Beachey's pistol, went back to the coach, and climbed inside.

From somewhere, a rock came sailing through the air and bounced off the coach's door. In the crowd, someone loudly urged that the territory be spared the expense of a trial. This was followed by shouts of approval. It seemed to Beachey that the mob of men who had arrived with the ropes was growing larger. He could see people separating from the crowd of bystanders and joining the lynch party—voting with their feet to hang the four here and be done with it. He didn't see anybody moving in the other direction. The sheriff's corps of deputies had shrunk from six to two, and Beachey could no longer see even the two. The town marshal had been swallowed up in the crowd, or left the scene entirely; he was nowhere in evidence. The four soldiers would be no match for this mob once it smelled blood. Here within a few feet of the Luna House veranda, everything was falling to pieces. If he didn't act soon, Beachey knew, it would be too late.

He took off his hat and raised it high above his head, signaling for attention. He asked the crowd for quiet and got it, grudgingly. Then he told the people who he was, in case there was anyone here who didn't know him. As he spoke he turned slowly from side to side so that everyone could see his face.

He told his audience that he thought the prisoners in the coach behind him were guilty of the murders of Lloyd Magruder and Charlie Allen. Otherwise, he wouldn't have followed them all the way to San Francisco and brought them back to Lewiston. But he said that was only his opinion; it would take a jury, after hearing the evidence, to say for sure. And he did not spend five weeks hunting and returning these four men to now stand quietly and see them hanged without a trial.

Beachey reminded the crowd that things had changed in the past year. This was no longer Washington Territory. It was Idaho Territory now and it had a court system of its own. Vigilante justice was all right in its time, but its time was past. What was the point of becoming a territory, he asked, and getting a system of laws and courts, if the people didn't use it? Standing in this crowd, Beachey said, were some of the jurors who would sit on this case. Let them hear the evidence, he demanded. Let them decide whether these prisoners were guilty or not. And then let the judge hand down the sentence according to law.

He was pretty sure what the verdict would be, Beachey said, speaking directly to the men carrying the ropes. You will get your hangings, but first we have to have a trial. He turned to the crowd. Mainly because the law required it, he said, but also because he had made a promise to the Governor of California.

Beachey sensed a growing restlessness around him and feared that if he did not hold the crowd's attention, everything would be lost.

He thrust his hand into a coat pocket and pulled out a creased newspaper clipping. He unfolded it and held it up, turning and displaying it to the crowd the way an itinerant preacher might lift up the Word. In his hand, he said, was an item clipped out of the *Oregonian*. It was a report of his visit to the Governor of California in an effort to gain custody of the four prisoners. He brought the clipping down to eye level and read to the crowd a paragraph saying that if Beachey got his way, the prisoners would soon be heading for "another necktie party" in Lewiston. He did not have to remind them, he said, what the newspaper meant by "another" necktie party. It had been only a year or so since the lynching in this very block of Peoples, English and Scott. That was a case of mob rule, Beachey said. And in the cities on the coast, that was Lewiston's reputation.

Governor Leland Stanford had read this item in Sacramento, Beachey declared, holding the clipping up again, and that had made his mission very hard indeed. In fact, he said, the governor had told him that he was not inclined to release these men if it meant they would be lynched the moment they reached Idaho. Beachey, shouting into a cold wind, then described his meeting with Governor Stanford. He recounted the argument of Lower's attorney,

Alexander Campbell, who had said the judicial system in this young territory was too new to be trusted. And Beachey gave again his counterargument: that the system could be trusted to work because it was new. The courts had not yet tried a criminal case in Idaho. The system had yet to prove itself and it would, because if it did not, no one would have any respect for the new territory, its courts or its government. Was that what the people of Lewiston wanted?

Beachey pointed to his left, down Third Street. There, he said, was the capitol of the Territory of Idaho. Here they all were, half a block from the territorial capitol, carrying ropes for a lynching party. Within the week, the first territorial legislature would meet less than a stone's throw from this spot. Would those delegates see much point in making laws in a city that cared nothing about the law?

Beachey was growing hoarse, but he had one more argument. He had made a promise to Governor Stanford that the prisoners would get a fair trial. He meant to keep that promise. His honor depended on it, and his honor was precious to him. He reminded his listeners that it was he, Hill Beachey, who had gone with Tom Farrell to San Francisco and he, Hill Beachey, who had jumped through all the hoops that were necessary to get custody of the prisoners. And that it was he, Hill Beachey, who had returned the fugitives to Lewiston alive and healthy despite certain indignities that he would not go into now. So if the people of Lewiston wanted these men they now had them, and they had him to thank for that. They could thank him by honoring his promise to the Governor of California. Or they could hang the culprits now and give him, Hill Beachey, a slap in the face for his trouble.

There was nothing more to say. Beachey felt spent and uncertain, not sure what sort of impression he had made on this crowd. But it was over for him. He had done everything he knew how to do and he was tired and cold and lonely. It was time to go home.

He started walking slowly toward the veranda of the Luna House. The quiet crowd of people parted ahead of him, leaving a path wide enough for the coach and four that followed behind. He mounted the two steps from the street and young Grigsby, who had been standing on the porch, held the door open for him. As the coach came abreast of the veranda, Beachey stepped into the lobby, drew Margaret toward him, and told her he could sure use a hot bath.

28 As soon as the coach stopped, on the C Street side of the Luna House, the onlookers crowded around, hoping to see the four prisoners. The men who had been carrying the ropes were still a part of the crowd but the ropes had disappeared and Sheriff Fisk now felt confident that the threat of a lynching was over at least temporarily. The sheriff's four missing deputies had materialized out of nowhere and the sheriff put them to work moving people back so the prisoners could be taken into the hotel. Captain LaFrancois was still inside the coach. The four soldiers, taking their orders from the sheriff, remained near the coach, rifles at the ready. The first two to emerge when the door on the hotel side was opened were Page and Lower, who were chained together. Both were pale and Page was trembling. They climbed down awkwardly and once on the ground stood looking at the crowd as though it were a monster that might spring on them at any moment.

The sheriff motioned to one of the soldiers, who barked an order to the two prisoners. They stood there looking dumbly at him until the sheriff prodded Lower with the barrel of his shotgun and got the pair moving toward the porch. Inside, with one soldier in the lead and the sheriff and another soldier following, the little group went clanking across the lobby, past the desk where Lower had booked seats on the stage that rainy night in October, and up the narrow stairway to the second floor. On the sheriff's orders, all the doors along the corridor had been closed except for two at the opposite end of the hotel. These were the rooms that served as the town jail. The lead soldier entered the room on the left side of the hallway, followed by Page and Lower and finally the sheriff and the second soldier. Sheriff Fisk picked up the end of a six-foot chain that was bolted to one wall and attached it to the chain that connected the two prisoners.

The sheriff then returned back down the long hallway, leaving the troopers on guard. Fisk lingered in the lobby only long enough to remind the desk clerk that nobody was to go up the stairs until all the prisoners had been moved. Then he went out to the veranda and the process was repeated, this time with Renton and Romain and the other two soldiers. These prisoners were deposited in the room opposite Lower and Page, the room that faced east, up the Clearwater River. The sheriff had no particular reason for giving Page and Lower a view to the west and the other two a view to the east, but it would make some difference later on. Both windows were barred and there was a small barred window cut in each door so that the prisoners could be seen from the hall. Each room contained two cots, a chamber pot, a bucket of water and a dipper to drink from.

There was no other furniture. When the "jail" was unoccupied, the two rooms were available to regular hotel guests—at a reduced price since some travelers preferred not to sleep behind bars.

With the last of the prisoners lodged, the sheriff posted an armed deputy in the hallway, then unlocked the chain in each room that connected the two occupants and backed out brandishing the shotgun. Fisk discharged the four soldiers, with thanks, and they returned to the *Tenino*. They had wanted to stop in the hotel bar first, thinking there might be drinks on the house in honor of the occasion. The sheriff said no. Get to the boat as quickly and as inconspicuously as possible, he told them; he didn't want anyone in the bar to get the notion the prisoners were unguarded. If Fisk could have had his way he would have ordered the bar closed at least until tomorrow. He could imagine a dozen angry men, inflamed by hard drink, deciding to storm the staircase to the second floor. Marshal Wickersham, appearing finally in the lobby, had reminded him that this was not the only bar in Lewiston; did the sheriff really think he could close them all?

For a jail, those two hotel rooms were a flimsy affair, and Lower was soon banging on his door and shouting that this place wouldn't hold him for long. A few moments ago he had been frozen with fear, thinking his end was at hand. But now, with the immediate threat of hanging gone, he was puffing up the old bluster again. He was sneering at the deputy when Renton came to the window of the door across the hall and told him to shut up. If the sheriff got tired of any one of them, Renton said, all he had to do was put the poor devil out on the street. They had just had a narrow escape, Renton said. Did Lower want to test this Lewiston crowd again? He should shut up, for God's sake, and be thankful he was still alive.

Renton's advice to Lower fell like a hammer on Page, who was still shaken by the ordeal in the coach. He'd thought he was a goner then, and his situation did not look much better to him now. The door that Lower had been banging on did not strike Page as very stout. How sturdy was the wall between this room and the sleeping room next to it? He looked at the bars on the outside window and tried to guess how long it would take a determined man on a ladder to tear them off. Twenty minutes? Thirty? Dear Lord, Page thought, if he could only have a drink. It had been so long.

*****

Beachey was up early the next morning, feeling fine except for a slight cold and happy to be home. He had missed Margaret and the Luna House more than he realized. Margaret had kept the accounts current and everything was running smoothly as far as he could tell. Some of the clientele, and Margaret herself, assured him that nothing had been the same while he was away. People did seem genuinely glad to have him back, and not just because he had brought the prisoners with him.

He was facing a busy time. Some of the legislators had been in town for a week or two and others were still arriving. Beachey fully expected his hotel to be full throughout the term, which probably would last into January. He wished now that he had not offered the county those two rooms upstairs. It made sense at the time, when business had been slow, because the price was right and Beachey needed the income. Now he could get twice as much for those two rooms as he was getting from the county and there wouldn't be the bother of having to put up with noisy, drunken miscreants.

As for the prisoners in those rooms now, Beachey was determined to have nothing to do with them. They were the sheriff's responsibility, and the sheriff was welcome to them. Beachey had no desire to look at any of them ever again. He would see them in court and no sooner.

Sheriff Fisk, however, was about to change Beachey's mind. Fisk had been huddling with Judge Berry and with E.F. Grey, the prosecutor, and both Berry and Grey were afraid there was not enough evidence to support a conviction. Two days after Beachey's return to Lewiston, the sheriff came to see him. Fisk told him that Grey needed more evidence than appeared to be available now. Since Beachey knew the four prisoners better than any of them, maybe he had some clue as to how they might proceed. To be specific: was there any chance that one of the four could be prevailed upon to squeal on the others? In other words, to turn state's evidence?

Yes, Beachey said, it might be possible. It had become clear to him, he told Fisk, that Page was the weak link in the chain. Renton was smart, Lower was defiant and Romain, although he was a crybaby, was loyal to Renton. In fact, Beachey said, he had never been able to figure out Page's involvement in the Magruder affair. He was an old muleteer and mountain man, not a desperado. And he seemed afraid of the other three. Page was the most likely witness against them, if they could find the right approach to him.

Fisk said he would think about that, and left. He returned an hour later saying he had talked with Grey and they had thought of a plan. The first thing they had to do, Fisk said, was separate Page from the others. They would simply move Lower out of the room he was in and put him in the room across the hall with Renton and Romain. Page would then be alone, and as long as he was alone perhaps he could be manipulated.

How? Beachey wanted to know. Well, the sheriff said, it may be a childish idea, but it could work. Grey thought that if Page could be convinced a lynching was imminent, he might be willing to do anything to save his own skin. There was a fair amount of traffic on Third Street, under Page's window, and it would be natural for a couple of men to just happen to stop on the sidewalk there and draw a small crowd. And it would be natural for some lynching talk to get started, since the jail was right overhead.

From what he knew of Page, Beachey thought it might work, and he agreed that it was at least worth a try. But he said he would rather not be involved in the scheme himself since he was sick and tired of all four of them, Page included.

The sheriff went upstairs and told the deputy on guard that they were going to move Lower across the hall. He would tell him why later, Fisk said. Lower objected, claiming he had a right to know what this was all about. Fisk told him it was none of his business, and hustled him rather roughly into the room with Renton and Romain, neither of whom welcomed the new arrangement. Lower demanded to know whether he was going to get his cot moved too, and Fisk said maybe. Romain whined about overcrowding. Renton said nothing until the sheriff had left and then, with the deputy out of earshot, he said quietly to the others that they were all in deep trouble now. They were going to pump Page, Renton said. That was why they wanted him in a room by himself.

They should have got rid of the old bastard a long time ago, Lower said, and Renton agreed with him. And to tell the truth, Renton added, he still wasn't quite sure why they didn't. He thought Page would be useful in the mountains, but once they reached the coast there was no longer any point in keeping him alive. Now he was in a position to hang them all.

Page had a story to tell, that Renton had given him in San Francisco, Lower pointed out. Maybe he would tell it.

Maybe, Renton said. And maybe not.

Page himself didn't know why the sheriff had moved Lower out until the next morning when Fisk and the prosecutor, Grey, paid him a visit. Grey told him that Renton, Lower and Romain were going to hang for sure because everybody knew they were guilty. But he said there was some question about Page. He said the evidence indicated that Page might not be as guilty as the others. In fact, Grey said, if Page would agree to testify against the others in court, they would drop all charges against him.

Page said he could not lie under oath because if he did he might be struck dead.

Grey assured him that he would not have to lie. Just tell the court the truth, he said.

The truth, Page said, was that he had been out in the mountains with Magruder, tracking down some mules, when these men came up and told him to go with them because Magruder didn't want him any more. And Page launched into the tale he had been sworn to tell, from which he had promised never to flinch.

Grey let the old man relate how he had passed through Lewiston in October with three other men and had later met Renton, Lower and Romain coming over the Mullan Road into Walla Walla. The three men in the room across the hall, he said, had never been with Magruder.

Grey heard the whole story and then told Page he didn't believe a word of it. Page insisted it was God's own truth.

The sheriff had been standing at the door while Grey and Page sat side by side on the cot. Grey stood up now and told Fisk it was time to go. As the deputy opened the door from the outside, Grey spoke again to Page, telling him the story he had just told would never save his skin. Think it over, Grey said; he would be back tomorrow for another chat. The prosecutor reached into a coat pocket and pulled out a small flask. He unscrewed the cap, picked up the tin dipper that was hanging on Page's water bucket, and poured out a bit of whiskey. He put the dipper carefully on the floor, gave Page a friendly smile, and walked out.

Page sat listening to the footsteps fading down the hall and staring at the dipper. It was all very bewildering, but one thing was sure. He hadn't had a sip of whiskey since the night he was arrested in San Francisco. He reached down and picked up the dipper with trembling fingers and held it up to his nose, breathing deeply. He would take a sip now, he thought, and save the rest for later. But once the liquor was crossing his lips he could not put it down. He drank it all. Then he lay on the cot, and with his eyes closed and the dipper across his breast, he let his old frame bask in the unaccustomed, thoroughly unexpected warmth.

The sheriff, meanwhile, was wasting no time. He went directly to the Luna House bar hoping that since it was only half past three in the afternoon he might find four or five fellows there who were still halfway sober. He did, and he steered them out into the lobby. There he outlined a plan to frighten Page out of his wits. If it worked, Fisk said, they could count themselves partly responsible for seeing justice done to the slayers of Lloyd Magruder; and they would have the thanks of his widow.

A December dusk had fallen when Page awoke from his nap. He lay on the cot listening to the sounds drifting up from the town below. A steamboat was whistling from the river—probably the *Tenino* departing, Page thought, wishing he had never seen the damn thing. There was buggy traffic on the street, men shouting, a pig squealing somewhere, and muffled snippets of conversation. The sounds washed over him like a fog too fragile to catch, until some words he barely could hear wafted into the room and stabbed him in the heart. Get them all, someone was saying, then other voices and sounds of agreement. Page rose from the cot and went to the window. If he opened it, he could hear better what was going on below. But would it open? He tried it, and the window did open part way up from the bottom, then stuck.

But it was enough. Page now could hear quite clearly the conversation that was taking place on the board sidewalk below his second-floor window.

You take the window on the other side, someone was saying, and we'll take this one. Them bars don't look too stout to me. From what Page could make out, there were a half dozen men or so, and they were planning to get the prisoners out through the windows sometime during the night. And he understood them to agree that the whole business would be taken care of by morning. They were going to save some people a lot of trouble and expense. He could hear laughter and someone apparently was passing a bottle around. He could hear the conversation fading as the men moved down the street, and he went back and sat on the cot, trembling.[74]

Should he tell the deputy what he had heard? Should he shout across the hall to the other three? He went to the door and tried to call for the deputy but no sound came out of his mouth. His throat felt dry and tight and useless. Finally he was able to cry Help! and the deputy came to the door, peering through the bars. Help for what? he wanted to know. Page was getting control of his voice and was able to squeeze out the gist of what he had heard from the sidewalk below. The deputy, who knew better, said he didn't know what Page was talking about. Forget it, he said. There wasn't going to be any assault on this jail.

Romain heard the exchange from his room and called Renton to the door to listen also. Renton asked Page, through the bars, what the hell he was talking about. Page told him. Renton told Page he should pay no attention to idle talk, but he turned to Lower and said someone was trying to spook Page. Lower understood, as well as Renton did, that this was bad news. Why didn't they get rid of Page when they had the chance? Lower wanted to know, but Renton had no answer. Romain demanded to know what was going on. Renton told him Uncle Billy was hearing things in his old age and not to worry about it. Romain wasn't fooled. He could smell the fear in the room and felt a swelling panic in his chest. He looked to Renton for assurance but found none. He looked to Lower, but Lower was clenching his fist and cursing to himself. He went to the window and looked out. It was dark now except for a last shaft of sunlight on the hill across the Clearwater River and the town was settling in for the night. Romain didn't know what he had expected to find out there, perhaps a man with a rope meant for him. But all he could see from his window was the Luna Stables, some horses, and an empty stagecoach that would be brought around later that evening and loaded for the run to Walla Walla.

Romain turned from the window and sat down on his cot. Renton paused in his pacing to dip a drink out of the water bucket. Lower, still standing at the barred door, shouted across the hall to Page, less in anger than despair, to keep his damn mouth shut.

29 Enos Grey, a small, thin man in his middle forties, had a fringe of brownish hair around the side of his head, but was bald as an egg on the top. He wore steel-rimmed glasses that he had bought out of a traveling salesman's tray and he had a nervous habit of taking them off, swinging them by an earpiece, and putting them on again. He was swinging them now, as he stood by the window in Page's room, apparently lost in thought. The window was still open, something for which he was grateful; yesterday during his initial conversation with Page, the room had been so stuffy and stale he was tempted to open it himself. He had not, for fear of offending Page, whose cooperation he most desperately needed. He was back for another little chat, as he called it, hoping that last evening's performance under Page's window had softened the old man up. Sheriff Fisk had accompanied Grey to the room and then left the two alone while he conferred with the deputy on guard—a different one today.

Page sat on his cot, visibly torn between misery and defiance. He had not told Grey what he heard last evening and Grey had given no sign he was aware of it. He made a careful scrutiny of Page's demeanor and appearance and concluded that it must have had some effect. There was no point in dangling the old fellow on a line of small talk, Grey decided, and he got right to the point.

Had Page given thought to the escape hatch the prosecutor had offered him yesterday? Grey asked. Page assured him that he had, but that his mind was unchanged. The tale he had told yesterday was the true one, he insisted, and if he changed it he would be lying under oath. He daren't do that, he said. Grey said again that yesterday's story was not credible; no one would believe it. He couldn't help that, Page told him, staring at the floor. His elbows were on his knees now and his chin in his hands.

The prosecutor put his glasses on, turned, and gazed out the window for a moment. It was an overcast, rain-threatening day, and Grey could feel a damp breeze on his face.

Billy ought to bear in mind, he said, turning back to Page, that his life would be in jeopardy if the three men across the hall should be acquitted of the murders they were charged with. Page looked up, puzzled, and told Grey he could not believe that. He had been with them all the way to San Francisco and back, and they had never laid a hand on him. But if he testified against them, then he would be in danger.

But if he testified against them, Grey pointed out, they would surely be convicted and hanged, and dead men do not pose a danger to anyone.

Page was not so sure, he said. What if they were not convicted? What if the jury did not believe him, and turned them loose in spite of his testimony against them? He would be a dead man as well as a liar.

Well, the prosecutor said, taking his glasses off and swinging them from his index finger, look at it this way: whether or not Page agreed to testify against his former companions, they had probably already asked themselves why he had been separated from them. And they probably had already figured out that it was so the prosecutor could talk to him alone. Since the men across the hall were not idiots, they could assume that Uncle Billy was going to squeal on them if he hadn't already.

Therefore, Grey continued, Uncle Billy could live to enjoy another summer only if the other three prisoners were convicted. And they probably could not be convicted without his testimony.

The prosecutor paused to let this sink in. Page, grasping for the meaning in what he had just heard, looked up at Grey in stony silence and found himself hypnotized by the daylight shooting off the rhythmically swinging lenses in the prosecutor's hand. For a long moment he could not think. Finally he dragged his eyes back to the floor, then to the water bucket and the dipper hanging from the rim of it, and he remembered the whiskey last evening. Page was no idiot either, when it came to the things that counted. He did not need to make this decision today.

He told Grey his head was so full of this problem that he would need time to sort it all out. Grey put his glasses on again. Very well, he told Page, he should think about it but the prosecutor couldn't wait long for an answer. Grey, preparing to leave, reached into his coat pocket for the flask and suddenly realized that another ounce of whiskey would only postpone the decision for another day. He buttoned his coat quickly, knocked three times on the door, and left.

Page was desolate. He rose from the cot and went to the window, and closed it. He was cold as well as scared. He took a dipper of water from the bucket and tried to drink it but the stuff stuck in his craw and he spat it out on the bare wooden floor. The prosecutor was no friend of his, he now realized, but the prosecutor was right: to save his own skin, Page would have to testify against the other three. He would have to flinch from the tale he had vowed to tell.

They had made him raise his right hand ten times in swearing to keep the faith. Ten times. But there had been no Bible. When he went into court, he would have to lay his left hand on the Bible. That probably meant that the oath he would swear in court outranked the one he swore in the jail cell in San Francisco. And anyway, it was Renton, Lower and Romain who had done the killing, no one else. And certainly not him. There was no reason why he should go to the gallows. Looking at it in those terms, Page found it easy to choose the path he would take. Once the trial was over, he would be a free man, and he would have the drink he was denied today.

Remembering yesterday's whiskey brought to mind last evening's conversation under Page's window. The men with the rope didn't know he was innocent and possibly didn't care. They could come for him tonight!

He went to the door and knocked for the deputy, who was trying to stay awake by strolling up and down the hall. When the deputy came to the door and opened the small window, Page told him he had to get word immediately to Mr. Grey. Immediately, he said, because it was a matter of life or death. Page noticed that the window in the door across the hall was open for some reason; he wondered if Renton, Lower and Romain were still in there and, if so, whether they had overheard any of the conversation in his room. What was the message? the deputy wanted to know; he would try to get it delivered. Page said he had to see Mr. Grey immediately.

He had something very important to tell him. It could not wait, he insisted.

The deputy walked down the hall to the head of the stairs and called to someone in the lobby below. The deputy returned and told Page that Mr. Beachey himself would deliver the message.

Page felt better now. As he thanked the deputy, he glanced past the man's shoulder and saw the eyes of David Renton looking at him from behind a little window in the door across the hall. He felt suddenly as though a cold vise had him by the chest and he was going to suffocate. Instead, he turned away from his own door, took three steps and collapsed upon his cot.

Prosecutor Grey, accompanied by Hill Beachey, arrived shortly a bit out of breath to find Page on the bed, eyes closed and breathing heavily. Beachey touched his forehead and found it clammy. He feared the old man was having a seizure of some kind, perhaps apoplexy, but Page seemed rational enough when he began to speak.

He looked up at Grey and said in a whisper that he had to be moved, immediately. He had heard plans being made for a lynching. Furthermore, he had reason to believe that Renton knew what was going on. Renton's window had been open. He must have seen the prosecutor come and go just moments before. He would testify against the other three, he said, but please get him out of here into some safer place.

Was there such a place? Grey turned to Beachey, who went quickly to the door and instructed the deputy to close the window across the hall. Then Beachey told Grey that Page must indeed be moved. But to where? In the whole town there was no really secure building. As a jail cell, the room they were in right now was a joke; so was the room across the hall.

Beachey considered for a moment and then asked Grey to join him in the lobby. They left Page alone and went downstairs, through the outer door, across the veranda and into the street. They would take a little stroll while talking, Beachey said, and that way they would not be overheard.

The two men turned down Third Street and walked slowly toward the Clearwater River two blocks away. Perhaps Beachey had some thoughts on old Billy's plight? Grey suggested. Yes, Beachey replied, an idea had occurred to him: why not move all four of the prisoners to Fort Lapwai? It would not be the first time the fort's guardhouse had been used to confine civilians. Major Truax had always been helpful on that score. The only question was whether the major had space available; they would have to find out.

Grey, with some relief, agreed to Beachey's plan. It was the perfect solution. But they would need to get word quickly to Truax. Beachey said he would ask young Grigsby, who liked to make himself useful, to ride directly to the fort with a message for Truax and return immediately. Once they had the major's permission, they would transport the prisoners, secretly and at night, from Lewiston to Lapwai. Nothing must be said to anyone who would not be directly involved in the move; they didn't want to expose the prisoners to a lynch mob.

Grey said he would notify Sheriff Fisk of the plan, and he would remain in his office, a block from the Luna House, until he received word that Grigsby was back. Then they would meet again. In the meantime, Beachey told him, he'd better ask Fisk to double the guard on the prisoners while they remained in their temporary cells.

The two turned and walked, faster now, back to the hotel and separated. Beachey went inside to the counter, found some paper, and scribbled a note to Major Truax asking if he could accommodate three dangerous prisoners and an endangered witness. He folded the paper, put it in an envelope, and went looking for Grigsby. He found the boy in the stables helping Chester Coburn calm a nervous horse. He gave him the sealed envelope and told him it was important that he hand it personally to Major Truax and return with the answer as soon as possible. He took the young man by the shoulder and whispered to him to please hurry.

Grigsby quickly saddled his own horse, and was gone. It was now mid-afternoon, and Grigsby would not be back until well after dark. Meanwhile they could be getting a rig ready, but what kind? There was a Concord coach in the stables that would not be needed for the Walla Walla run until the day after tomorrow. It would carry six people plus luggage, but for this kind of trip it would require a six-horse team. Beachey feared that a coach and six driving out of Lewiston going east in the dark of night would arouse entirely too much curiosity. Freight wagons, on the other hand, were a common sight on the road to Lapwai. They could put all four of the prisoners, securely shackled, in the bottom of a freight wagon and cover them with canvas, or burlap, or something else. They could make the trip in fairly good time with four horses. No one would be surprised to see a freight wagon go by, accompanied by a few riders, on this road even at night.

Beachey sent word to Fisk, who went to the White Front Livery Stable and said he needed a wagon that evening for county business; he said he had to move some equipment for the district court and didn't want to do it during business hours. He got the wagon and team and drove them down to the Luna House.

The sheriff then made a tour of several business establishments—a blacksmith, a saddler, two general stores, the assay office and a butcher shop—looking for people he knew and trusted. He found several and deputized four of them. He told them to meet him in two hours at the Luna House, and to stay out of the saloons in the meantime.

Beachey, who had determined not to get further involved with the prisoners who had already taken too much time out of his life, found he could not keep the promise he had made to himself. He had been deputized to go in pursuit of the four; was he a deputy still? He asked the sheriff. Fisk said he must be, since he had not got around to changing his status. In that case, Beachey told him, he would go along on this move as a guard and general helper. He could not possibly remain in Lewiston, not knowing what might be happening to the sheriff's party on the road to Fort Lapwai.

It was a long evening. Beachey busied himself with his books and his customers, doing his best to act as though nothing unusual was afoot. He told Margaret what was planned but no one else. The sheriff was handling things; he was only going along for the ride, so to speak. The prisoners upstairs had been given their supper as usual, unaware they would be spending the night some twelve miles away. That was, if Major Truax had room for them. If he didn't, all these arrangements would have been in vain and some other haven would have to be found for Page and the others.

But when Grigsby arrived at the hotel on a tired horse, and burst into the lobby with the envelope, Beachey's doubts vanished. Bring your prisoners, Truax had written under Beachey's message to him. He sent Grigsby to notify Grey, who was waiting in his office reading law by the light of a coal oil lamp. Grey hurried to the hotel and joined Beachey, the sheriff, and the sheriff's deputies.

The sheriff had advised everyone to behave as though nothing was going on. So after a while, one by one, they all left and gathered quietly in the Luna Stables where the freight wagon had been parked. There was a backstairs down from the hotel's second floor to the back of the building, and the streets were quiet. Beachey left his registration desk and went upstairs to stand by while the prisoners were moved. The two deputies now on guard took Renton, Romain and Lower down the stairs one at a time, in the pitch darkness, and hustled them into the stable. Then they brought down Page. All four were ordered into the straw-covered wagon bed, their hands and feet chained together. Then Chester Coburn and one of the deputies pulled a canvas over them and secured it loosely at the sides and the four corners.

The sheriff told the prisoners there was only one way they could be sure of arriving at their destination alive, and that was to keep quiet. There were a lot of people in the district, he reminded them, who would love to know where they were this night.

Fisk himself would drive, he said. The others would ride in front and behind, but not so close to the wagon as to appear to be guarding it. Fisk sent two of the horsemen out into C Street heading east, and within a minute drove the wagon out behind them. In ones and twos, the other riders followed, and the caravan was on its way.

On Fisk's orders, the deputies who had been guarding the prisoners in the hotel remained at their posts on the second floor. That way, it would appear to anyone coming upstairs that the prisoners were still there. It would be a long night for them, but the sheriff had told them they could come downstairs in the morning; by then it would make no difference.

A light, short shower had fallen in the late afternoon, but the primitive dirt road had dried out and the traveling was good. It was the route Magruder had taken back in August—east out of town, then to the right up a grade to the bench above the city, then up still another grade to the wide flat that stretched all the way to the Lapwai Valley. Across this grassy plain the party was going east again, with the Clearwater on its left and Craig's Mountain in the distance on its right but invisible in the darkness. The lead rider, chosen because he knew the road the best, held a lantern. Another

lantern swung from the back of the wagon to guide the riders behind. It was slow going, and quiet, for the sheriff had said the less
the prisoners knew of what was happening the better.

Beachey, following the wagon's lantern, couldn't help wondering what the prisoners might be thinking. He felt a bit sorry for
Page, who must be terrified, but it was Page, after all, who had
insisted he be moved to a safer place. They were going to the only
safer place Beachey could think of, and he was pleased with
himself for having thought of it.

No sound came from the wagon. After seven or eight miles,
that began to concern the sheriff, who called for a halt and stopped.
He asked the deputies to loosen the canvas on one side and check
on the prisoners with a lantern. Page was lying curled up in the
rear under a heavy coat, apparently all right. Renton and Romain
were lying near the front, scowling. Lower peered at the lantern,
poured out a curse and demanded to know where in the hell they
were taking him. Satisfied, the sheriff ordered the canvas closed
again and the journey continued.

The darkness on either side was unbroken. But when the sheriff and his men reached the head of the canyon that wound down to
Lapwai Creek, they could see several lights ahead on the valley
floor. There were lantern lights shining at the fort, although the
fort itself could not be seen in the distance. There was a light on
the left, probably the Indian agency. The lead rider led the way
down a twisting trail from the plateau to the valley, very slowly. The
sheriff had to brake the wagon to avoid running into the horses,
and the brakes squealed in the darkness.

A trooper met the travelers at the entrance of the fort and waved
them inside. Major Truax, who had been waiting up, came out of
the officers' quarters to greet the sheriff and his party with hand-
shakes. He had several soldiers on hand ready to escort the prisoners to the guardhouse so Beachey, Fisk and the others accepted
the major's invitation to come inside and get warm. But first, Truax
said, he would like to have a look at his four new guests. By the
light of a couple of lanterns, the canvas was pulled off and the prisoners prodded to their feet. They were taken down from the wagon
with difficulty, stiffened by two hours on the wagon bed and
partially immobilized by their chains.

The sheriff's deputies lined them up beside the wagon bed and Fisk held a lantern up in front of each one. When the lantern shone on Lower's face, the major said to no one in particular that this man looked familiar. He couldn't remember offhand where it was he'd seen him before, but he knew he had. What was he charged with?

Beachey said he was going on trial for the murder of Lloyd Magruder. Hearing that, Truax recalled again the last time he had seen his friend Magruder, that August evening when he and Magruder and the Indian agent had spent an evening here at the fort in pleasant talk.

But why did he remember this man? he wondered, staring at Lower's face. And what was the connection?

30 When Frank Creely arrived in Lewiston on the stage from Walla Walla, and learned what had happened to Lloyd Magruder, he went into the bar of the Luna House and had a quick one to steady his nerves. Thank God he had decided not to return with Magruder and to go prospecting instead. But his relief quickly turned sour. Several people who knew him noticed that he seemed to have more money to spend than he had ever had before, and within hours he was under arrest. It was well known that he had left Lewiston with Magruder on the trip east, and it was clear that he was still alive. That could mean the money he was spending had once belonged to Magruder.

Creely told the sheriff, and anyone else who would listen, that he had left Magruder in Virginia City to go prospecting and was not a part of Magruder's crew on the return. He said he had done pretty well on the Beaverhead and then had gone to Boise City, thinking to spend the winter there. But he had run into a couple of legislators who were heading for Lewiston by way of Walla Walla, and decided to join them. He thought his friends here would be glad to see him, he told Sheriff Fisk. The sheriff was inclined to believe him and so were Beachey and the prosecutor, but Fisk insisted he should be charged anyhow and let the grand jury decide where to take it from there.

So when the grand jury met it had to consider murder and robbery charges against not only Renton, Lower and Romain but Frank Creely as well. The charges against Page had been dropped. The hastily organized panel considered the evidence and quickly dismissed all charges against Creely. But it handed up indictments against the other three and bound them over for trial in the district court.[75]

The prosecutor told Beachey and Sheriff Fisk that he didn't care to spend all of his time traveling between Lewiston and Fort Lapwai, and asked that the prisoners be brought back to Lewiston where he could interview them more easily. Grey was joined in the plea by the two attorneys for the defense. Beachey didn't like the idea. He knew the prisoners were safe at Lapwai; he couldn't be so sure if they were brought to town. Fisk felt the same way, but he also thought the lawyers had a point. The sheriff had acquired a wood frame building near the Snake River that he was using as a jail, and he told the others that he could house the prisoners safely there.

Beachey agreed, on condition that the move be made swiftly and as quietly as possible. He would ride out to the fort himself, he said, and make the necessary arrangements with Major Truax.

The major by now had made the connection between the man who climbed out of the freight wagon with three others that December night and the man who had come to the fort in August with a bad case of dysentery. What this would be worth as evidence, he did not know. He would be able to testify only that Renton and Romain had brought Lower to the fort that day and left him there for treatment while they rode on toward the Camas Prairie. He had never seen Page before, but he was not surprised that Page was being held apart from the other three; the old scoundrel didn't seem to belong with them.

When Beachey arrived at the fort, Truax kept him there long enough to hear the whole story of the pursuit of the suspects. Truax recalled for Beachey his last meeting with Magruder, when the pack string had stopped for the night last summer on the way to Bannack. And Beachey reminded Truax of the times he and Margaret, together with Lloyd and Caroline, had enjoyed the major's hospitality at the fort's occasional military balls. By this time, Beachey could feel the visit turning into a memorial service, and said that he had better get back to town. The wagon would be here the next day to pick up the prisoners, and they would be taken back the way they had come—unannounced, but this time with a military guard and in daylight.

The move was made quietly and without incident, and the prisoners were housed in the sheriff's new jail. The building had three rooms—two cells with a guardroom between them and a narrow corridor that ran across the front. On each end there was a narrow, barred slit up near the eaves that served for ventilation. The walls that separated the guardroom from the cell on either side went only to within three feet of the ceiling; the space from there on up was barred. A small wood stove in the guardroom heated the whole building, after a fashion. Lower complained constantly that he was cold, but it couldn't be helped because the guard could not adequately heat the cells without overheating his own small space.

When Enos Grey or the lawyers for the defense needed to talk with a prisoner, a couple of deputies would escort the accused, in chains, to the lawyer's office and stand guard during the interview. Page was kept in confinement in another place because if he panicked and fled the country, the people would lose their chief witness. Page did not complain. He had no wish to be turned loose to face a passel of would-be lynchers, and as long as he was in jail preparing to testify, he could count on the prosecutor coming around once a day to pour him an ounce of whiskey.

Judge Alexander (Alleck) Smith, who represented the First District on the Territorial Supreme Court, was to preside, but as trial date neared, Judge Smith could not be found. On the day the trial was to begin, Judge Smith was still absent. He apparently was away on other business somewhere in the winter vastness of the territory and unable to get back. He failed to show up the next day or the day after that, and after a week had passed Samuel Parks, the Second District judge, offered to preside in Smith's place.

Court convened several days later in a building on First Street that served as the county courthouse. Assisting Enos Grey, the prosecutor, were William C. Rheems, the Bannack legislator, and Milton Kelly, a legislator from Boise. The attorneys for the defense were J.W. Anderson and W.W. Thayer. The jury that was seated January 19, after considerable skirmishing among the lawyers, included George H. Sandy, Henry Harsel, Joseph Wagner, Ezekiel

Beam, Samuel Ramsey, N.B. Holbrook, Richard Leitch, Nathan W. Earl, John Mooney, Henry Myers, Francis Cabe and J.P. Shockley. Several of these men, as Beachey had predicted, were in the crowd that had earlier threatened to lynch the prisoners. They chose George Sandy as their foreman.

The formalities opened with the usual pre-trial legal skirmishing. Anderson and Thayer, for the defense, moved that the indictments be quashed on the grounds that the place of the alleged crime had not definitely been given. If there had been a crime, where was it committed? Grey responded that the precise location, while it was not known to the prosecution at the time the indictments were sought, was known to one of the witnesses and would be revealed in his testimony. The motion to quash was denied. The defense then moved to quash the indictments on the ground that the defendants themselves had not been properly identified. Grey replied that they had been identified as thoroughly as they could be and adequately for the purpose at hand. That motion also was denied. Counsel for the defense, throwing their cards on the table one at a time, then moved to quash on the grounds that the indictments could not have been issued in Nez Perce County since there was no such county; because of a quirk in the bill creating the new territory, Nez Perce County had been left out. At this point Enos Grey, swinging his spectacles in agitation, urged that the judge put an end to this nonsense. The motion was denied.

When testimony began, Mose Druillard said he saw Renton (whom he knew as Howard) at the "French house" on the morning of October 19. He was acquainted with both Renton and Lower, but did not mention seeing Lower there.[76]

L.C. Miller said he saw Magruder in Virginia City and knew he was preparing to leave for Lewiston. He said Magruder had bought some government mules from a party from Minnesota. Miller also was present when Magruder and Charlie Allen were making arrangements to come back together.

W.W. McCarty testified that he saw Lower at the Luna House buying the tickets for the stage.

Leo Guion, the night watchman at the Luna House, said he saw the defendants get into the stage, "all except Page. I don't know where Page was at the time . . . I seen Page when I was calling eleven o'clock. He spoke to me and I called him by name. He asked me if I knew where Mr. Goodrich was, and I told him he was down in the Luna House."

Guion also said that the animals left at the Goodrich ranch by the defendants had been taken into town and turned over to the sheriff. (They then were taken to the Luna Stables.)

Louis Holt reported his dealings with Magruder in Virginia City, explaining how he had served as a sort of broker in obtaining mules for the packer. Holt, who helped Magruder pack for the journey home, also described how they packed the gold dust and protected it with sealing wax. He identified Renton (whom he knew as Doc Howard) and Romain, and said they both had been hanging around Magruder's store in Virginia City. But he never saw Lower there.

"I never saw him at the store. Romain and myself fixed up a lot of saddles one day," Holt testified, but he never saw anything of Lower at that time.

Holt also said he recognized a mule and a horse that belonged to Magruder "here in Beachey's stable" and he had seen a saddle at the stable that Magruder had loaned to William Phillips.

Timothy Lee said he and another man met the prisoners east of Elk City on October 15, about a week after the murders. He recognized Renton, "and we stopped and talked. I noticed a horse and brown mule, I think I have seen since in Beachey's stable. I walked up to the mule and put my hand on it, and said it looked like the one Howard rode. Someone said it was the same. Lower rode up on another brown mule, I think it was him; I have not seen that mule since. There was one man who was larger and rode a horse, leading a gray mule. I have seen the horse since. He kept to my left. They all did (but) Howard did not appear to be avoiding me . . . I remember that the animals looked well."

Several of the witnesses agreed that the three defendants boarded the stage at the Luna House on the early morning of October 19 and that all were "muffled up." They appeared to have established that some animals and equipment left with Goodrich by the defendants had once belonged to Magruder. And the testimony of Holt and others seemed to confirm that Renton and Romain, at least, had been with Magruder in Virginia City. But the evidence thus far was circumstantial. It was clear to Beachey and Grey that it was not enough for a conviction. Their case would hang on the testimony of William Page.

*****

In the bars of the Luna House and the Hotel De France, where a round of drinks could cost a whole day's legislative pay, the delegates grumbled loudly about the time and expense of serving the territory. One of the first things they had to do, they agreed, was raise their pay from four to six dollars a day. They did that. Some of those who had come the farthest hoped to locate the capital in a more accessible place. They would get to work on that too, and wasted little time.

Although Lewiston was host to the legislature, it was not yet officially the capital. The bill that would put the capital in Boise City instead of Lewiston was one of the first in the hopper, and it was offered by none other than R.P. Campbell, who had been all over the territory trying to round up support for his plan. L.C. Miller of East Bannack would go along, he said, with one change: make that Virginia City. Milton Kelly of Boise argued for the bill as Campbell had written it. Alonzo Leland of Lewiston urged "indefinite postponement" of the capital question, calling it an unwelcome distraction that was keeping the lawmakers from more important work. Others agreed with Leland, and Campbell's bill was temporarily set aside.

Then someone brought up the terrible truth that the new territory had no legal code. The Washington code no longer applied here. It was possible to get by to some degree on the laws of the United States, but they didn't have much to do with criminal offenses short of high treason. It would take some time to produce a territorial criminal code and meanwhile there were no laws in the territory against assault, robbery or murder.

This came as a shock to Beachey, who had promised the Governor of California that the law would ensure justice for Renton, Lower, Page and Romain. If there was no law against it, all four could be lynched with impunity. In the absence of a criminal code, they could not be brought to trial. If convicted, they could not be executed. In strictly legal terms, they probably could not even be held. To Beachey the whole thing seemed absurd. How could a territory bigger than Texas come into being without any means of protecting itself against thieves and murderers? Sitting on the high stool behind his registration counter, he harangued legislators coming and going, demanding to know what kind of government would let a thing like this go on.

But Beachey underestimated his paying guests. The lawmakers solved the problem by adopting the English Common Law in all matters where it did not conflict with the U.S. Constitution. That law would apply only to future offenses, not to any already committed. Still, Beachey could relax, his promise still in force, his honor secure. In gratitude, he offered drinks on the house.[77]

31 Enos Grey, adjusting his glasses, announced that the people would now call Mr. William Page to the witness chair. He turned anxiously toward the door, half afraid that his chief witness might have died or run off or disappeared in a puff of smoke. But Page came in, accompanied by a burly deputy sheriff, looking uneasy. Judge Parks had agreed with Sheriff Fisk that Page would be safer elsewhere under guard than sitting exposed in the courtroom.

The room was small. It could accommodate some thirty spectators on benches plus the jury and the principals on chairs. Judge Parks sat on a similar plain chair behind a small table and the defendants sat with their lawyers at a larger table—as did the prosecutor and his two assistants. At a small table of his own sat Charles Frush, the court reporter, prepared with a writing pad and a handful of pencils to take down the proceedings.

To reach the witness chair, Page had to walk between the building wall and the benches, then past the defendants' table where sat Renton, Lower and Romain. As he passed them, prodded along by the deputy, Lower whispered to him to be careful now, Uncle Billy. Page gave his head a shake, as if to clear it of something, and halted in front of the judge. He took the oath and sat down, fiddling with his hands. He looked at the jurors, he looked at the prosecutor, he let his eyes roam over the spectators, but he avoided even a glance at the defendants.

He was gazing at his boots when Enos Grey asked him to explain where he had met Mr. Magruder and under what circumstances.

He said he had known of Magruder in Lewiston but had not met him until he had seen him in Virginia City in the previous September. He was sleeping in a stable where he had gone to sell a mule, when Magruder and Holt arrived there. Page awoke when they called the stableman out, and that was where he had made Mr. Magruder's acquaintance. He later had looked Magruder up in Virginia City.

"It might be somewhere about the 24th of September. He had goods in a store. I seen him some days a time or two and some days not so often. I had no heavy conversation, only bid him good day."

Grey wanted to know how Page had come to go with Magruder from Virginia City to Lewiston.

Page said he was planning to come back over the Bitterroots to Lewiston on his way to The Dalles: "Mr. Magruder asked me if I was coming over the mountain and I told him yes. He told me he wanted me to look after the animals and that he would furnish me a good animal to ride and everything, so I agreed to come with him."

In response to lawyers' questions, Page testified that he and Magruder had been talking in Skinner's saloon when those arrangements were made. He said he knew that Renton and Romain would be returning with Magruder because Renton had told him so that morning. But he hadn't heard what Lower was going to do.

Page said he, Renton and Romain left Virginia City with Magruder on October 3 and camped the first night at Beaverhead Rock. The party reached Bannack the next night and spent a couple of days there.

While the four of them were at Bannack they were joined by the Chalmers brothers, who were heading west from Missouri with a small pack string. They asked Magruder if they could join their string with his, and Magruder agreed. Lower also showed up there as did William Phillips, who had become friendly with Romain in Virginia City. According to Page, Romain tried to talk Phillips out of joining the party but Phillips insisted. Later, Phillips would die as Romain screamed at him, "You son of a bitch . . . I told you not to come!"

According to the testimony of L. C. Miller, Charles Allen had traveled with Magruder from Bannack to Virginia City and back to Bannack. Page testified that the group leaving Bannack en route to Lewiston included himself, Magruder, the Chalmers brothers, Allen, Phillips, Renton, Lower and Romain—nine men and some 70 pack animals.

Page remained in the witness chair for parts of three days. He recounted the journey from Bannack into the mountains, describing the lay of the land at each night's camp and recalling who stood guard duty. He could hardly believe it, he said, when Renton told him what he and his companions were planning. And in surprising detail, he described the events of the night that Magruder, Allen, Phillips and the Chalmers brothers were killed.

Prosecutor Grey was more than pleased with this witness. He now realized that all the trouble he had gone to with Page was well worth the effort. In deference to Thayer and Anderson, whose clients already could smell the hemp, Grey tried not to look smug.

Thayer, recalling for Page his testimony that Renton had told him of the defendants' murder plans, asked Page: "Why did you not inform Magruder?"

"I was a little afraid to inform him," Page said. "I was afraid that he was not much acquainted and would not believe me. And again, I thought (the defendants) were the greatest friends Magruder had in the world up to this time." Later, Grey brought the matter up again. This time, Page explained, "I was afraid that if I did mention it to Magruder that some of them would kill me."

Anderson and Thayer realized from the start that their clients were probably doomed unless they could stain the character of the prosecution's chief witness. Thus, from time to time they bore in on Page.

Question: "Have you dealt in any (stock) that did not belong to you?"

Page refused to answer.

Question: "When you went to Bitterroot, did you take any stock with you that did not belong to you?"

Page: "I had not a hoof that did not belong to me."

Question: "Have you ever been on trial before?"

Page: "Never. I never had a sheriff take hold of me before."

Page testified that when he and the defendants arrived in Lewiston on the night of October 18, Renton and Romain went in search of a boat while he set out to find Bishop Goodrich. He found Goodrich at the Luna House, he said, and made arrangements to leave some animals and equipment with him.

When no boat could be found, "Renton came back and said that the stage was going to leave early that morning. So he said we would all go down on it. Lower said he had no coin enough to pay the passage. I gave him fifty dollars."

Page recalled that at the Luna House, before entering the coach, "I seen Judge Berry, then I seen Mose the expressman, Mr. Beachey and Leo the watchman. Passed them in the house and passed outside. I seen Goodrich there, and I seen that they took notice of us as we passed out of the room."

After describing the flight from Lewiston to Walla Walla, Wallula, The Dalles, Portland and San Francisco, Page commented, "We stopped in Frisco two nights before we were arrested. The first night at the Rosetta House, the second night in a private house."

He said he and Lower were in the private house when they were arrested by Captain Lees of the San Francisco police: "After the arrest, we were put up in a private room . . . Then there was arrangements to get out a writ of habeas corpus . . . After this, we were all put in together. So we could all tell one tale." Page then recounted the story they were to tell.

"They made me hold up my hand ten times that I would never flinch from this tale."

Page identified several weapons and some camp equipment left behind in the care of Bishop Goodrich.

On January 22, after four days of testimony, the jurors retired to consider the facts and returned the next morning with a verdict. Foreman George Sandy delivered it, reading from a penciled sheet of paper.

"We find the following, to wit: That the persons named, to wit: David Renton, James P. Romain and Christopher Lower, are guilty of the crime of murder in the first degree as charged in the indictment and that the punishment therefore shall be death."

*****

Caroline Magruder told the Beacheys that she wanted to see the murderers and look them in the eye; she could do that, she said, now that the verdict was in. She did not know why, but it was important to her that she stand face to face with them one time before they went to the gallows. Beachey told her it was not a good idea, and Margaret agreed. Both assured her that the sight of those three faces would only add to her pain. But Caroline insisted. She asked Beachey to take her to the jail; if he refused she would go there alone.

Beachey was thinking not only of Caroline's distress but of his own; he had no wish to lay eyes on those men again except possibly at the hanging. But he suspected that she must have some deep need, that she could not explain, to see them. Perhaps she had to let them see her, to make them face Magruder's widow, this further consequence of their sin. Beachey told her he would take her to the jail as soon as he had made arrangements with the sheriff, and he did.

Renton and Romain were in one of the cells and Lower was in the other. While Beachey remained in the central guardroom, the guard escorted Caroline to a barred door on the south end of the tiny building and told Renton and Romain they had a visitor. She had no trouble telling which one was Romain; he looked like a badly whipped schoolboy. She wasted hardly a glance on him but stared intently into the blue-gray eyes of David Renton. She was Caroline Magruder, she said, the wife of Lloyd Magruder, and she had come to see the man who killed her husband. Renton meant to say he was innocent but he couldn't get the words out. Something in the farthest depths of the woman's brown eyes held him speechless. Her look was direct and accusing and, yes, serene. He felt himself impaled upon it, unable to speak, to move or to look away.

After a long moment Caroline turned and walked down the short hallway to the cell where Lower was standing and watching. She told him what she had told Renton, but before she could get it all out, Lower whirled around, turning his back on her, and put his hands against the wall. She stood staring silently at the back of his head for a long moment, then turned and marched down the hall to where Beachey stood waiting for her. As the two left the building together they could hear Lower shouting curses at the guard and screaming that he never wanted that woman anywhere near him again.[78]

*****

East of the Bitterroots, meanwhile, all mining had ended. The miners who had been unable to find or build snug cabins had left, most of them heading south toward the emigrant trail and the towns of the Boise Basin. With the cold hand of winter on the land, there were few people traveling and therefore not much work for road agents. In Bannack, Sheriff Plummer was single again. His wife Electa, had returned to her home in Iowa and Plummer was living at the Goodrich Hotel and taking his meals with Electa's sister and brother-in-law, Martha and James Vail, who lived in a cabin just off the main street. He continued to spend his time wandering amiably from office to shop to saloon, maintaining his pose as a law-abiding officer and businessman and keeping in touch with his "deputies."

These included Red Yeager, Buck Stinson and Ned Ray. Stinson was sharing a cabin with John Toland, an apparently decent man who had befriended him. Ray, who had not left town in time to avoid the winter, was keeping warm by moving among the town's saloons. Yeager, whom Plummer had lost track of, evidently got into trouble somewhere, because Plummer's boys had picked up a rumor that Yeager, under duress, had spilled his guts and named some other members of the gang. Plummer himself got wind of the report and was uncertain what to do about it. He was alarmed enough at first to try to check it out, and roamed about town sniffing the wind and listening for clues. He appeared to be as respected as always among the good people of Bannack, and within a few days he was feeling as safe and self-assured as ever.

But Yeager had indeed got into trouble. He had botched a robbery and was caught, and when a party of vigilantes produced a hanging rope, Yeager had broken down and named names. Since the vigilantes worked secretly and did not often bother to report their executions, hardly anybody knew that Yeager had died or what he had said.[79]

On a bitter cold Sunday evening in early January, three small vigilante parties went out in separate directions in search of three of the men whom Yeager had mentioned. One group went to John Toland's cabin and arrested Buck Stinson. The men told Stinson to put on his coat and come with them. He did. Another group went down the main street of Bannack and found Ned Ray in one of the saloons asleep on a card table, wrapped in a buffalo robe. The third group, at about the same time, went to the door of the Vails' house and knocked. Plummer, who had complained of a headache, was lying on a couch with his coat and pistol on a chair within reach.

Mrs. Vail was sitting and chatting with Francis Thompson and Joseph Swift, who boarded there; her husband was not at home. At the sound of the knock, she got out of her chair and went to the door, and Plummer rose quickly from the couch. John Lott, the leader of the party, entered the room and told Plummer that he was to come with him. Plummer said he would be glad to, after he had slipped on his coat. He reached for the pistol, but Lott snatched the coat off the chair and grabbed the gun first. He gave Plummer the coat and Plummer put it on, quietly and gravely, then he and Lott stepped out the door and the vigilantes closed in on either side.

The three groups, each escorting the man it had arrested, met a little way outside the town where the sheriff had put up a gallows that was to be used for the execution of one John Horan, condemned by a miners' court for murder. The vigilantes used it instead to hang Plummer, Stinson and Ray. They let the three corpses twist slowly in the freezing night for an hour, and then allowed the friends and relatives of the deceased to cut them down. The ground was frozen too hard for burial and so the corpses were stored temporarily in a small shed.[80]

Several of the sheriff's other "deputies" followed him to that same gallows. As January drew to a close, the Plummer gang ceased to exist except for a few cutthroats who had left the Beaverhead. And three of these—Renton, Lower and Romain—were on trial for their lives in a real court with a duly sworn jury and a genuine judge.

The three defendants could not have known that Plummer was now dead since winter had made communication across the Bitter-roots impossible. Nor would they have cared. To Cy Skinner, how-ever, the news would have brought considerable comfort. Skinner, who had found temporary employment tending bar in a saloon in Vancouver, had learned from various customers that Hill Beachey had delivered Renton, Lower and Romain safely to the authorities in Lewiston.

Since Skinner had fumbled his assignment to silence them in the most effective way, his remaining hope was that they would be lynched on arrival in Idaho. They had not been, according to the news traveling down the river, and as long as they were alive, Skinner himself was in danger. So what to do? Nothing, he decided. He would go on pouring drinks, washing glasses and keeping his head down. Come spring, he might find out whether or not he could safely return to Bannack and the money he had left there.[81]

32 Judge Samuel Parks had little doubt, after William Page's first day in the witness chair, that the prosecution in this case would prevail. Despite a reputation for drinking and idling, Page was a credible witness. The grizzled old mountaineer had an air of simple innocence about him, and Parks was confident the jurors would believe what he told them. Thus the judge was prepared for a verdict of guilty. After hearing it read, he dismissed the jury with thanks for its patience and the quality of its deliberations. Then he told the crowded courtroom that he would pronounce sentence three days later, on January 26.

He could have delivered the sentence at that moment; he was so certain of the outcome that he already had prepared the statement he would make in pronouncing it. But he wanted to be sure the date he had in mind would satisfy the sheriff and others. And Judge Parks had a feeling for history. He considered this trial and its consequences so memorable that it deserved all the newspaper coverage it could get. By delaying the sentencing for three days he could keep the reporters in town that much longer and enhance the prospects of a place in the history books for Idaho, for this honorable court, and for himself.

On the day of the sentencing, despite the cold and a fitful snowfall, Judge Parks faced a full courtroom as he sat down at his table in the front. He ordered the prisoners to stand, and asked each if he wished to say why the sentence of death should not be passed upon him.

Romain complained that he had not had time to get witnesses.

Lower said he was innocent and hoped God would forgive his persecutors.

Renton blamed Page and declared: "I stand before the world innocent of this bloody deed. I have nothing more to say."

The judge then reached into a file folder lying on the table, drew out several sheets of paper, and without further ceremony began to read: "The duty which I am now called upon to perform is one of the most painful of my life. I am to pronounce a sentence which will consign to an early and infamous death three young men, each in the prime of his life and strength."

The judge paused long enough to look eye to eye with each of the defendants, and turned again to his paper.

"A few years since you left your homes, all respectable; all with useful and honorable occupations; all with high hopes and all with the love of relatives and friends. You had more than ordinary energy and intelligence and might have made useful and influential men in your day and generation; been respected and upheld by all good citizens.

"How different is the picture you present today. You are degraded and abandoned outcasts, universally regarded as the implacable enemies of humanity. You have not only the Territory of Idaho but all civilized society combined against you. I do not say these things to reproach you but from a sense of duty. Punishment is inflicted even upon the worst criminals not in a spirit of vengeance, nor to expiate or atone for the crimes, but to prevent such offenses in the future."

He recalled the events that had brought the defendants into this courtroom and the motivations that might have prompted them. Then he added:

"Your history demonstrates clearly the ruinous effects of idleness and bad company. You abandoned your occupations to hang around saloons, gambling houses and low haunts of vice. You became the associates of gamblers then gamblers yourselves. As there is but a single step from gambling to stealing, you soon became thieves, then robbers, and then murderers, of course. And you have closed your careers by one of the most awful tragedies ever recorded; one which, when it shall be known in its horrible details, will cause the ear of humanity to tingle.

"What a warning is this to all men, to follow respectable pursuits and to avoid the haunts of vice and dens of the gambler. Upon all these sinks of iniquity should be written in letters of fire, 'This is the way to hell, going down to the chambers of death.'

"Another thing your history illustrates: . . . It is that there is no security to any man in the commission of such crimes, no matter how wild or remote the place of commission. You vainly thought by murder of all your fellow travelers you secured silence and safety. You burned the blood of Magruder, that it might not reveal your guilt; but like the blood of Abel it cried to God against you and the cry was heard and answered . . .

"It is a strange coincidence that your conduct first excited the suspicion of one of Magruder's friends; that he followed and brought you back here; that you have been tried and been convicted close to the desolate home of the murdered man and in sight and hearing of his widowed wife and orphan children. The robber and murderer may learn from your fate that there is no safety for them and that the way of the transgressor is indeed hard. If such men have expected immunity in crime here, let them know now that the reign of law and order has commenced, even in this remote region; that where bad men array themselves against society they encounter a power which they can neither resist nor escape, and that the punishment of the law will be visited upon them.

"You have had a fair trial and been legally convicted, and your punishment will be just. It is my duty to tell you that there is no hope of pardon or escape. The law gives you but a few days to live. Let me advise you to employ that time in making what reparation you can for the evil you have done, and in preparing for trial before that Great Judge at whose bar you will soon stand; whose laws, as well as those of man, you have violated; whose goodness you have abused, and whose power you have defied. And it will be the prayer of all good men that in your final trial you may find a merciful judge and that your crimes, numerous and great as they have been, may be forgiven."

Judge Parks then announced that the three would be hanged by the neck until dead on the fourth day of March next.[82]

The judge addressed his final remarks to the packed benches. This was not a time for celebration, he said, knowing that half his audience would be drunk within the hour, but of contemplation. He said he suspected there was more than one man in the courtroom today who had escaped the noose only by craft or blind luck. Temptation is strong, he said, and man is weak. This sad occasion called for humility in the face of human folly, not prideful revelry.

He dismissed the court and the spectators scrambled quickly into the cold outdoors, heading for the stores, the saloons and the assembly hall where there was still the territory's business to be done.

Sheriff Fisk was pleased with the verdict and the sentence for professional reasons. He needed the jail for other prisoners now and the death sentence, he explained to Beachey, meant that these three were no longer in danger of being abducted and lynched. Therefore, they could be safely held in that upstairs room at the Luna House. He could confine his new prisoners, a couple of accused claim jumpers, in the jail. Otherwise, he would have to transport them to Fort Lapwai and he never knew whether there would be room for his prisoners in the guardhouse there.

Beachey objected. He had paying guests, a couple of legislators, in that room. Fisk assured him he would be amply compensated by the county for any loss he might incur and besides, these three would be using the room for only a little more than a month. Beachey reminded Fisk that in a month's time, two legislators could run up a considerable bar bill. If they did their drinking in another hotel, the Luna House would be out much more than just the room rent. Would the county compensate him for that? Fisk didn't think so. But he had an idea. If Beachey would rent him one room for five weeks, Fisk would pay for every glass that Billy Page downed in the Luna House bar during that period. All Page had to do was sign for each drink and after the executions Fisk would come in and pay up.

Beachey, now ashamed of himself for putting a bit of profit ahead of his duty to the county, told the sheriff he couldn't ask him to do that. But Sheriff Fisk assured Beachey that he didn't mind. After all, he said, the territory had Page to thank for these convictions, and as an officer of the law he felt he owed the old man something.

Beachey began remembering things: Page in that cell in San Francisco, frightened and miserable. Page in the brig aboard the *Pacific*, seasick on the shifting deck. Page scared out of his wits by Enos Grey's make-believe lynch plot. He imagined Page that night in the Bitterroots, lying in the dark as murder erupted around him. Yes, they owed Page something for all that he had been through, for helping to see justice done. And there wasn't much you could do for the old fellow beyond buying him a drink when he was thirsty.

Never mind, he told the sheriff, he could have the room. Beachey would take care of Billy Page.

It was what the Sheriff expected to hear. He knew Beachey too well to be fooled by that business-is-business nonsense. He went to get his prisoners.

*****

Judge Parks had been right about the reporters. They stayed in Lewiston long enough to cover the sentencing and then some. The Magruder case wasn't the only story in town, after all. The legislative session was winding down a couple of blocks from the courthouse, and the lawmakers hadn't yet decided whether or where to move the capital. Lewiston's Alonzo Leland, who had argued in December for postponement of the question, was walking on eggs, hoping the session would end before it came up. But if it didn't, Leland was preparing for the grandest filibuster of his career.

Campbell's bill finally was resurrected on February 4, the last day of the session. The Boise City delegation argued eloquently that the territorial capital belonged in some place more accessible than Lewiston and in some place that had a future; Lewiston was losing population and Boise City was gaining. Then Leland took the floor and began to talk. And talk, and talk. He talked about the glorious, if brief, history of the town, and he talked about the sturdy, honest citizens who had put their stamp upon the great Clearwater region. He talked about the mighty rivers that gave the city access to the sea. He talked about the great wealth of gold in the mountains that would ensure a future worthy of the territory and, ultimately, a state. Others tried to get the floor, but Leland would not give it up. People began to doze, or leave the room. Somebody put out one of the lanterns, joking that it would make sleeping easier. Finally Stanford Capps of Pierce City, feeling the moment had come, rose and, catching a pause in Leland's speech, moved that the question be indefinitely postponed. His move was answered by a weary chorus of ayes, and the session ended.[83]

Lewiston was still the capital, and the reporters who had come mainly to cover the trial, joined in the celebration. They had come from Walla Walla, Boise City, Portland and Salem, and Leland, though now a legislator, was still filing reports to his old newspaper, the *Times* of Portland. Beachey had hoped that Gerald Schwartz might come from San Francisco for the *Bulletin*. He would be pleased to entertain the reporter whose interview in California had been a great help in persuading Governor Stanford to send the prisoners back to Idaho. But Schwartz did not come. As Leland explained it to Beachey, the *San Francisco Bulletin* would copy its story out of the Portland papers or the *Oregon Statesman* at Salem. From San Francisco to Lewiston, I.T., was simply too far to send a reporter in the middle of winter.

Although Beachey missed Schwartz, he found the reporters an engaging lot, and they spent their money freely. They would gather of an evening in the bar of the Luna House or the Hotel De France to swap yarns and talk politics, and when they were in the De France they made a great fuss over Madame Bonhore. She enjoyed the attention, while pretending not to, because of its effect on Captain LaFrancois. The captain by now had made it clear he had no desire to move on. This suited Madame, but she wished he would be a bit more definite about his plans for the future. He had some mining interests and had invested in cattle, but as far as she could tell, his prospects were uncertain. Most important of all, he had made no mention of marriage, and as far as Madame was concerned, it was past time. Her own mind was made up: the captain, despite his shaky financial condition, was by far the most eligible bachelor in the district. And he liked her, she was sure. She would do the proposing if necessary, but in the meantime she would enjoy the company of other men and trust that the captain noticed their attentions.

He did. And it pleased him to note that the woman he planned to marry had not only a head for business, and a good business at that, but a touch of the coquette. He would propose in due course, and in the meantime enjoy the sight of other men competing for the favor of his bride-to-be.

Captain LaFrancois, like Beachey, found pleasure in the company of the newspaper reporters because they were full of news from the "outside." He spent as much time with them as he could, which was considerable for they found him charming and faintly exotic. They also found that he knew everyone in the region worth knowing and had a knack for getting things done. So it was natural for them to turn to the captain when they needed help in finding a photographer.

No one in Lewiston owned a camera, but there was a photographer in Walla Walla named Brown who traveled around the region once a year taking pictures by appointment. But Brown did not travel in the winter. By the end of January, there was too much ice in the rivers to permit travel by steamboat. Travel by stagecoach at that time of year was miserable, and Brown's equipment was both bulky and expensive. If there was a picture to be taken, he would say, it could wait until summer.

But this one, of course, could not wait. Some of the reporters had asked Sheriff Fisk to get the prisoners' permission to have their pictures taken. Absolutely not, said Renton and Romain, using somewhat more colorful language. But Lower said it would be all right with him. All they needed was a photographer, and the only one available wouldn't come. Captain LaFrancois, on hearing the problem, told the reporters he would see what he could do. He sent a letter to Brown in Walla Walla reminding him that he, the captain, had set up several appointments for Brown in the previous summer and was prepared to do the same again, assuming Brown was willing to return the favor. He knew it was asking a lot, he wrote, considering the weather, but the captain would be most eager to show his gratitude. And Brown would have the only photograph of one of the most heinous villains in the annals of frontier crime.

Brown wrote back that he would come. He said he would need a building or a tent that he could use as a makeshift studio. The captain found a sticks-and-canvas former saloon that had been abandoned by its owner and sent word to Brown that the studio was ready. A few days later, the captain met the stage at the Luna House and took Brown directly to his tent studio. The photographer threw his bedroll down on the rough board floor and set up his camera, a large, boxy contraption on three legs. Brown carried with him a portable darkroom, a black cloth mini-tent in which he processed the emulsion-coated glass plates that served as his negatives.

Captain LaFrancois had fired up the small wood stove that occupied one corner of the tent, using as fuel the wood from the packing cases that had once supported the bar. Brown had to get his glass plates warm before he could expose them, and in the meantime the sheriff would go and fetch the prisoner.

Lower, Renton and Romain were occupying the same room that had held them when they were first returned to Lewiston, before they had been taken to Fort Lapwai. A deputy once again stood in the corridor outside the room. Sheriff Fisk, reminding Beachey that he was still deputized, asked the innkeeper to help him move Lower from the hotel to the photo studio. Since the former saloon was only two blocks away, they walked there, with Lower between them in chains. The captain had brought a chair over from the De France, and they sat Lower down in it. The photographer fussed with his camera, peering through the lens under the cloth head cover and shifting his position. He wanted a straight-on shot of Lower, but Lower kept moving in the chair and laughing. A couple of the reporters were there, and Lower started joking with them, saying that if they stuck around until he arose from the grave, they'd have a real story. Then, he said he wanted to be buried face down "so the whole world can kiss my ass."[84]

The reporters were taking notes and chuckling, and Lower appeared to be enjoying this moment on stage. The sheriff was not. Fisk was nervous. This was taking too long, and the prisoner was both dangerous and unpredictable. He turned to Beachey with a frown, and Beachey nodded. He also was wondering why they had taken this chance. Here they were, in a tent with a condemned man who had nothing to lose, and who might have friends nearby. What was the point of taking the picture anyway, he wondered, glancing toward the reporters. They were enjoying the episode at least as much as Lower was. Only Beachey and the sheriff seemed to care about security, and Beachey was in favor of halting the whole silly business right here and taking the prisoner back to his cell.

He flexed his hand on the pistol grip, half wishing Lower would make a sudden move and praying that he wouldn't. Lower must live until his execution date, Beachey knew, to make these last four months worth while.

Brown had the rubber bulb in his hand and seemed ready at last to snap the shutter. Lower sat in the chair, looking straight into the lens, and grinning. Brown held up his left hand, holding the stick of powder which would ignite when he pressed the bulb. Suddenly it lit the room, and as it did Lower leaped from the chair, lifted the camera high in the air and smashed it on the floor.

Brown reeled backwards against the wall. The sheriff threw himself at Lower, pinned his arms and wrestled him to the boards. Beachey and the reporters stood where they were, in shock. Beachey recovered quickly, and put a knee in Lower's back so that Fisk could get up. Then the two of them pulled Lower to his feet. Why in hell did he do that? Fisk asked Lower.

"I didn't know it was loaded," Lower said, bursting into laughter.[85]

33 Captain LaFrancois, who had not been present for the picture taking in Brown's tent studio, came by later to find Lower in the chair the captain had provided and both Beachey and Fisk standing over him, guns drawn. Brown was on the floor, picking up the pieces of his broken camera. The two reporters were scribbling in their notebooks and trying to control their laughter. The captain asked Beachey what in the name of Heaven was going on, and then knelt beside the photographer and began picking at some shards of glass, all that remained of Brown's film plates. Beachey told him what had happened. The captain glanced up at Lower, who was grinning broadly, and then, touching the photographer's shoulder in sympathy, said he was very sorry. Brown said nothing but after a moment turned his attention from the broken camera for the first time and looked up at the others, with tears on his cheeks.

The sight of Brown's woe so infuriated LaFrancois that he leaped up and lunged at Lower, spewing a stream of French curses that left the prisoner slack-jawed and white. While Beachey and Fisk were pulling the captain away from Lower, the two reporters, shamed by Brown's tears, stuffed their notebooks into their coat pockets and joined the photographer on the rough wooden floor.

Having fired his salvo of profane French, the captain reverted to English and tried to console the photographer. It was his fault, he said, that this had happened. He was the one who had persuaded Brown to come here against his better judgment. Brown could be sure that he would take responsibility for the broken camera, the broken film plates, and the indignity to which he had been subjected. Send him the bill for everything, he told the photographer.

Brown had uttered only a few words during the episode and none since he had started to focus his camera. Now he stood up and declared, in a professional voice, that it would be impossible to proceed. The subject, he said, seemed unwilling to sit. He declared the session at an end and asked the captain to arrange a seat for him on the next stage to Walla Walla.

Back in his Luna House cell, Lower bragged to Renton and Romain that no one was going to use his picture for profit. The other two were unimpressed. Renton found no humor in what he considered a childish, impetuous act. Romain was so full of the horror of his own impending death that he could not react to anything else. For the first few days after the sentencing, Romain had refused to accept the import of Judge Parks' pronouncement. Then he had looked to Renton to assure him that all was not lost, but Renton had no assurances left. Now, realizing he was doomed, Romain cried in the night and in the daylight hours stared through the bars of his window at the bleak outdoors.

Several times, as the days counted down through February, Lower told Romain to stop wallowing in his misery; it was depressing the others, he said. Renton said they all had plenty to be depressed about, but he agreed that there was no point in dwelling on the future. Renton spent much of his time reading the newspapers while Romain stood at the window or slumped on his cot. Lower asked the guard to get him a writing tablet and a pencil, and he wrote letters. He gave them to the guard, who promised him they would be mailed—after the executions. It didn't matter to him, Lower said. He also was writing something else, which he told Renton would be read by the sheriff after the hanging to all the people who had come to watch him die. He wouldn't say what it was. But apparently he had a hard time getting it right, because he kept destroying pages and starting over again. He would crumple a page, then flatten it out between his knee and the palm of his hand, then he would tear it into tiny pieces. He would throw the pieces into the chamber pot, saying there they were, for anyone who wanted to dig them out. He told Renton that in case he forgot to do it, Renton should tell the sheriff at the final hour to look in Lower's coat pocket as soon as he stopped twitching. His statement would be there.

Renton scolded Lower, as he had done many times, for talking so candidly about his final moments; he would get Jimmie to bawling again, and they didn't need that.

Page had become something of a curiosity in the Luna House bar. Turning state's evidence, and testifying against his former companions, had not made him universally popular, as Beachey told him more than once. Renton and Lower had friends in the region. If any of them should find Page in the bar, Beachey would feel partly responsible; if he weren't supplying the old man's liquor, Page wouldn't be hanging around.

As for Page, he seemed not to comprehend the danger. He wasn't worried, he said, because here he was among friends. Some of Beachey's other customers would walk out when Page came in, hoping to avoid trouble. Some others would stay, on the off chance that later they'd be able to say they were present when the man fell off the high wire. Beachey finally gave up, telling Margaret that Billy Page was no longer his responsibility. To hell with him.

By the end of February, Sheriff Fisk had completed arrangements for the executions. Major Truax had agreed to provide a company of soldiers to keep order and lend some pomp to the occasion. The Rev. J.B.A. Brouilette, a Catholic priest, was coming from Walla Walla to offer the condemned the solace of religion.

The Indian agent, Hutchins, suggested to the Nez Perces that some of them might wish to attend this demonstration of the white man's law, no doubt thinking they would be impressed by its power and majesty. Several chiefs said they would come, and that guaranteed a large Indian turnout. Like most Indians, the Nez Perces had no conception of capital punishment. When one of them behaved in a manner intolerable to the rest, he would be told that he was no longer welcome in the village. To become a social outcast was the worst punishment imaginable to a Nez Perce. So a lot of them were planning to come to the hangings to witness this odd, incomprehensible custom of the whites.

The scaffold already had been built in a glen some little distance out of town at the foot of one of the trails leading up to the bench above. Even in the blustery chill of early March, it offered a fine view of the hills across the Clearwater to the north, whitened near the tops by thin skiffs of snow.

The builders had raised the platform some eight feet above the ground to provide the guests of honor with a good drop once the trap was sprung. They had hung the ropes from a large beam running the length of the platform, some twenty feet. Under the ropes where the prisoners would stand, they had put the single, hinged trap that would drop all three at the same time when the executioner jerked out the pin. They had stretched a cloth across the front, from the platform to the ground, so the onlookers would not see the victims kicking and twitching at the ends of their ropes.

The preparations gave no comfort to Caroline Magruder, and she refused to let the children go with other youngsters to the execution site. Hill and Margaret Beachey were with her much of the time, wishing along with Caroline that they could speed the dirty business and get it over with. Even now, in March, Caroline could not bring herself to accept the certainty that Lloyd was dead. Even with the guilty verdicts in hand, she clung to the fact that no one had produced a corpse. Billy Page was an old drunk, she told Margaret, and he could be confused about what happened on that trail. Margaret, knowing it would do no good, reminded her of the other evidence and the jury's conviction that Page had told the truth. Still Caroline tortured herself with baseless hope, refusing to let go of the husband she had kissed goodbye last August.

Once, walking back to the Luna House after one of these visits, Beachey told Margaret he thought he knew what Caroline needed. She would not be able to accept her loss until she had a corpse to show for it—or part of one. And come spring, he said, he planned to do something about that. Margaret had no doubt what he meant. But he probably could never find the place, she told him. Not by himself, he agreed, but Page knew where it was. All he had to do was keep the old buzzard alive until spring.

*****

The Nez Perces began arriving on horseback on the morning of March 3rd, and set up tepees on the broad flat between the Clearwater River and the execution site. By evening there were several hundred men, women and children milling about among the tepees in a festive mood. They were here out of curiosity and to relieve for a couple of days the monotony of winter. The weather on the third was cold and windy with occasional light rain in the valley turning to snow on the prairies. On the morning of the fourth, the clouds thinned and a pale sun rose dimly in the sky. At mid morning, the soldiers arrived from Fort Lapwai, by wagon and horseback and wearing dress uniforms. Without pausing, they rode past the scaffold, past the Indian village, and into town.

Upstairs in the Luna House, Father Brouilette sat with the three prisoners, asking them how they had spent the night. They had slept well, they said, thanks to the morphine they'd been given.

At 11:30, the wagon that was to take them to the scaffold drew up to the front of the Luna House and the troops formed a hollow square around it. The door of the hotel opened and the prisoners emerged, not in chains but simply handcuffed, and got into the wagon. Lieutenant Purdy, the commander of the company, shouted an order and the troops began to march, before, behind and beside the moving wagon. Lower and Romain stared straight ahead and Renton dropped his face briefly into his hands, then lifted it again.

Caroline Magruder sat in her kitchen, saying no, no, no to the children, who wanted to march with the soldiers. They would pass near the house, and she was determined neither to see nor to hear them. Finally she told the children they could do as they pleased. Then she stood up and went into a back room and locked the door. John, James and little Eliza ran out into the street and followed the soldiers toward the outskirts of town.[86]

When the soldiers reached the gallows they formed a square around it. The prisoners stepped down from the wagon and Sheriff Fisk together with Beachey, a deputy sheriff, a deputy U. S. marshal and two guards, accompanied them up the stairs to the scaffold. Renton went up first, quickly, followed by the sheriff. Then came Lower, with a bit of a swagger, and then Romain, unsteadily as though feeling his way. There were three chairs on the platform, and the prisoners sat down. Almost immediately, Father Brouilette began his prayer and the three went down on their knees.[87]

Beachey, standing beside the sheriff and behind Renton, looked out beyond the soldiers at a great, milling throng of people. He had never seen so many Indians at one time and he wondered what had brought them all here from their villages up the Clearwater. There were even more whites, crowded as close as the soldiers would permit, and children on the fringes of the crowd. Beyond them all were the tepees, shedding the smoke from cooking fires into the cold March air, and a great jumble of buggies and horses.

The prisoners were invited to speak and Renton rose first. He held up the rope that was meant for him and declared that it would strangle an innocent man. And that was all he had to say. Lower then startled the crowd by declaring that he could easily have cleared the other two but only by implicating someone who was dearer to him than his life. He said that Page had plotted the murders and that he, Lower, had murdered two innocent men by his silence. He then turned to Renton and Romain and asked them to forgive him.

Renton asked Lower why he hadn't said all this before and cleared them.

Lower replied that he couldn't and wouldn't, and that he was now ready to "launch the boat."

Romain stood up and tried to speak, but couldn't get the words out at first. He finally managed to say that "I am an innocent man. I want you to distinctly understand that." Then, as the noose was being adjusted and his hands tied, he started to cry.

With the ropes all in place, the sheriff asked if the prisoners were ready.

"All ready," Renton replied.

"Launch your boat," Lower said, "She's only an old mud scow anyhow."

Romain said nothing until Lower turned toward him, and he muttered simply, "yes."[88]

Then all three dropped through the floor and out of sight, leaving on the platform three chairs, the priest and the officers gazing solemnly ahead, and three ropes, two of them swinging quietly and one convulsively jerking. The drop had not broken Renton's neck, and his rope continued to flop erratically. The crowd watched it in silence, as though stunned, for a few seconds and then some of the people began to shout their approval. Father Brouilette raised a hand as if for quiet, thought better of it, and hurried down the steps to the ground. Most of the spectators were still there twenty minutes later when Dr. Madison A. Kelly pronounced the prisoners dead. That prompted more applause and started more bottles passing around. Sheriff Fisk went immediately to where Lower was hanging and reached into one coat pocket then the other, and finally pulled out a folded sheet of paper. He read it to himself quickly, turned red, and shoved it into his pants pocket.

Beachey, who was watching, asked him what it was. Never mind, the sheriff told Beachey, he didn't need to know. The sheriff said it was something Lower had wanted him to read aloud from the scaffold, but he would not. No, by God, he would not. He glared at the suspended corpse and turned to Beachey in puzzled fury. It was the nastiest, most obscene, blasphemous filth he had ever read, he declared, and he added, nodding toward the body: but about what you'd expect.

Cut it down, he told a guard, and get the damn thing buried.[89]

*****

Chester Coburn got up from the box he was sitting on and pushed another piece of wood into the tiny stove that heated his cubbyhole of an office. He was glad this winter was about over, he told Beachey. It wasn't the kind he'd choose to live through again.

Beachey said nothing, and Coburn mused on. Of course it could have been worse, he said. At least three of the season's worst villains met their fair reward.

Beachey looked up at Coburn and raised a questioning eyebrow. That traitor Campbell from Boise City deserved to be hanged too, Coburn said, sitting back down, and Beachey realized he was half serious. Well, he was right, Beachey thought. The filthy schemer had accepted their hospitality and then double-crossed them—or tried to.

Thank God for Alonzo Leland, Coburn said, and Beachey had to remind him that Leland's fine filibuster had only postponed the inevitable. The capital question would come up again, he said, and he didn't expect Lewiston would win next time around.

Coburn asked Beachey if he could remember how it had been only a year ago when Lewiston was the most promising city in the Pacific Northwest, before the miners started moving east to the Beaverhead and south to the Boise Basin. Of course Beachey remembered. He remembered the excitement of watching a territory born, the dances at Fort Lapwai, the good times at the Luna House with the Magruders. He remembered Caroline playing a sweet, sad song on Madame Bonhore's new piano and wondered if she would ever feel like playing again. Of course she would, he thought, as would they all. It had been a bad winter but spring was on the way. The ice was breaking up in the downriver sloughs, and before long they would be hearing north-bound geese chattering overhead.

In the meantime, it was comfortable here in the stable. Beachey told Coburn that if he could find the cards they might as well have a game of cribbage.

Epilogue

Part Four

In late May, a little less than three months after the executions of Renton, Lower and Romain, William Page led Hill Beachey and some others to Lloyd Magruder's last camp— the site of the crime. What they found there is best described in their own words, written in a letter to the editor and published by *The Golden Age* in June 1864:

"For the satisfaction of the reading public, we thought it proper to give a little history of facts in regards to a journey made in search of Magruder and party, or of what little remained of those who were once our dear friends. We left Elk City 29th of May, made Red River Meadows and spent the evening with our friend George Zeigel.

"May 30th—Made what is known as the Mountain Meadows, where we camped. The snow had nearly disappeared but we were obliged to tie our horses, as there was scarcely a vestige of anything green to be seen.

"May 31st.—Made a start at four o'clock in the morning; we made Little Salmon about 11 a.m. where we camped and prospected for grass. In the afternoon we moved camp some three miles up the Little Salmon, where we camped for the night. Page expressed some uneasiness, for he hardly knew where he was, but he left camp and was absent some three hours. While gone, he discovered the little prairie where they camped the first night after the murder of Magruder and party. There he found the leggins they left and knew where he was.

"June 1st—We made a start at half past four a.m. After some eight or ten miles travel, we met a Mr. Adams on his way from Bitter Root, and, as he had had the misfortune to lose his provisions in crossing the Bitter Root River, he was as much pleased to meet us as we were him. He returned with us to the fatal spot where

Magruder and party fell victims to the demons in human shape. We arrived at the spot after a long and tedious ride. At about four o'clock p.m. we unsaddled our animals, and proceeded to search for the remains. The first thing discovered was the gunnysack of tin cups, coffee pots, etc., which all who heard the evidence of Page at the trial of Renton, Lowry and Romain, will remember as being described by him. The next discovery was the blankets which were wound 'round the bodies of the two brothers. The next discovery was the tent and blankets which Allen and Phillips were lashed up in. These we searched with care. We found in the pockets of Allen a portmonie [a small traveling case] in which we found two 25-cent pieces, American coin, a gold ring, a thimble and some needles. We also found Allen's watch. We found Phillips' hat; Holt knew it to be Phillips'. Page knew the pants to be Allen's, in which was found the portmonie. We also found pieces of skull bones in this particular spot, and some hair said to be, by those who knew, Allen's. Also the under jaw of Allen or Phillips. We also found the under jaw of one of the brothers, or supposed to be, as it was near the blankets which once encased their bodies. We also found two blue jean coats in one of which was found the memorandum book which shows that the two brothers had $1,658.78 on their persons when they started for Oregon with Magruder and party. We found in camp, near the spot where Page saw Allen shot, a piece of his skull, supposed to have been blown off with the shot-gun. We found the quartz specimens which were taken from Magruder's cantinas, and thrown away by one of the villains. We found the rings, buckles, etc., as described by Page, buried in the ashes. We then repaired to the spot where Magruder received that fatal blow, or, we may say, blows, for we found several pieces of his skull, which had been literally hacked to pieces. Oh, what an awful sight! He was murdered nearly a half mile from the others. His coat and vest were somewhat torn by the wolves, but enough was left so that they looked quite natural. We then went with Page to the spot where he had thrown the guns. We there found Mr. Beachy's gun, the one he had loaned to Magruder, and found it to be loaded but the caps had been removed. We also found the gun which Page said belonged to one of the brothers, also one rifle and the shot-gun which Page said was once Romain's. We found other relics and things much as described by

Page. It makes the heart sink to think of this terrible tragedy. On our return, we went to the spot which had been described by Page, and found the remains of the slaughtered animals. We hope never to witness such a sight again."

The letter was signed by A.J. Coffin, David Reese, Matthew Adams, Hill Beachy, L.O. Holt, James Smith and Joel D. Martin.

The reference to the Little Salmon River on May 31st will puzzle readers familiar with the region, for the Little Salmon as it is called today is far to the west of the southern Nez Perce Trail. It is most probable the writer was referring to another tributary of the Salmon that is now known as Bargamin Creek.

One of the party scratched the significance of the spot on a board and nailed it to a tree. Beachey salvaged some of Magruder's broken skull and brought it back to Lewiston for Magruder's widow, Caroline. Caroline was pleased to have it, according to a granddaughter, and she carried it with her to her grave.[90]

The territorial legislature appropriated $6,240 to compensate Beachey for his expenses in the pursuit and return of the murderers. The money the killers had not squandered in spending sprees in Portland and San Francisco—some $17,000—was retrieved from the San Francisco Mint, where it had been placed for coining, and given to Mrs. Magruder. At any rate, that was the plan. Some of the relatives say the money passed through so many hands that Caroline received little or none and lived in such poverty that she had to put the children in foster homes. In February 1866, she married Hiram Burt, a laborer from Vermont who died in 1881, leaving her widowed for the second time. We know almost nothing about her later life except that she spent some of it trying in vain to get the money due her from Lloyd Magruder's army pension. She died in Hillsboro, Oregon, in 1900.

The Beacheys' two-year-old son, Early, died of typhoid fever, September 28, 1864. Beachey sold the Luna House that November to T. J. Bunker, a saloon operator and early-day sheriff, and A.W. Sweeney, a former Presbyterian minister, for $5,000. Shortly thereafter, Beachey moved with his family to Nevada, where he built stagecoach lines and where, on October 10, 1867, Margaret died.

The *North-Idaho Radiator*, of Lewiston, reported on March 18, 1865: "Hill Beachey left San Francisco in the latter part of January for Star City, N.T., with stages and teams, to start a stage line from Star City to Owyhee [Idaho Territory]. If such line can be made a permanent and paying institution, Mr. Beachey is the man to do it."

When railroads began replacing stagecoaches, Beachey moved to San Francisco to manage another hotel, the Lick House, apparently with considerable success. On April 6, 1872, the *Idaho Signal*, a successor to *The Golden Age*, reprinted a report from San Francisco that "The Lick House catches most of the mountain people since Hill Beachey became the managing spirit. Beachey is widely known in Oregon, Idaho and Nevada and his numerous friends who visit the city from these regions make straight for the 'Lick.' The house is doing a rushing business under the present management. It is the place of all others to find the 'Sagebrushers.'"

This was the hotel in which Romain was arrested. Also in that issue, the *Signal* noted that John Denny, the current owner of the Luna House, "is improving the outside of his hotel by whitewashing, and has changed the name from Luna House to City Hotel."

Beachey suffered a stroke on a San Francisco street on Thursday, May 20, 1875. On Friday, although paralyzed on the left side and unable to speak, he managed to write out a will. On Sunday, May 23, he died and was buried in Marysville alongside his wife and several children.

*****

There is a hidden irony in Beachey's argument in San Francisco that the law and the courts of Idaho Territory would guarantee the prisoners a fair trial, and in his appeal to the people of Lewiston that the law would see justice done without the aid of a lynch mob. For as we have seen, there was no law in Idaho Territory from March 4, 1863, until January 4, 1864. Beachey didn't know this in November 1863 when he was trying to get his prisoners out of California, or in December of that year when he returned them to Lewiston and put them in jail, first at the Luna House and later at Fort Lapwai.

The statute that created Idaho Territory out of parts of the territories of Washington, Dakota, Utah and Nebraska in March 1863 did not provide Idaho with a criminal code. Because of an oversight, none of the codes of the other four territories continued in effect in the new one. Later, when this came to the attention of the courts, it allowed one accused criminal to escape trial, and released two convicts on the grounds that their crimes had violated no law. The territorial legislature hastily put a code of sorts in place by adopting the English Common Law in January 1864. The absence of a law to hold them did not help Renton, Lower and Romain, however. If their attorneys, Anderson and Thayer, had realized the county had no right to hold their clients, they could have demanded their release. Perhaps they did find out and decided that if there was no law preventing the accused from going free, there also was no law preventing others from stringing them up. At Fort Lapwai, they were at least safe.

Almost a century later in Lewiston, two members of the Idaho Supreme Court, after watching a dramatized version of the trial on May 12, 1961, issued an informal opinion declaring that Renton, Lower and Romain had been illegally executed. They based their argument partly on an 1866 decision of the territorial supreme court involving a man named Williams. He had been accused of armed robbery, allegedly committed in 1863. The indictment was returned in 1865, and in 1866 the court ruled that Williams could not be tried. "The Williams case being the precedent," the two justices wrote in 1961, "it follows that [Renton, Lower and Romain] were hanged for an act which did not constitute a crime. It then follows that they were unlawfully hung."

*****

William Page, who bought his freedom with his testimony, did not live long to enjoy it. He befriended a woman named Eliza Wilson, and had on occasion bought food for her and defended her against the rough advances of her boyfriend, a young ne'er-do-well named Albert Igo. On Christmas Eve 1865, Page got drunk and at 2 o'clock the next morning went to Eliza's house and knocked on the door. Eliza, who was in bed with Albert, gave no response. Page then broke the door down and came in, calling Igo "you son of a bitch." According to Eliza's later statement to Judge John Berry, Page knocked Igo down and pummeled him until Eliza feared he was dead. Page then left. Eliza washed the blood off Igo and the two went back to bed. Later in the morning, Page returned and complained to Eliza that "you don't want to let me in your house any more." He demanded to see Igo, who then stepped in through the back door saying, "Here I am. Now, Page, defend yourself." Eliza went out into the yard. She heard a shot, and when she came back into the house she saw Page on the floor. He was dead.

Igo told Judge Berry he had fired his shotgun when Page came at him with a pistol. The authorities considered it self-defense, and Igo was never charged. Some writers, including Julia Conway Welch, suggest that Igo would have been prosecuted had Page not been despised by the people of Lewiston. This presumes that Page, despite his testimony, was considered a murderer who had escaped punishment by tattling on his pals. That may have been the case, but it seems odd that Page's fellow citizens, if they hated him that much, would have suffered his presence in the community for almost a full year after the trial. Besides, by the standards of the time, perhaps it was a clear case of self-defense; Page had started the fight that ended in his death.

*****

Captain Charles LaFrancois did propose to Madame Melaine Bonhore (or perhaps it was the other way around) later in 1864, and they were married that year. The date is uncertain, but her name is listed as Madame LaFrancois in an ad in *The Golden Age* on November 19. The captain's obituary, published in the *Idaho Signal* of Lewiston on February 7, 1874, gives the year of the marriage as 1861, but that is probably a typographical error. LaFrancois was in the Florence mining district at that time and didn't settle in Lewiston until 1863.

If Madame expected him to share the burden of running the De France, she was disappointed, for the captain was of little practical use around the place. He did, however, continue to charm the guests and enliven the bar, and he served the community in various ways. The *Idaho Signal* in April 1872 lists him as an election judge for the Lewiston Precinct of Nez Perce County. He died of a heart ailment on February 2, 1874. Madame carried on, building her hotel's reputation as "the finest in the north country." The De France was noted for sumptuous meals and elegant accommodations surpassing anything else in the region.

Another Frenchman, Raymond Saux (pronounced Soo), arrived in Lewiston shortly after the captain's death and approached Madame with an offer to buy the De France. She declined. Then she decided she would like a vacation, and leased the hotel to him. She spent some months in California and Paris, and when she returned to Lewiston she resumed operation of the De France, leaving Saux without a business.

Saux bought a lot at the corner of Fifth and Montgomery streets and in 1879 built the Raymond House, a handsome three-story hotel. Times were not so good by now and the De France was losing money. Madame kept things going by pinching pennies but she was unable to pay her chef, Baptiste Escude. He continued to work even so, but by 1895 he was running out of patience and demanded back wages. Madame signed a promissory note but could not make the payments to Escude, and after her death on April 14, 1897, the chef gained ownership of the building.

Escude's health too was failing, so he put a manager in charge and retired. He died in 1898 after dining at the home of Madame's son, Eugene.

The De France, gradually deteriorating, passed through several hands and finally was torn down in 1945 to make way for a garage and service station.

Chester Coburn remained a prominent citizen of Nez Perce County for many years. Scattered items in *The Golden Age, Lewiston Journal, Idaho Signal,* and the *Northerner* tell of Coburn running the Luna Livery Stables, serving as a deputy U.S. marshal, then U.S. marshal, running for the Lewiston City Council, dealing in cattle, serving as a delegate to the Republican county convention, becoming a father, serving as a fire warden and school trustee, and opening the Lewiston Market with a partner, D. Waldrip. The Coburn family home in the 1870s was on First Street across from the present Lewis-Clark Plaza, overlooking the confluence of the Snake and Clearwater rivers.

*****

The bones of Henry Plummer, who was hanged by vigilantes in January 1864, apparently did not rest easy. The bullet that Sheriff Crawford had fired at Plummer in 1863 in Bannack had hit him in the right arm. Plummer had been treated by Dr. John Glick, a Bannack physician. Here is what happened then, paraphrased from Jean Davis' book, *Shallow Diggin's: Tales from Montana's Ghost Towns* (1962; see page 46):

Dr. Glick tried to remove the bullet from Plummer's forearm, but couldn't find it, and gave up. He continued to wonder where the bullet was, and some five weeks after Plummer's execution, the doctor decided to examine the arm and find out. On his way to a dance, he opened the box in which Plummer's corpse was awaiting the spring thaw and burial, removed the arm, and cached it in a snowdrift. Dr. Glick went on to the dance, after which a dog came by, pulled the arm out of the snow and carried it into the dance hall. In the confusion that followed, Glick managed to retrieve the arm, took it away with him, and found the bullet.

Some time after this, a couple of drunks dug up the corpse, took off the skull and played catch with it. After tiring of the game, they presented Plummer's skull to the proprietor of the Bank Exchange Saloon in Bannack, where it graced the bar for several years.

One or more of Magruder's murderers apparently suffered postmortem indignities that were not much different. Years later, a Lewiston citizen told Robert G. Bailey, a Lewiston printer and historian, that some time after the executions, he and two friends had disintered the remains of Renton, Lower and Romain, and stored the skeletons in a warehouse on the bank of the Snake River. The three belonged to a secret society which needed a new skeleton for its ritualistic work. The three corpses remained in the warehouse until the stench became so bad that the owner demanded they be removed. According to this version, the bones were then thrown into the river.

Bailey, trying to check this story out, found another citizen who said it was only partly true. He claimed it was his secret society that needed a new skeleton and that it was he who conceived the idea of digging up one of the corpses, cleaning the bones, and putting them in shape for his lodge. The skull, he said, was the only thing worth saving, so he threw the rest of the remains away and took the skull to his room. After a few days it began to smell bad, so he carried the skull down to the river, went aboard a steamboat, and threw the thing as far as he could into the Snake.

If this latter tale is true, there are still two skeletons lying under the parking lot of a Lewiston grocery store that now stands near the site of the hangings.

*****

By the summer of 1864, Bannack and Virginia City were no longer in Idaho Territory; Bannack, in fact, was the first capital of the new Territory of Montana (Virginia City would be the second). And by the following summer, Lewiston no longer was the capital of Idaho— if the capital can be defined as the actual seat of government. Governor Wallace had located a temporary capital at Lewiston in 1863. According to directives, both the governor and the legislature later would have to decide where a permanent capital would be located. But in 1864 Governor Wallace was no longer around, and a majority of the legislators decided they would rather meet in Boise because it was easier to get to. Thus, the people who had almost managed to get the capital established at Boise in the first session of the legislature, succeeded during the second. But it was a messy and complicated business.

The second legislature passed the capital relocation bill early in the session, before all of its members were formally sworn in. That cast a cloud over the action and gave the people of Nez Perce County some hope that they might win this battle after all. But the new territorial governor, Caleb Lyon, had arrived that summer with every intention of settling at Boise, where he had made prominent friends. Nez Perce County went to court, and District Judge Alexander Smith ruled that Lewiston was still the capital. Thus armed, the people of Nez Perce County vowed to resist "the Boise Gang" in every possible way.

Governor Lyon was placed under a sort of house arrest to prevent him from absconding, but he escaped to Walla Walla and from there directed his henchmen at Lewiston. With the help of a military force from Fort Lapwai, they captured the territorial seal and records, and spirited them off to Boise, effectively moving the seat of government.

The territorial supreme court later held that the bill establishing the capital at Boise was legal. Even so, the people of Lewiston considered it a case of outright theft, and many of them still do.

The territorial capitol building in Lewiston served a number of purposes after the permanent capital was established at Boise, then fell into disuse. While the burghers of the town talked of preserving the landmark, it was gradually picked apart by people looking for firewood.

Ferryman John Silcott's house, on the north side of the Clearwater, survived many decades until it too succumbed to fire in 1971. Silcott died in 1902, but his ferry continued to ply the Clearwater until 1913, when a new bridge put the ferry out of business. (At the dawning of the automobile age, the 18th Street bridge was built for wagons, and it quickly became obsolete.)

Steamboats continued to serve Lewiston until well after the arrival of the railroad and automobile. The last sternwheeler, and the last of four to bear the name *Lewiston*, left its Snake River dock on a dark and drizzly day in February 1940, and went to work as a tug on the Willamette River.

*****

The Nez Perce Trail that Magruder followed over the Bitterroots in 1863 was known then—and still is by historians—as the southern Nez Perce Trail to distinguish it from the more famous Lolo Trail north of the Clearwater. It was on the Lolo Trail that the retreating Nez Perce warriors and their women and children crossed over the Bitterroots into Montana during the 1877 war.

A primitive Forest Service route, called the Magruder Corridor Road, now follows in a general way the old southern trail. Some parts of the trail itself are still evident, but most of it fell into disuse and disappeared under ground cover after Indians, miners, and packers stopped traveling this way in the late nineteenth century.

At its western end, the road begins near Elk City, Idaho (still in some ways a mining camp), climbs to the high ridge, and winds its way some ninety miles to the Selway River and beyond, into Montana. The author drove the route in a passenger car in late September 1990, in order to view the terrain as Magruder would have seen it. The vistas are spectacular. On either side, forested ridges fall away, one after another, toward the Clearwater and Salmon drainages. In late September, near the time of year when Magruder passed this way, brush turns to autumnal colors—the vegetation under the fir and cedar is a mass of yellows, greens and reds.

The Magruder Corridor Road itself is narrow, and rough and steep in places, but passable in good weather without the need of a four-wheel-drive vehicle. Much of the route forms a narrow dividing line between two great National Forest Service wilderness areas—the Frank Church-River of No Return Wilderness on the south, and the Selway-Bitterroot Wilderness to the north. This is prime elk hunting country and the traveler driving this way in the fall should be prepared to share the road with pickup trucks and horse trailers.

At one point, the Forest Service has erected a sign and cleared a trail leading to the spot where Magruder supposedly made his last camp. It is within easy walking distance of the road, but no one can be sure that this is in fact the murder site. It doesn't quite fit William Page's description in his trial testimony. The Forest Service can only speculate that this is exactly where the bloody deed took place.

The route is paved over Nez Perce Pass into Montana, where it becomes dirt again for awhile, but then is paved the rest of the way in the Bitterroot Valley. From there, a modern highway crosses over the Continental Divide into the Big Hole Valley, which is lush with ranchers' hay. The state route continues south through the western Montana towns of Wisdom and Jackson. Not far after the highway crosses Big Hole Pass into the Grasshopper Creek drainage, a side road turns off the highway to the now-deserted mining camp of Bannack. The last few miles to the old ghost town are gravel and dirt, a fitting approach to what must surely be one of the best preserved of the historic old gold camps in western North America.

When our party arrived there, on a Saturday afternoon, Bannack was deserted. The State of Montana protects the town as a heritage site. The park attendant had taken the weekend off, so we had the dusty streets to ourselves. There is a small house for the park attendant and picnic tables beside Grasshopper Creek; otherwise Bannack has not been "civilized." The buildings, mainly built of squared logs, are genuinely authentic. Many of the doors are ajar, as if the occupants just stepped out, and visitors are free to explore them inside and out.

It was a warm, quiet, late-summer afternoon. The sagebrush in the front yards and behind the houses stood head high, and the soil was rocky and almost white. The place was absolutely silent, dozing in the sun and full of ghosts.

Not so in Virginia City, some eighty miles to the northeast, where Magruder spent a couple of busy weeks in 1863. Virginia City is a tourist town on a well-traveled highway, whose ghosts have long since been exorcized by automobile traffic and souvenir shops.

Even here, however, Henry Plummer lives on in myth and mystery. If half the things said about him are true, he must have died a rich man. Then what happened to all that gold? One story has it that the sheriff cached it in various places between Bannack and Virginia City, and that it is still there in buried cans and bottles, waiting to be found.

Endnotes

Chapter 1

1. Craig's Mountain was named for William Craig, a Rocky Mountain beaver hunter who settled in the area in 1840. Craig, along with hundreds of other "mountain men," had been forced to give up the life of a roaming "free trapper" when the fur trade collapsed by 1840, due to the depletion of fur resources and because beaver hats went out of fashion in the East and Europe. Being married to a Nez Perce woman, he settled among his wife's people on Lapwai Creek, which drains the northern portion of Craig's Mountain. Craig was not the first white settler in the area, however. Four years earlier, the missionaries Henry and Eliza Spalding had established a mission station lower down on the same drainage. The name Craig's Mountain has evolved slightly over the years and these broad heights now are commonly called the Craig Mountains.
2. The files of the *Lewiston Morning Tribune* contain photographs of the Hotel De France taken in 1945 just before the building was torn down. The pictures reveal the building's interior, particularly remnants of its decorative woodwork which testified to the old inn's faded elegance.
3. Margaret Day Allen, *Lewiston Country* (1990), p. 60.

Chapter 2

4. Lloyd Magruder's background and some of Caroline Magruder's later life are described in a letter written by a granddaughter, Mrs. Carl Braun, and printed in the *Idaho Statesman* (Boise), October 11, 1942. Reprinted in R.G. Bailey, *Hell's Canyon* (1943), pp. 541-43.
5. The trail Magruder probably took out of town became a gravel road, and later a paved arterial leading to present Lewiston Orchards. The original road almost entirely disappeared when the gully was filled in for a new highway (Thain Grade) and for commercial development.
6. The Spalding Mission site now is part of the Nez Perce National Historical Park. Much of the ditch that carried water to the mill wheel can still be seen.
7. The Indian agent's fears were well-founded. Hostilities did break out in June 1877 between a portion of the Nez Perce bands and white settlers and soldiers.
8. Today, the town of Culdesac is situated here.
9. Hoffman Birney, in *Vigilantes* (1929), p. 66, locates one shebang "between Alpowai and Pataha Creeks, some twenty-five miles from Lewiston on the road towards Walla Walla," and another "at the foot of Craig's Mountain, between Lewiston and Oro Fino." According to some writers, there was still another shebang on the road to Florence in the Salmon River country; see Julia Conway Welch, *The Magruder Murders* (1991), p. 32.

Chapter 3

10. The Luna House register, opened to this page, is on display at the Luna House Museum, Lewiston. A month later, on August 23, 1862, Plummer again registered at the Luna House, this time with his name spelled with two "m"s— Plummer—and checking in as coming from Florence. Charles Reeves and Charles Ridgely, members of the so-called Plummer gang, checked in from Florence on the same day. A few days later, all three were involved in a shoot-out at Oro Fino in which Ridgely was wounded.
11. Welch, *The Magruder Murders*, p. 91.
12. Birney, *Vigilantes*, 62. This quote evidently is based on an extensive interview with Martha Edgerton Plassman, who was still alive and living in Great Falls, Montana, when Birney was writing. He quotes her recollection of Henry Plummer further: "He never wore buckskins and his clothes were always clean and pressed. He kept his hands clean, too, and I never saw him when he seemed to need a shave. Of course I saw him only when he was, you might say, on his good behavior; but I can remember that his voice was low and pleasant and that he never used any of the slangy talk of the miners or their rough expressions. He had a bow and a pleasant smile for every woman he met on the street, and the same for the men . . . Yes, Henry Plummer was a bandit—there's no doubt about that. He was a thief and a killer, but he was a gentleman as well."
13. Thomas Dimsdale, *The Vigilantes of Montana* (1866), p. 29, describes the man in the chair as seated there to get a shave. According to Birney, he was dozing.
14. R.E. Mather and F.E. Boswell, *Hanging the Sheriff* (1987), p. 35.
15. Birney, in *Vigilantes*, pp. 66-67, describes Cyrus Skinner as a saloonkeeper who had been ordered out of California following a shoot-out in San Francisco, and who later ran saloons in Walla Walla and Lewiston: "He was primarily a plotter, planning coups which other men executed, but he possessed an abundance of courage and frequently rode with the road-agents on their missions." The vigilante John Xavier Beidler described Skinner in his memoirs as "the great slugger and knock-down champion of [Plummer's] gang"; see *X. Beidler: Vigilante*, ed. by Helen Fitzgerald Sanders, p. 93.

Chapter 4

16. Mrs. Carl Braun letter; in Bailey, *Hell's Canyon*, pp. 541-43.
17. Ibid.
18. Allen, *Lewiston Country*, p. 5.
19. Welch, *The Magruder Murders*, p. 29.
20. Dorothy M. Johnson, *The Bloody Bozeman* (1971), p. 5.
21. Ibid.

Chapter 7

22. *The Golden Age*, September 5, 1863, printed an advertisement announcing that L. Bacon was now carrying the express from Lewiston to Elk City.
23. *The Golden Age,* September 5, 1863.
24. Ibid.

Chapter 8

25. Welch, *The Magruder Murders*, p. 93, quotes an acquaintance of Renton as saying that Renton had served time on a prison brig in Sacramento. According to an item in the *San Francisco Journal*, reprinted in the *Oregon Statesman* (Salem), November 23, 1863: "The man Lowry is a state prison convict who was pardoned by Gov. Downey on condition of his leaving the state. Failing to do that he was re-arrested and taken back to San Quentin, but was soon after again released."
26. See Welch, Ibid.
27. Joe Baily, "The Magruder Murder," *Spokesman-Review* (Spokane), March 17, 1963.
28. Louis Holt, who worked with Magruder in Bannack and Virginia City, testified in court that Lower was a heavy-set man of light complexion (see trial transcript).

Chapter 9

29. Baily in "The Magruder Murder," *Spokesman-Review*, March 17, 1963, presents a detailed description of the route of the southern Nez Perce Trail.
30. *The Golden Age*, September 5, 1863.

Chapter 10

31. Beaverhead Rock was a landmark on the road from Bannack to Virginia City. Lewis and Clark called the large natural stone feature "Rattlesnake Cliffs," and today it commonly is known as Point of Rocks. It stands 14 miles northeast of Dillon, next to State Route 41.
32. Bannack has been preserved as a Montana state park and Skinner's saloon still stands on the main street.

Chapter 11

33. Mather and Boswell, *Hanging the Sheriff*, p. 47.
34. Ibid.
35. Johnson, *The Bloody Bozeman,* p. 5.
36. Ibid, p. 7.
37. Ibid.

Chapter 12

38. Michael P. Malone and Richard B. Roeder, *Montana: A History of Two Centuries* (1976), p. 52.
39. Magruder by this time evidently had a campaign flyer printed up; Dimsdale in *The Vigilantes of Montana* (1866), p. 121, stated that a man he knew in nearby Nevada City still had a copy of the "circular."

Chapter 13

40. William Page's trial testimony.
41. Ibid.
42. Louis Holt's trial testimony.
43. Page's testimony.
44. Ibid.

Chapter 14

45. The information in this chapter is based upon Page's testimony.

Chapter 15

46. The trial transcript is confusing and barely legible at this point, but it is clear that a stop was made here for whiskey.
47. If Lower suggested robbing the ferryman, there is no mention of it in Page's testimony; but the author would be surprised if he didn't.
48. Page's testimony.
49. Although Page did not mention this episode in his testimony, several writers have claimed that a crossing of the Clearwater was attempted some 50 miles above Lewiston: e.g., Byron Defenbach, *Idaho, the Place and Its People* (1933), vol. 1, p. 330.
50. Page's testimony.
51. Chester Coburn, quoted by William Shiach in *An Illustrated History of North Idaho* (1903), p. 35.

Chapter 16

52. Defenbach, *Idaho, the Place and Its People*, vol. 1, p. 331.
53. Alvin M. Josephy, Jr., "The Blood of Abel," *Journal of the Nez Perce County Historical Society* (Spring-Summer 1985).
54. Ibid.
55. Affidavit of Associate Supreme Court Justice Alleck C. Smith, October 31, 1863. The affidavit accompanied an arrest warrant signed by W.H. Wickersham, certifying that Wickersham was a credible witness acting with full legal authority.
56. Official Records of Idaho Territory.
57. Allen, *Lewiston Country*, p. 61.
58. According to some accounts, Thomas Farrell returned with Ankeny to Lewiston; according to others, he caught the next steamer south and joined Beachey in San Francisco. We know he continued on to California because of a document signed by Governor Leland Stanford on November 2, 1863, ordering that the fugitives be arrested and delivered "into the custody of Hill Beachy and Thomas Farrell."

Chapter 17

59. *San Francisco Bulletin* article reprinted in the *Oregon Statesman* (Salem), November 16, 1863.
60. Ibid.
61. Page's testimony.
62. Ibid.

Chapter 18

63. Betty K. Beachy, "Hill Beachey," *Journal of the Nez Perce County Historical Society* (Spring/Summer 1985). Thomas Donaldson, in *Idaho of Yesterday* (1941), described Beachey as "a thickset man . . . with brown hair and blue eyes . . . He was a man of intense energy, indomitable when aroused."
64. Victor Goodwin, "William C. (Hill) Beachey, Nevada-California-Idaho Stagecoach King," *Nevada Historical Society Quarterly* (Spring 1967).
65. Allen, *Lewiston Country*, p. 31.
66. See Joe Baily article in the *Spokesman-Review* (Spokane), March 17, 1963.

Chapter 19

67. Information from Captain Charles LaFrancois obituary, *Idaho Signal*, February 7, 1874.

Chapter 20

68. Early Beachey died September 28, 1864, according to a brief notice in the *Oregon Statesman* (Salem), October 31, 1864.
69. Oscar Lewis, *The Big Four: The Story of Huntington, Stanford, Hopkins, and Crocker, and of the Building of the Central Pacific* (1938), p. 113. Lewis describes Stanford as "a large, heavy man, deliberate in thought and motion."

Chapter 22

70. *Sacramento Daily Union*, November 12, 1863.

Chapter 23

71. *Oregon Statesman* (Salem), December 14, 1863.
72. The "Laramie Fraud" poisoned Idaho territorial politics for many years. According to Defenbach in *Idaho, the Place and Its People*, vol. 1, p. 372: "The Democrats have never quit condemning that count; Governor [James H.] Hawley expressed his feelings at least 50 years after the election."

Chapter 26

73. According to the editor of the *The Golden Age*, Beachey's party arrived by stage, not boat, and there was no threat of violence (however, see the Bibliography for a discussion of why *The Golden Age* report can be discounted). Most historians claim the party arrived by steamboat and faced a lynch mob. See *An Illustrated History of North Idaho*, p. 35: also Nathaniel P. Langford, *Vigilante Days and Ways,* vol. 2 (1890); Welch, *The Magruder Murders*; and John Hailey, *History of Idaho* (1910).

Chapter 28

74. According to another version of this episode, in Langford, *Vigilante Days and Ways,* vol. 2, and R.G. Bailey, *River of No Return* (1935), Page broke down after being led past the open door of a room in which he could see four ropes hanging from a ceiling beam.

Chapter 30

75. Docket of the District Court, December 1863.
76. This and the testimony that follows are taken from the transcript of the trial.
77. Ronald H. Limbaugh, "The Year without a Code," *Idaho Yesterdays* (Spring 1987).

Chapter 31

78. Caroline Magruder's visit to the jail is mentioned by her granddaughter, Mrs. Carl Braun: letter to the *Idaho Statesman*, October 11, 1942, and reprinted in Bailey, *Hell's Canyon*, pp. 541-43.
79. For a detailed description of the hangings, see Mather and Boswell, *Hanging the Sheriff*, beginning on p. 84.
80. Ibid.
81. Fairness compels the author to remind the reader that Cyrus Skinner's pursuit of the murderers, including his presence in the Portland area, is a product of the author's imagination. Skinner could have been there, but not for long: he was hanged by vigilantes at Deer Lodge early in 1864.

Chapter 32

82. The text of Judge Parker's statement was published by *The Golden Ages;* and reprinted in the *Oregon Statesman* (Salem), February 8, 1864.
83. W.A. Goulder, *Reminiscences* (1909), p. 332.
84. This quote has been widely attributed to Lower, but the author cannot vouch for its authenticity.
85. This incident was reported by *The Golden Age* and other papers of the day, and later in *An Illustrated History of North Idaho*, among others. Lower's exact words have been variously recorded, but the import was that he "thought

it was loaded," "didn't know it was loaded," or "thought it was going to go off." See Welch, *The Magruder Murders*, p. 88.

Chapter 33

86. Mrs. Carl Braun letter; in Bailey, *Hell's Canyon*, pp. 541-43.
87. *The Golden Age*, March 5, 1864.
88. Ibid.
89. Although Thomas Dimsdale identifies Romain as the author of the note that infuriated Sheriff Fisk, *The Golden Age* and all of the other sources consulted by the author say it was Lower.

Epilogue

90. Mrs. Carl Braun letter; in Bailey, *Hell's Canyon*, p. 541.

Bibliography

Although much has been published concerning the Magruder affair, all that we know for certain about it after more than 130 years are the facts that we can glean from the testimony of William Page and other witnesses in the trial, plus information from several other legal documents and from contemporary newspaper reports and personal reminiscences.

The many accounts that authors have written over the years vary so much in interpretation—and often this literature is so divided against itself—that the more one reads the more one longs to know what really happened regarding many aspects of the story. Did the murderers travel with Magruder at least part of the way from Elk City to Bannack, or did they first join Magruder on the way back? If they followed Magruder out of Lewiston, were there three of them? Or five? Or eight? Was Bill Page an accomplice or an innocent bystander swept up in the plot? Was Henry Plummer a gang leader masquerading as sheriff, or a talented and dedicated lawman? What role, if any, did he play in the Magruder incident? One can find sources in the literature for either answer to any one of those questions. Thus hardly *any* version of this tale can be said with certainty either to be absolutely false or surely true.

Listed here are the major sources consulted in the preparation of this narrative, with brief summaries of their contents and, where applicable, their points of view.

Books

Allen, Margaret Day. *Lewiston Country: An Armchair History*. Lewiston, Idaho: Nez Perce County Historical Society, 1990.
  This book contains a one-chapter "traditional" recounting of the tale and in the main accepts Dimsdale's version of events (see Dimsdale, below). The author also treats Henry Plummer as a scoundrel and suggests that he may have been involved in the Magruder massacre.

Bailey, Robert G. *River of No Return (The Great Salmon River of Idaho)* . . . Lewiston, Idaho: Bailey-Blake Printing, 1935.
  In this collection of tales of the Salmon River country, Bailey includes a version of the Magruder incident generally following the accounts by Dimsdale and Langford (see Dimsdale and Langford, below).

Birney, Hoffman. *Vigilantes: A Chronicle of the Rise and Fall of the Plummer Gang of Outlaws in and about Virginia City, Montana, in the Early '60's*. Philadelphia: Penn Publishing, 1929.

Although the vigilantes had nothing to do with the apprehension and execution of Magruder's killers, Birney devotes some space to the Magruder incident. He locates the Plummer gang's hideaways, or "shebangs," and has the murderers trailing the pack train from Lewiston and joining it before its arrival in Bannack.

Callaway, Lew L., edited by Lew L. Callaway, Jr. *Montana's Righteous Hangmen: The Vigilantes in Action*. Norman: University of Oklahoma Press, 1982.

As a young man, the elder Callaway knew many of his subjects intimately, including Captain James Williams, the executive officer of the Montana vigilantes. This book, not surprisingly, is a justification of the vigilante system. Callaway describes Plummer as a desperado and his election as sheriff as "one of the strangest episodes in American history."

Davis, Jean Walton. *Shallow Diggin's: Tales from Montana's Ghost Towns*. Caldwell, Idaho: Caxton Printers, 1962.

This is a collection of tales about the Montana mining camps, including an account of the exhumation of Henry Plummer's arm.

Defenbach, Byron. *Idaho, the Place and Its People: A History of the Gem State from Prehistoric to Present Days*, vol. I. Chicago-New York: American Historical Society, 1933.

In a laudatory account of the Idaho vigilance committee, Defenbach gives the number of its hangings at twenty-seven and notes: "The men thus punished had been guilty of murdering more than 100 people, besides committing almost innumerable other crimes."

Dimsdale, Thomas J., *The Vigilantes of Montana: Or, Popular Justice in the Rocky Mountains*. Norman: University of Oklahoma Press, 1953.

Originally published in 1866 by the *Montana Post*, this was the first book printed in Montana and copies of the original edition are extremely rare today. Professor Thomas J. Dimsdale, a teacher and editor, originally researched and wrote this account as a series of newspaper articles for the *Montana Post* (Virginia City), beginning with the August 26, 1865, issue. Dimsdale personally knew persons involved in the vigilante movement. In general terms, Dimsdale's account constitutes the traditional version of the Magruder incident as opposed to the revisionist accounts of some more recent authors. It is the primary source for the connection of Plummer and Cyrus Skinner to the murders. Many later historians consider the book biased and therefore not always reliable, because Dimsdale's articles were written in praise of the vigilantes and to justify their existence. A well-educated Englishman afflicted with consumption, Dimsdale had come west hoping to improve his health and arrived in Bannack from Canada in the summer of 1863. He died September 22, 1866, at the age of thirty-five.

Donaldson, Thomas. *Idaho of Yesterday.* Caldwell, Idaho: Caxton Printers, 1941.
Donaldson, a one-time vigilante himself, describes the people and life of frontier Idaho. He writes: "In my own personal recollection I never knew but one man hanged unjustly by the vigilantes," and he was hanged in Arizona. Donaldson also recalls: "Many a yarn did I hear spun of Henry Plummer and his murderous gang."

Fisher, Vardis, and Opal Laurel Holmes. *Gold Rushes and Mining Camps of the Early American West.* Caldwell, Idaho: Caxton Printers, 1968.
Fisher and Holmes blame Plummer for the murder of the Magruder crew, saying the massacre "was typical of Henry Plummer's methods." They believe that William Page was one of the bandits. (That doesn't fit with Page's own testimony, but Page had agreed only to impeach the other three suspects, not himself.)

Goulder, W. A. *Reminiscenses: Incidents in the Life of a Pioneer in Oregon and Idaho.* Boise: Timothy Regan, 1909.
This is an on-the-scene description of mining camps, frontier politics and the hazards of the trail by a school teacher, legislator and historian. The writing style is dated but the book is informative, engaging and sometimes eloquent.

Hailey, John. *History of Idaho.* Boise: Syms-York, 1910.
Of all the authors listed here, Hailey had the advantage of personally knowing Hill Beachey, whom he describes as a man of honesty, intelligence and courage. In my narrative, Beachey takes his Kentucky rifle to where Magruder is loading his mules for the trail; Hailey says that Magruder, after loading the mules, went to the Luna House to say goodbye to Beachey and that he received the rifle there. According to Hailey, eight men followed Magruder out of Lewiston, including William Page and Bob Zachary.

Hunt, William R. *Dictionary of Rogues.* New York: Philosophical Library, 1970.
Hunt describes Plummer as a western bad man and says he planned 102 robberies and murders that were carried out by his gang. That number is Dimsdale's figure and is too precise to be credible, given the casual manner in which such crimes were recorded on the frontier.

(An) Illustrated History of North Idaho, Embracing Nez Perces, Idaho, Latah, Kootenai and Shoshone Counties, State of Idaho. N.p.: Western Historical Publishing Company, 1903.
The author of the chapter on Nez Perce County, William S. Shiach, visited Lewiston, examined the trial transcript, and interviewed several old-timers including Chester Coburn, who described certain events of the night the fugitives passed through town. According to Shiach, "There is reason to believe that [Renton, Lower and Romain] left Lewiston with no other intent than to murder Magruder and take his money." He writes also that Beachey and the prisoners arrived at Lewiston by boat and that Beachey had to dissuade an angry crowd from lynching his charges. Since Shiach took pains not only to read the trial

transcript (which he found brief and confusing) but to conduct interviews, his version should be given considerable credence.

Johnson, Dorothy M. *The Bloody Bozeman: The Perilous Trail to Montana's Gold.* New York: McGraw-Hill, 1971.
    Johnson describes the origin and significance of the Bozeman Trail, one of the key routes connecting the Oregon Trail with Bannack, Deer Lodge and Virginia City. The book is well researched and full of intimate glimpses into the lives of the miners and their families.

Langford, Nathaniel P. *Vigilante Days and Ways: The Pioneers of the Rockies; the Makers and Making of Montana, Idaho, Oregon, Washington, and Wyoming,* 2 vols. Boston: J. G. Cupples, 1890.
    Next to Dimsdale, Nathaniel P. Langford (1832-1911) has been the most-quoted "authority" on the vigilantes and the Magruder incident—although his authority, like Dimsdale's, has been questioned by modern historians. Langford says that David Renton, Christopher Lower and James Romain left Lewiston one day after Magruder did, heading west, then turned and followed the pack train. He says Bob Zachary was along and that they met Page on the trail before joining Magruder. He says it was Howard (Renton) who suggested fording the Clearwater east of Lewiston after stealing the gold, and that Hill Beachey and the prisoners encountered a lynch mob on arriving at Lewiston from San Francisco. Langford does not connect Plummer to the murders but says that Renton, Lower and Romain were members of Plummer's gang. Langford also states that George Wright, the commander of the Department of the Pacific in San Francisco, issued orders for a military escort to meet the prisoners on the lower Columbia.

Lewis, Oscar. *The Big Four: The Story of Huntington, Stanford, Hopkins, and Crocker, and of the Building of the Central Pacific.* New York: A.A. Knopf, 1938.
    An engrossing examination of Leland Stanford, railroad tycoon and the first Governor of California—the man with whom Beachey dealt in gaining control of the prisoners. The section on Stanford is only slightly germane to the Beachey story, but it is worth reading as a portrait of a corruptible man in a corrupt time. Stanford emerges less benignly from Lewis's book than from this one.

Malone, Michael P., and Richard B. Roeder. *Montana: A History of Two Centuries.* Seattle: University of Washington Press, 1976.
    A solid, readable history covering the opening of the mining camps at Bannack, Alder Gulch and Virginia City, descriptions of mining methods, and the development of transportation routes.

Mather, Ruth E., and F.E. Boswell. *Hanging the Sheriff: A Biography of Henry Plummer.* Salt Lake City: University of Utah Press, 1987.
    This revisionist biography of Henry Plummer argues that he was not the desperado that history has painted but a decent, law-abiding young man trying his best to civilize the mining camps. The authors acknowledge his scrapes with the law in California, where he killed two men, but insist that the killings were not his fault. And his hanging, they say, was inspired by powerful men whose

careers he threatened. These authors also argue that the number of crimes committed by road gangs has been wildly exaggerated.

Miller, Joaquin. *Unwritten History: Life Amongst the Modocs.* Hartford: American Publishing, 1873. [Reprinted by Orion Press, Eugene, Oregon, 1972.]
This book by Joaquin Miller (1837-1913), the famous Western poet, describes his years among the Modoc Indians of northern California, but in a digression he devotes a chapter to some time he spent in the Lewiston region in 1861-62 as an expressman. He describes the execution of Dave English, Nelson Scott and William Peoples for the armed robbery of the Berry brothers, and says English's followers also included Renton, Lower and Romain. And he adds that all six were buried in the same place. No one else, it appears, has mentioned this. Most historians are skeptical about the reliability of Miller's recollections.

Pierce, Elias Davidson. *The Pierce Chronicle: Personal Reminiscenses of E.D. Pierce.* Moscow: Idaho Research Foundation, 1975.
Captain E.D. Pierce (1824-1897), a veteran of the Mexican War, led a band of prospectors into the Clearwater Mountains in the summer of 1860, where they discovered gold on about September 28 at a place called Canal Gulch near the present town of Pierce. These reminiscenses, dictated years later by Pierce, describe the hardships of the trail and the gold strikes that launched the great rush of prospectors into the region in the following spring.

Powell, Barbara V. *Citizens of North Idaho, Vol. II: Newspaper Abstracts, 1862-1875.* Medical Lake, Washington: Self-published, 1986.
This handy volume describes the contents of the newspapers published in Lewiston from 1862 through 1875. It is useful not only for the news these papers contained but also for the advertisements, which tell us much about early-day Nez Perce County.

Sanders, Helen Fitzgerald, ed. *X. Beidler: Vigilante.* Norman: University of Oklahoma Press, 1957.
Helen Sanders (b. 1883) was the daughter-in-law of Wilbur Sanders, who had come out in 1863 from Ohio with his uncle, Sidney Edgerton, newly appointed member of the Idaho territorial supreme court. (Edgerton never traveled west of the Bitterroot Range, however, and eventually was elected the first Governor of Montana Territory. Edgerton and his nephew became influential in the mining districts and actively supported the vigilante system there.) John Xavier "X" Beidler was one of the vigilantes who hanged Plummer and other road agents in 1864. This book is a collection of Beidler's memoirs, dictated late in his life and edited by Helen Sanders. According to Beidler, both Page and Romain were members of Plummer's gang. Sanders writes, in an editorial note, that "Plummer and his gang met in Alder Gulch and planned the robbery of the pack train and the murder of Magruder and his friends." And, the book claims, Page "incriminated Henry Plummer." If the latter happened, it isn't clear whether it was before or after Plummer was hanged. Page made no reference to Plummer in what remains of the trial testimony.

Simon-Smolinski, Carole. *Journal 1862: Timothy Nolan's 1862 Account of His Riverboat and Overland Journey to the Salmon River Mines, Washington Territory.* Clarkston, Washington: Northwest Historical Consultants, 1983.

A fictional account of a diarist's journey from San Francisco to Lewiston and the Salmon River diggings in 1862, based on extensive research into actual historical sources concerning the people, places, and transportation network en route. The "journal" describes in detail the coastal steamers of the day, as well as the riverboats and portages of the Columbia-Snake waterway.

Welch, Julia Conway. *The Magruder Murders: Coping with Violence on the Idaho Frontier.* Helena, Montana: Falcon Press, 1991.
A valuable recent addition to the Magruder literature. Welch offers considerable detail about Magruder's service in the Mexican War, his activities in the California legislature, and the financial difficulties that led him to strike out for Washington Territory. Welch speculates on the accuracy of various versions of the Magruder incident and concludes that the murderers could not have followed Magruder's pack string out of Lewiston, despite many accounts to the contrary, because they were known to have been in the Beaverhead country at the time. She says this version was seized upon and preserved by people on the west side of the mountains who wanted "a piece of the action." Yet Mose Druillard at the trial testified that he had seen either Renton or Lower—the transcript is not clear which—at Lewiston in August 1863, the month Magruder started east toward Elk City and Bannack. It seems likely that if one of the three was in Lewiston at that time, the other two were there also. Welch writes that Beachey "delivered the men safely at the dock in Lewiston," and that he had to talk a crowd of vigilantes out of hanging his prisoners on the spot. And she doubts that Henry Plummer had any connection to the crime.

Journal and Magazine Articles

Dakis, Mike and Ruth. "Vigilantes on Trial." *Idaho Yesterdays* (Winter 1968-69).
The authors provide an enlightening and well-documented account of the debate carried on within the press over the vigilante system as it operated in Idaho and western Montana. Various contemporary editors defended the vigilantes as a necessary force for law and order, while others condemned them as more dangerous than the villains they were supposedly trying to control.

Goodwin, Victor."William C. (Hill) Beachey, Nevada-California-Idaho Stagecoach King." *Nevada Historical Society Quarterly* (Spring 1967).
Although Goodwin has the name wrong (William C. actually was Hill's nephew), he provides a detailed account of Beachey's career, after Beachey left Lewiston, as a builder of stagecoach routes and railroad lines in Nevada and southern Idaho. It is worth remembering that Beachey is as well known in Nevada for his involvement in transportation development as he is in the Pacific Northwest for his role in the Magruder affair.

Josephy, Alvin M., Jr. "The Blood of Abel." *Journal of the Nez Perce County Historical Society* (Spring/Summer 1985); reprinted from *American West* magazine (May/June 1983).

Josephy states there was a lynch mob waiting on the riverbank when Beachey arrived at Lewiston with the prisoners, and that Beachey's oratory saved the day. This issue of the *Journal of the Nez Perce County Historical Society* also has an article about Hill Beachey by Betty K. Beachy (apparently a relative but not identified as such) and a report on the executions from the *Walla Walla States-man*, March 26, 1864.

Limbaugh, Ronald H. "The Year without a Code." *Idaho Yesterdays* (Spring 1987).
Limbaugh focuses on the period between the passage of the organic act creating Idaho Territory and the development of a criminal code. For a time, in fact, the new territory was without any law.

Nordhoff, Charles. "The Columbia River and Puget Sound." *Harper's New Monthly Magazine* (February 1874); reprinted in *Readings in Pacific Northwest History—Washington, 1790-1895*. Seattle: University Bookstore, 1941.
Nordhoff's impression of Astoria and the Columbia River estuary, and his vivid description of the scenery on the lower river, were useful in describing that part of Beachey's journey. Nordhoff recalls the Astoria shoreline as being "a dreary continuity of shade."

Legal Documents

Nez Perce County Courthouse records—affadavits, indictments, subpoena, trial testimony.
The testimony from the Renton, Lower and Romain trial is the key source for the Magruder story. Not all authors who have written about Magruder, however, knew about or had the opportunity to examine these documents.

Newspapers

The following newspapers reported the Magruder affair and associated events as they occurred. As was the custom in this era, editors frequently borrowed and reprinted articles from other newspapers.

The Dalles Journal
The Golden Age (Lewiston)
Idaho Statesman (Boise)
Oregon Statesman (Salem)
Oregonian (Portland)
Sacramento Daily Union
San Francisco Bulletin
San Francisco Call
Walla Walla Statesman

The Golden Age, in early December 1863, reported that Beachey and his prisoners had arrived in Lewiston by stage, not by boat, and no lynch mob was waiting. *The Golden Age* claimed that: "not the least excitement was manifested except the natural elation felt by the people at the success of Mr. Beachey . . . We have not heard a single expression that would tend to excite mob violence. Everyone appears willing that the prisoners shall have a fair and impartial trial before our legally established tribunals. We are a law-abiding people, and as long as we have legally established courts to try criminals, no one need fear mob violence—our contemporaries in San Francisco, Portland and The Dalles to the contrary notwithstanding."

This may be a better example of protecting Lewiston's civic image than of good reporting. If there had been no need to fear mob violence, then it would have been unnecessary to move the prisoners out of the Luna House jail rooms to the relative security of Fort Lapwai.

The newspapers of the time are an essential source of information, but sometimes they are unreliable. For example, when the *Sacramento Daily Union* of November 3, 1863, reported the murders, it had the date wrong by a month and erroneously claimed that Magruder had met his killers at a political meeting. *The Dalles Journal* of November 2 carried the following inaccurate report: "A stranger who came from the upper country last Saturday states that the body of Magruder, who is supposed to have been murdered by Romaine and his party, has been found. The gentleman says that he was well acquainted with Magruder and recognized the body at once. Magruder lay as he was shot from his horse, with his watch and pocket money undisturbed. He had a shotgun grasped in his hand, as if in the act of raising it to his shoulder to fire."

The following newspapers came into existence after 1863-64, but each later printed material pertinent to the Magruder/Beachey story.

Idaho Signal (Lewiston; 1872-74)
Lewiston Journal (1867-72)
Lewiston Morning Tribune (1892-to present)
North-Idaho Radiator (Lewiston; 1865-66)
Northerner (Lewiston)
Spokesman-Review (Spokane; 1883-to present)

The *North-Idaho Radiator* reported on some of Hill Beachey's activities after he left Lewiston and on some post-Magruder political doings, and the *Lewiston Morning Tribune* has carried numerous articles over the years relating to the Magruder story, as has the *Spokesman-Review*.

Letters

Mrs. Carl Braun (daughter of James Pelham Magruder and the granddaughter of Lloyd and Caroline Magruder), letter in the *Idaho Statesman* (Boise), October 11, 1942; reprinted in R.G. Bailey, *Hell's Canyon* (1943), p.p 541-43.

An important source of information about Magruder's early years and Caroline's reactions to the criminals and the executions.

Thomas Morgan, letter to the editor, *True West* (1963; undated clipping in author's collection).

Morgan claims he had been in communication with two other Magruder granddaughters and had learned that an Idaho lawyer had once offered to get back the money stolen from Magruder, but was not heard from again. Reportedly, Morgan also said he had learned that "Lloyd's widow finally became so poor she had to put two of her boys out under the old 'Bound Child' law. So it is without question that the family got little of the stolen money."

Appendix

When History and Folklore Intertwine
By Carole Simon-Smolinski*

A cosmopolitan army of would-be millionaires once ranged throughout the American West, temporarily assembling in wild and remote places in a relentless search for "color." Mining was hard, dirty, unglamorous, and usually unprofitable work, and related professions often fared none better, but some individual experiences of that era have evolved into bigger-than-life stories remembered and treasured today. Readily identifiable heroes and villains seem destined for good or evil as shades of gray disappear. Human events gain mythical dimensions in which coincidence looses its relevance. With time the telling and retelling of what once was fact becomes so confused with fantasy that regional mythology evolves.

The story of Lloyd Magruder has become such a story. Magruder was a packer and merchant whose 1863 travels took him from the supply town of Lewiston, Idaho Territory, across the territory's rugged Bitterroot Range to the gold camps of Bannack and Virginia City. There was nothing unique about him or the work he was doing. It was also probable that nefarious men might murder him in the mountains on his return trip to Lewiston, given the mood of the times and the circumstances of his trip.

What then was special about his story; what caused the events surrounding his murder to be remembered from generation to generation while time forgot other stories from that era? Why have we transformed this tale from a regional historic event to a piece of central Idaho and western Montana folklore? Perhaps, as James Oliver Robertson suggests in *American Myth: American Reality,* there is something about the story that helps us better understand or identify with our region.

Robertson explains that "myths are 'the way things are' as people in a particular society believe them to be: and they are the models people refer to when they try to understand their world and its behavior."[1] If that is true, then maybe in the Magruder story—the character of the man and the events that surrounded his death—are attitudes, behavior traits, and characteristics which help identify people of this land and their mythology.

For one thing, Magruder, like others who ventured into the gold camps of the West, no doubt accepted the belief that individual effort alone dictated one's success or failure. At a time when a man—maybe even a woman—"pulled himself up by his bootstraps," why else would he pursue the uncertain life of the western wilderness? People then believed anyone could begin with a clean slate, even though we now know many faced closed doors. That notion of individualism remains deeply rooted in local lore and belief, and continues to dictate regional behavior. It is a model, as Robertson points out, which helps us better understand our world today.

Magruder also did as many other townspeople—he contributed to the taming of the West by helping to establish a permanent, "civilized" society. Along with his work as merchant, he threw his hat into the political ring to represent the newly created Territory of Idaho at the nation's capital. Others contributed in different ways; together they transformed the West in a relatively short time. Westerners continue to view that accomplishment with some degree of pride as they ignore its many negative aspects, and believe strongly in the potential for community, state, or even national change through individual effort.

Magruder exhibited other character traits upheld through western lore and custom. He operated on a basis of trust. Local lore is replete with stories of unlocked cabins or homes, supplied with provisions and open to a passerby should he or she need food and shelter. Magruder trusted those he put in his employ, a trust that may seem unreasonable to us today, but a trust as natural then as leaving one's door unlocked. Do people today look only to the past—the good old days—to find that type of trust?

It wasn't logical to be so trusting, as Magruder's experience so graphically shows. It was an era of contradictions; lawless days of bandits and robbers, when some lay in wait at shebangs for unsuspecting, innocent, gold-bearing miners and packers to pass their way. Others covered their tracks in the guise of gamblers, fellow miners, even sheriffs or capitalized upon that inherent trust of the West and schemed their way into the employ of an unsuspecting person like Magruder. Nevertheless, we ignore those contradictions today to look back upon a seemingly black and white, uncomplicated time when you simply applauded the hero and hung the villain.

Westerners also can be fiercely and sometimes unreasonably loyal. It is that type of loyalty Hill Beachey showed towards his friend Magruder that seems to most captivate our interest today. Beachey's dream of Magruder's impending death ultimately took him from the shores of the Clearwater and Snake rivers in Idaho Territory to the streets of San Francisco. It was as though he was destined to avenge his friend's murder and symbolically usher in law and order to the new territory in the process. Beachey's dream may have been nothing more than his telling a friend, "I had a hunch something would happen to him," a statement we have all said from time to time? What matters is that the dream's mystical qualities helped set the stage for the tale's conversion from historical fact to lore.

The violent murder happened during a snowstorm in one of the most inaccessible sections of the intermountain West. Beachey, missing opportunities to identify and apprehend the criminals while in Lewiston, relentlessly pursued the suspects to California with nothing to go on but his presumed dream and a strong set of suspicions. In San Francisco intrigue followed his every move. After his nerve-wracking return to Lewiston with the fugitives, one of the territory's biggest trials and hangings ensued. The trial became a public spectacle and Beachey a territorial hero. Good triumphed over evil for all to see, and was confirmed during a concluding return visit to the crime scene. Every stage of the drama reminds us of the lessons to be learned: an individual and loyal friend emerges victorious, good prevails over evil, and the territory becomes a better place. With all of those ingredients in play, you not only get a best-seller, you get a story that captivates a region for decades.

Why, then, has the Magruder story not moved beyond a regional folktale and become a popular addition to Western American folklore? For one thing, it happened in a relatively underpopulated section of the country long overshadowed in both literature and history by more populous or glamorous areas. For many years local residents have been aware that few outsiders knew about their region or its history. Some have felt apologetic about it; others are satisfied to live in an "undiscovered" land and hope its isolation continues. We know our history parallels the greater drama of the American West in countless ways and Magruder's experiences are but one example. But because this particular story is unique to us, that might be another explanation of its popularity in a limited geographic area.

Also by remaining a part of local history, the story has undergone more transformation than an event subjected to outside scrutiny. Local history frequently absorbs such an interweaving of fact and fiction that the true story becomes obscured with time. That is partially because of the sources used. "Old timers," people whose experiences provide an invaluable, personal perspective on specific events or incidents, are often cited as the final authority for all the events from "the olden days." (Never mind that the "olden days" happened decades even generations earlier.) Many local historians fall into the trap of using those people as their prime source and contribute to the perpetuation and, unfortunately, authentication of incorrect information. Magruder's story is a good example.

Although Nathaniel Langford's 1890 reminiscences, *Vigilante Days and Ways*, and a 1903 publication, *An Illustrated History of North Idaho*, both included references to the Magruder murder, the story wasn't widely known until 1947 when Lewiston historian Robert G. Bailey published *River of No Return*. He claimed that he first became aware of the murder while hiking across the southern Nez Perce Trail (often called the Magruder Corridor) years earlier with fellow traveler Vic Bargamin. He noticed a grave marker on which he deciphered "October, 1863, one Lloyd Magruder had been murdered in this place."

He asked Bargamin about the murder and was told, "Oh, a fellow who had a store in Elk City in the early days . . . was killed and robbed while returning from the mining camps in Montana."[2]

Bailey's interest again perked while going over some 1863 issues of the early Lewiston newspaper, *The Golden Age,* where he found references to Magruder. He then "talked with old timers" and got details of events connected to the murder, including Beachey's now-famous dream, which he learned from James Witt, "an old timer who died in Lewiston about 1925."[3] Witt "knew all the actors in the tragedy" causing Bailey to believe the dream occurred. Bailey corroborated Witt's version by claiming, "Other persons who lived in Lewiston at the time of the tragedy have expressed the same belief."[4] There is no evidence that he consulted any of the earlier published accounts.

Bailey deserves credit for recording some of the interesting history of north central Idaho. He also deserves credit for interviewing and preserving stories from older citizens of the area, many of whom dated back to the heady days of the gold rush era. His intent was simply to tell the stories of his region before they were lost; but in doing so, he did not differentiate between documented fact and assumed or remembered information, his research was not very extensive, nor did he provide a reference guide for his sources.

Another regional historian whose work appeared shortly after Bailey's was Sister Alfreda Elsensohn. She looked at the murder in a broader perspective, noting it was the Magruder murder that "started the purge of Idaho's early day outlaws." She, however, repeats the dream as fact. "It was after a dream that Hill Beachey, who operated the Luna House, informed friends he had seen Lowry kill Magruder with an ax."[5] Her brief account of the murder includes daily entries from the Luna House Hotel register, where the prisoners were held during their trial, and concludes with a reference to a later packer. While encamped in the wilderness with considerable money and at least one suspicious member of his party, his thoughts went back to the recent Magruder murder. He claimed that had any of his men come towards him in the dead of night, "he probably would have been killed as I was wrought up to the highest pitch."[6]

Of course people were wrought up to the highest pitch, and of course they told and retold the story from campfire to parlor room. It was ripe for the embellishments of an active imagination and it was those embellishments reported by Bailey and Elsensohn and others that gave the story all the dimensions it needed to become a popular, often repeated legend.

What then is fact and what is folklore? How does one write a good story, capturing all the drama and suspense of a made-for-Hollywood historic event and still remain true to the integrity of history? Must the telling of fact imply that the flavor of the story be removed to insure its accuracy? And how does the historian or writer know for sure that the works he or she so carefully researched and the words so laboriously selected and connected hold true to the actual events?

Perhaps the writer does as Ladd Hamilton has done in this book. First, he is as true to the historic events as is possible and, by supporting his research with a bibliographic essay and endnotes, provides valuable documentation. He respects the moods of the land, and knows the role of the region's geography in dictating human activities. He clearly demonstrates an understanding and appreciation of the complexity of the times. It was the Civil War era and Idaho, a newly created territory, was a direct by-product of Civil War politics. People of the West took as keen an interest in national events as anyone on the Eastern battlefields and, as Hamilton shows, many of their actions were dictated by national and territorial politics. He also shows how circumstances of the times made it difficult to apprehend and try a criminal under the confusion of a new territorial structure. Perhaps less significant but equally important to the historical sense of the story is the way Hamilton described travel and communication of the times.

By using limited editorial comment within the narrative, Hamilton shows the reader information that he or others may have embellished, but he does it in a non-obtrusive way. His "Author's Note" and "Endnotes" lets the reader know when he is assuming a chain of events or fabricating supporting characters, thus losing none of the drama's flavor. A good example is his reenactment of Beachey's return trip from San Francisco, all fabricated but with a distinct understanding of what might logically have transpired, including Cyrus Skinner's very realistic bout with seasickness. His characters are extremely real, not Paul Bunyons of mythical proportions but people you could be as comfortable with now as then. Throughout the book Hamilton has neither compromised history nor his storytelling abilities. His version of the Magruder episode provides not only a good perspective on Idaho Territory in the 1860s, it's a good read.

The Magruder story will remain an important part of regional folklore. Possibly generations from now its retelling will include some of the additions Hamilton made in this book. That's good, for each generation contributes a part of itself to its lore.

Notes

1. James Oliver Robertson, *American Myth: American Reality* (1980), p. xv.
2. Robert G. Bailey, *River of No Return (The Great Salmon River of Idaho)* . . . (1935), p. 123.
3. Ibid.
4. Ibid.
5. Sister Alfreda Elsensohn, *Pioneer Days in Idaho County, Vol. 2* (1951), p. 222.
6. Ibid., p. 223.

---

*Carole Simon-Smolinski is the author of *Journal 1862: Timothy Nolan's 1862 Account of His Riverboat and Overland Journey to the Salmon River Mines, Washington Territory* (Clarkston, Washington: Northwest Historical Consultants, 1983).